HOME
ORCHID GROWING

by

REBECCA TYSON NORTHEN

D. VAN NOSTRAND COMPANY, INC.

TORONTO   NEW YORK   LONDON

NEW YORK

D. Van Nostrand Company, Inc., 250 Fourth Avenue, New York 3

TORONTO

D. Van Nostrand Company (Canada), Ltd., 25 Hollinger Road, Toronto

LONDON

Macmillan & Company, Ltd., St. Martin's Street, London, W.C. 2

02544a25

PRINTED IN THE UNITED STATES OF AMERICA

PREFACE

Orchid literature of the last few decades has done its job well in proving that orchids are plants that any flower lover can grow, and in giving beginners a start in orchid culture. Where once there were few orchid growers, now there are thousands; where once orchids were owned only by those who could afford an elaborate greenhouse and a trained grower, now there are little backyard greenhouses springing up everywhere. Busy people from all walks of life, as well as those who have retired, are finding relaxation, joy, and excitement in their orchids.

But beginners need more than a start. Once a person has tried his hand with a few plants, his enthusiasm grows to unlimited proportions. He finds himself seeking more and more information. Even after becoming a successful grower he will find himself faced with problems now and again. Often an amateur has had to wait for years to find a grower who has solved the problem with which he needs help, or he has had to dig through research papers or study textbooks to find the answer.

It has been my endeavor to help the amateur with his problems as far as possible. This book is designed not only to give the beginner a start but to advance him through the years into every phase of orchid growing. More than that, it gives him, along with the methods, a background in the functions and needs of the plants so that he will be able both to recognize problems and to solve them on the basis of his knowledge. It is sometimes thought that amateurs cannot be given scientific information lest it scare them away from their project. But in this age when people insist on knowing the "why" behind everything they come in contact with, certainly orchid growers are entitled to every fact that can be of help to them. A good deal of the information which has been accumulated here has not been presented to amateur growers before.

It is my hope that the book will encourage many to venture into this fascinating hobby, and that it will be of help to all orchid lovers, both beginner and professional.

R. T. N.

Laramie, Wyoming
December, 1949

ACKNOWLEDGMENTS

A book is seldom the product of one mind alone. Not only do the experiences of others go into the actual making of the book, but they are absorbed by the author in the subtle forming of the background that comes before the book. I should like therefore to express my grateful indebtedness to the following for information obtained personally or through their published works, for encouragement and criticism, or for the use of photographs or color plates: Const. J. Alexopoulos, Oakes Ames, Peter A. Ark, Frederick T. Bonham, Ernest Cory, J. T. Curtis, Gordon W. Dillon, Robert E. Duncan, H. A. Dunn, David C. Fairburn, B. A. Friedman, D. D. Jensen, Rodney Wilcox Jones, Lewis Knudson, Alex Laurie, Donald P. Limber, H. F. Loomis, Mary E. Marx, R. A. MacLeod, G. A. L. Mehlquist, Henry T. Northen, G. H. Pring, H. D. Sawyer, Jack Sweet, H. E. Thomas, Joseph Urmston, Mrs. J. J. Waring, W. G. Waterman, Louis O. Williams, Carl Withner; Armacost and Royston, Inc., Clarelen Orchids, Flower Grower Magazine, Jones and Scully, Inc., Lord and Burnham, University of Maryland, Clint McDade and Sons, Ohio State University, H. Patterson and Sons, The Smithsonian Institution, Stuart Low Company, University of Wyoming.

CONTENTS

CHAPTER   PAGE

I Orchids as a Hobby 1

II Adult Cattleyas and Their Care 12

III Adult Cattleyas and Their Care (continued) 24

IV The Cattleya Species 36

V Hybrids 52

VI Seedlings from Flask to Community Pot 78

VII Seedlings from Community Pot to First Bloom 89

VIII Growing and Sowing Your Own Seed 99

IX The Orchid Tribes; The Aërides Tribe 120

X The Cattleya Tribe 135

XI The Cymbidium Tribe 141

XII The Cypripedium Tribe 154

XIII The Dendrobium Tribe 169

XIV The Odontoglossum Tribe 175

XV Collectors' Items 189

XVI Mineral Nutrition 212

XVII Diagnosing Orchid Ailments 224

XVIII Housing Your Orchids 241

XIX The Care and Use of Cut Flowers 255

Bibliography 265

Appendix A—Key to the Tribes and Genera of the Orchid
Family 267

Appendix B—Sources of Orchid Plants and Supplies 277

Index 279

LIST OF COLOR PLATES

FACING PAGE

1. *Sophrolaeliocattleya Anzac*   10

2. *Cattleya Bow Bells*   26

3. *Laeliocattleya Clint McDade*   58

4. *Laeliocattleya Snowdrift*   74

5. *Laeliocattleya Gold Gleam*   106

6. *Laeliocattleya Derna*   122

7. *Cymbidium Jocosity*   154

7a *Cymbidium Nell Gwynne*   170

8. *Cypripedium Tonbridge*   202

9. *Miltonia Marietta Armacost*   234

10. Orchids in their native habitat   250

Chapter I

ORCHIDS AS A HOBBY

My excitement ran high when I set my first little pots of orchid seedlings on the kitchen window sill. I could imagine myself someday becoming a real orchid grower, but everything I had read about orchids sounded so difficult that I was half afraid I couldn't do it. But those first little plants grew and were the beginning of a hobby that has thrilled me more and more each day, each year.

Gradually I learned how to manage plants of all ages and conditions, getting what help I could from books and research papers, but mostly learning by experience. My orchids laid a magic spell on me so that I had to go on and on adding to my collection. The joy of watching them grow was climaxed whenever a plant bloomed. And one of the most exciting experiences was when the first of those original kitchen-window-sill babies produced two beautiful, pure white flowers.

Now the orchids are becoming a family hobby. There is plenty to do in the two greenhouses with their more than two thousand plants. Even the children are becoming young orchid growers. Seven-year-old Philip and ten-year-old Betty have learned how to pot seedlings and back bulbs and take pleasure in finding jobs they can do to help. Both can give visitors a comprehensive description of orchid growing from flask to bloom. Thomas, now three, made his first contribution by postponing his arrival for two days, so that his mother could transplant four flasks of seedlings that came without warning on the day he himself was expected.

Orchid growing has been an adventure. This field of wonders opened itself to me bit by bit, and each new thing learned about the care of the plants and their fascinating history gave me a sense of achievement. Most wonderful was the discovery that orchids are really just plain plants. Their requirements differ only slightly from those of other plants. And for learning their few simple needs I can have these exotic things from the tropics of the world all in my own backyard. They even make themselves at home in the house along with ordinary house plants.

A legend of mystery once surrounded orchid culture. It grew from the uncertainties and hazards that confused man's first attempts to tame the wild plants. The early growers found that they could not just bring orchids down from their perches in jungle trees and grow them in ordinary soil in flower pots. Nor could they grow them from seed by the usual methods. Orchids spent tens of thousands of years developing the specialized structure that enabled them to survive under crowded conditions. Many problems had to be solved before they could be made to feel at home under human care. But those problems have been solved by the patient work of generations of

A thoroughly satisfactory plant for greenhouse or home is the Cypripedium. Its waxy flowers also make stunning corsages.

commercial growers and devoted amateurs, and orchid culture has at last been brought to the point where everyone can share its thrills.

Cattleyas are the largest and showiest of the 15,000 species of orchids, the most familiar of corsage orchids, and the easiest to grow. They bloom year after year, giving two or more flowers at a time. Mature plants may be had for no more than the price of a single orchid corsage, and some as cheaply as the usual kinds of potted plants. Young seedlings are very inexpensive. Osmundine, the potting medium, is about $3.00 a bag, and one bag goes a long way. You can start your collection for a small investment, even without a greenhouse. Once you have ventured into orchid growing you will not be able to stop. Increasing the size of your collection need not be the extravagance you might think, for if you can bear to part with some of the blooms to a local florist, the plants will soon pay for themselves, even become quite a profitable hobby.

Cattleyas come from the tropical regions of Central and South America, largely from Venezuela, Brazil, and Colombia. Their native conditions give the best hint as to their needs under cultivation. Their home is the tropical rain-forest, where vegetation is dense and competition at its keenest. Plants grow so thickly that the jungles are really forests upon forests. Giant ferns and other plants completely cover the ground. Plants that need more light than they can get on the ground contrive in some manner to reach up above the undergrowth. The struggle for light is almost vicious. Great vines grow up the tree trunks and form a tangled network among the branches. Some trees whose seedlings would die on the ground send their seed to germinate on branches of other trees, and when a seedling is developed it sends roots

The plant bearing the two white flowers in the foreground was the first of the kitchen-window-sill seedlings to bloom. Behind it are two jungle orchids in flower, both *Cattleya Trianaei*.

down into the ground and eventually smothers the tree that gave it support. Light- and air-loving orchids would have been pushed out of existence if they had not moved up and away from the stifling mass of undergrowth.

The whole top of a rain forest is an aerial garden. Orchids and some other plants have learned to cling to tree trunks, in the crotches, and along the branches. Sometimes the burden of plants grows so heavy that a great thick branch may break under its weight. Plants that live thus on other plants are called "epiphytes," "epi-" meaning "above or on," and "-phyte" meaning "plant." They are not parasitic. They merely grow where they can find support and a collection of nutrient material, even sometimes, outside of the forest, on roof tops or in rock crevices. They obtain minerals from decaying vegetable matter and make their own food from carbon dioxide and water, as do all independent plants.

The orchids have cleverly adapted their structure to their needs as air-dwellers. Clinging as they do to sparse deposits of decaying debris, they do not have access to the continuous water supply they would have on the ground. They must depend on catching rain and dew, and for this purpose their roots have a spongy covering that soaks up water quickly like blotting paper. The central conducting tissue of the root then conveys it slowly to the rest of the plant. Some of the roots fasten the plant to its perch, and the rest hang out in the air. When an orchid plant is grown in a flower pot, the potting medium must be porous in order to allow the roots to be well aerated. Osmunda fibre, or osmundine, a fern root, is ideal for this purpose. The fibres hold water and have spaces for air between them. As the osmundine decays, it gives off minerals needed for the nutrition of the plant. Having such a substance in which to pot orchids is a great convenience, too, for it does away with the bother of sifting soil and mixing a compost.

Orchids have developed reservoirs in the form of thickened stems and fleshy leaves, which store both food and water, and keep the plants from drying out between rains. They are really quite like cacti, which have to store what water they get for use over a long period. It is this characteristic that makes it possible to ship orchid plants all over the world.

In the aerial gardens of the jungles, the plants that can resist drying most efficiently inhabit the topmost branches. Those that do not have as large water reservoirs live on branches lower down where they are less exposed. High up in the airiest places, live the Cattleyas.

The temperature in the high altitudes where Cattleyas abound is quite moderate, with little difference between day and night temperatures. Under cultivation these orchids like about the same temperature range as human beings. They can thrive indoors where people are comfortable, and in greenhouses that are well ventilated and not too hot.

To collect wild Cattleyas men hack their way through the jungles to the high regions, climb the trees, and chop the plants off the branches. Wild plants are also grown on plantations whose chief business is to export them. To prepare them for shipment, the rootless plants are dried for a time to put them in a dormant condition, because dormant plants travel better. Then they are crated and shipped, nowadays frequently by air, to this country. On arrival, they are inspected, fumigated to rid them of any insect pests, and sent on to their importers. The importers sell them, a few here and there to amateurs, thousands at a time to commercial growers.

These wild Cattleyas consist almost entirely of species, though a few natural hybrids occur. The species are the progenitors of all artificial or man-made hybrids. Colors range from dark purple to pale rosy lavender, with rare fuchsia, yellow, and white. The lip is usually a darker shade than the petals, with yellow or gold markings in the throat, and perhaps a light ruffle around

Orchid collecting in the Province of Chiriqui, Panama. Rich in orchids, Panama is the southern limit of Central American and the northern limit of South American species. Altitudes from sea level to 12,000 feet offer habitats for a wide variety of genera.

Rio Chiriqui Viejo flows from 12,000 foot El Volcan down to the Pacific Ocean, cutting a swathe through the orchid country. (Courtesy of H. A. Dunn)

An Epidendrum growing on a tree. (Courtesy of H. A. Dunn)

An agile native orchid collector. (Courtesy of H. A. Dunn)

Native collectors returning to camp. (Courtesy of H. A. Dunn)

Two thousand plants of *Cattleya Skinneri*, collected by Mr. Dunn and grown on this tree at his home in Ancon. (Courtesy of H. A. Dunn)

Sorting plants for transportation to base camp. (Courtesy of H. A. Dunn)

its edge. The variety in any one species is untold, as no two flowers are identical. Outstandingly beautiful varieties are sought as parents of hybrids. A grower will choose one with a particularly beautiful lip and cross it with another that has wide petals. When this hybrid matures and blooms, its choicest offsprings are crossed with other outstanding blooms in the hope of combining all the fine characters in one flower. Wide petals with a generous ruffle to them, broad sepals that stand out straight from the center, a wide, frilled, richly colored lip, the whole flower holding up its head like an aristocrat, these are the qualities that make show orchids and win prizes for them here and abroad. Though there is a definite lure to the hybrids, many members of the species are lovely enough to win medals and are as highly prized as the hybrids.

Each species has its own blooming season, which may not be the same in this country as in the tropics. For instance, *Cattleya Trianaei* blooms twice a year in its native home, and once a year here. It is *Cattleya Trianaei* you see in most corsages at Christmas time, and *Cattleya Mossiae* at Easter. In June it is *Cattleya gigas* that is worn by brides and girl graduates. There is a species for every season. Some hybrids have a regular blooming time, too, but often do not adhere to the regularity shown by the species.

A small orchid collection can be planned to give infinite variety and year round blooms. One each of a few of the species, and a few hybrids, possibly the hybrids made by crossing members of the species you choose, will give unending pleasure. For instance, if you choose *Trianaei, Mossiae,* and *gigas,* you may want *Cattleya Trimos* (*Trianaei* by *Mossiae*) and *Cattleya Ballantineana* (*Trianaei* by *gigas*).

Except for young seedlings, Cattleyas are fairly tough. They can stand a good bit of abuse, though, as is true of any plant, will do best with good care. They grow slowly and give you time to learn their needs. Happily they are resistant to most plant diseases and pests. If you love them in bloom and out, and watch them carefully from day to day, you will catch their signals when something is not quite right.

Hybrid seedlings are a gamble, but a gamble in which you gain whether you win the top prize or not. When a grower makes a cross, he plans it with the hope that it may produce a prize orchid. If he sells seedlings before they bloom, he does so without knowing which ones will grow up to give the choicest flowers. Three-year-old seedlings are $3 to $5, two-year-olds are $1 to $2. If you buy them still in the flask in which they are germinated, they cost even less. A flask costs somewhere around $25, and may have a hundred plants in it. That means that each tiny plant costs about 25 cents. The thrilling part of the gamble is that with your few dollars, or your 25 cents, you may buy the prize orchid the grower was hoping for when he made the cross. And a prize orchid for anything under a hundred dollars is a bargain. Even if you do not have a show plant, the seedlings hold in store for you variety and beauty well worth your waiting.

Tiny seedlings just out of the flask are delicate, really incubator babies even though they are a year old when they are ready to be transplanted. They are about ½ inch long, so small that they are put in "community" pots, about twenty-five to a 3-inch pot. Their growth for the next year is slow, still a formative stage, and many do not survive. During the third and fourth years, they grow to be large vigorous young plants. The most vigorous may bloom in their fifth year, those that grow more slowly may take a year or two longer. It is fun to watch them develop from month to month under your tender care. As a new growth appears you watch it grow larger than the one before it. You can see it put out its own new little roots, watch the bud swell where the next growth will develop, and exult in its size as it grows. Then when the plant nears maturity, you watch each new growth with added excitement, for maybe this one or the next will bloom. Finally, when one appears with a sheath, and flower buds come up in the sheath, the great moment is near.

The suspense of waiting for the new hybrid to reveal its secret is beyond description, for no man has yet seen that which you are about to witness. Day by day the buds grow larger and fatter, until one day the point of the bud begins to separate. It takes 12 to 24 hours for the bloom to open. You can almost see the flower parts move as the sepals swing out, the petals spread wide, and the lip unfurls its ruffles. The colors are pale when the flower begins to open, but grow more intense as the hours pass. Even when the flower is wide open the colors continue to deepen. You wonder how much longer you can stand the steady crescendo, and then, after another 24 hours, you suddenly realize that it is finished, it is perfect. And this lovely thing, the result of man's thoughtful combination of individually lovely flowers, is yours.

Many amateurs have ventured into orchid growing by buying seedlings in flasks or community pots. While raising them this way is ultimately the most fun, it might be safer to begin with a few mature plants to learn the general structure and growth processes of orchids. And, too, in this way you won't have to wait so long for blooms. Then, when you are familiar with the older plants, try some two- and three-year-old seedlings, and then a flask.

Eventually you will want to create a new hybrid from some of your own fine plants. To get ready for this you should set a seed pod when you have

The variety to be found among orchids is half of their charm. Gathered together here from this varied collection are Cattleya, Odontoglossum, Vanda, and Miltonia. (Courtesy of Lord and Burnham)

Orchids in your home. Three plants by a south window, a little away from the glass. Left, a plant in sheath. Center, a four-year-old seedling. Right, *Cattleya Mossiae* in flower.

some blooms and use the seed to practice sowing flasks, a technique you can perform in the kitchen. Just for the fun of seeing what combinations of characters they may have, you will want to carry on some of your first seedlings to maturity. But before you raise a quantity of seedlings, be sure the cross you make has really fine parents behind it.

There are many genera of orchids besides Cattleyas that have attractive flowers, Cypripediums, the ladyslipper kind, and some of the spray orchids. Many will grow under the same con-

COLOR PLATE 1. *Sophrolaeliocattleya Anzac*, Orchidhurst Variety.

ditions as Cattleyas. When you have become familiar with the latter, you will want to try some of the others. Their needs are essentially the same, with only slight modifications one way or another. There is truly no end to orchids as a hobby, and no plants can give you deeper satisfaction. For a little patient care they reward you with the most artful flowers yet designed by nature.

Chapter II

ADULT CATTLEYAS AND THEIR CARE

Treatment of Cattleyas in cultivation is planned to match as nearly as possible their native conditions. If you wonder what is behind some of the rules for growing them, look back at the plants in nature and all will prove logical. Even the process of growing seedlings in flasks, which seems so strange when you first hear of it, has its own very simple explanation. Orchids in pots, grown in the shelter of a greenhouse with artificial heat, are in strange circumstances, and success with them depends on learning to understand their needs and tempering their treatment accordingly.

STRUCTURE OF THE PLANTS

The mature Cattleya plant is built for endurance. There is nothing delicate in its appearance to suggest the exquisite beauty of the flowers to come. Its thick, spatula-shaped leaves remain on the plant for a number of years, bright, shiny green at first, growing a bit dull with age, until finally they turn yellow and drop off. The leaves stand up stiffly from their upright thickened stems, or pseudobulbs, capable of resisting the forces of the elements. Their leathery texture makes them resistant to drying and discouraging to insects. But they are subject to burning if they receive direct sunlight for too long or too suddenly. Although the plants live on high branches in the jungle, the sunlight is filtered by the moving branches above them. So in cultivation they like their light bright, but broken up or diffused.

A Cattleya is made up of a tough, creeping, ground stem called a "rhizome" that rests on the surface of the osmundine, from which grow the thick, brittle roots, and which gives rise at intervals to the pseudobulbs topped by their leaves. Each successive growth, or "lead," comes from the one preceding it, in the following manner. At the base of a mature "lead" there occurs a swelling, which is the developing bud or "eye." This soon breaks the dry scales, grows out horizontally for about an inch, and then curves upward. The horizontal part is a new section of the rhizome, and the upward growing part will bring forth pseudobulb, leaf, and blooms. It takes about six months

12

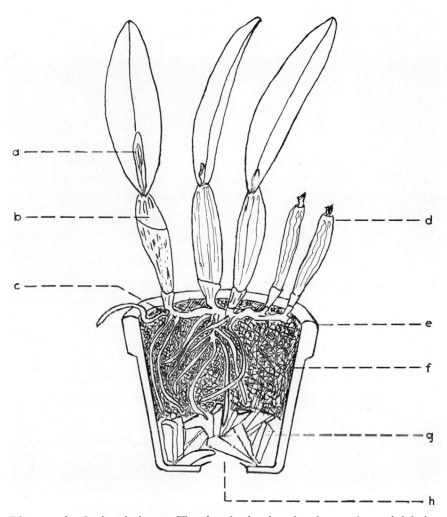

Diagram of a Cattleya in its pot. The plant is placed so that the growing end, left, has room for new leads. The old end, right, is set close to the rim. a, sheath with flower buds. b, pseudobulb. c, new roots growing from the rhizome at the base of the new lead. d, old pseudobulb from which leaf has fallen. e, rhizome, the cut end of which can be seen below the oldest pseudobulb. f, osmunda fibre, packed hard, and with the rhizome just at its surface. g, broken crock to provide drainage. h, drainage hole, enlarged.

for a growth to reach full size, after which it flowers, produces its own set of roots, and completes the cycle by giving rise to another new lead.

The pseudobulb, the thickened part of the stem, is a storage place for water and food. It is not a true bulb, since it is a stem structure, hence the

Cattleya Trianaei, one of the most useful and best known of the genus.

addition of the prefix "pseudo-." When you read about orchid "bulbs," the term is just shortened for convenience. New plants can be grown from pseudobulbs separated from the rest of the plant, the young growths arising from dormant buds at the base of a pseudobulb.

From the top of the pseudobulb, along with the leaf, there grows a thin envelope or "sheath," in which the flower buds appear. The sheath protects the buds until they are well formed. When the buds start to grow larger they soon fill the sheath, and break out through the top. From this time they mature rapidly, and in ten days or so will open to prove to you that they are well worth the careful planning nature gave them.

When a growth has finished blooming, it is ready to give rise to a new lead. Plants vary in the length of time between flowering and breaking a new bud. Some wait awhile, others produce it immediately. Just before this activity takes place, or simultaneously with it, the growth that has just flowered puts out its own set of roots. When you see the new roots starting, you can know that the fat green bud will soon appear. Sometimes two buds will start at once, with the promise of double the number of flowers next season.

The roots will surprise you. Except for the little green growing tip, they are white, brittle, and thick, about the diameter of a lollypop stick. Some grow straight into the osmundine, others wander over the surface and out over the edge of the pot. Still others will come back up out of the fibre to travel down the outside of the pot. At first they are single, but later branch and re-branch. Older roots from the back part of the plant go through stages of renewed activity from time to time. You may think an old brown root is dead, yet suddenly it will burst out with new white roots all along its length. If you break a root, you will see the spongy outer part differentiated from the slender central fibre of the conductive tissue.

When you buy mature orchid plants, you have a choice of propagations made from older plants, mature seedlings that have just bloomed or are ready to bloom, or wild plants fresh from the jungles. Propagations are made by dividing a large plant into several smaller ones, or removing the older pseudobulbs from a plant that has outgrown its pot. It takes such a division just a short time to re-root (become established), but about two years to be ready to bloom again. They are less expensive if you buy them newly established, but if these are to be your first orchids, it would be worth the additional cost in order to have flowers sooner. Mature seedlings are far more expensive, partly because they are new hybrids, and partly because seven years of care have gone into their raising without any return to the grower. If you are going to buy seedlings, it would seem more thrifty to get them younger when they cost only a fraction of what they would sell for later on.

Jungle plants are an experience that you must give yourself some time, though perhaps not right at first unless you buy them already potted and with growth started. It is exciting enough to receive them this way, but they are a real challenge when they come to you right out of the box in which they traveled from South America. They are dried and shriveled, their leaves

Cattleya gigas, collected in the jungle. Its large, heavily ruffled lip is rich purple with bright yellow eyes. (Courtesy of H. A. Dunn and H. Griffin)

somewhat battered and chewed. Instead of the neat orderly shape possessed by greenhouse-grown plants, they have taken the shape of their branch or tree-crotch perch, and their rhizomes have grown in loops or spirals or humps. They will make a striking contrast to the smooth, evenly green plants already on your greenhouse bench. Their blooms may not be all of the same quality you would get from growers who have bred selected plants, but they will show you the wide variety of coloring possible in any one species and may give you some excellent flowers, perhaps even a white one. Even if you cannot go to the jungles yourself, you can have the thrill of handling the wild plants, and of persuading them to bloom for you as they once did only for jungle creatures and the few people who have invaded the solitude of their tropical home.

CARE OF THE PLANTS

Temperature. Plants do not keep accounts, but if balance sheets were published for them, they would be quite similar to those you receive from the bank every month. If you spend more than you earn, you end up in debt. If you earn more than you spend, you have money left for savings. And philosophically, savings mean better living. The earnings of plants are the food they make, and their spending is the food they use in respiration, just as human beings use food for energy. Their savings go into growth and development. If a plant is kept at such a high temperature that it has to use more food for respiration than it can make, it will have nothing left for growth. The reason behind a so-called optimal range of temperature for any particular kind of plant, is that within this range food manufacture is greater than food expenditure, leaving a good reserve for plant growth and flower production.

Cattleya Dowiana, a striking yellow, with a deep purple lip veined with gold. (Courtesy of H. A. Dunn and H. Griffin)

During the day a plant carries on three activities, the making of food, respiration, and growth. At night no food is made, but respiration and growth continue. A nicely balanced relationship between day and night temperatures is important.

On a bright day, the warmer the temperature up to about 85° F. the more food is made. But it does not follow that the plants should be grown at that temperature, because respiration will catch up to food manufacture, even use the food as fast as it is made. Some lower temperature, that allows the plant to make food faster than it is used, is better. For Cattleyas the best day temperature, in the winter with artificial heat, is between 65° and 70° F. This is the temperature at which they grow natively all year round. In the rain-forests there is little difference between winter and summer. In our latitude we can let the summer temperature in the greenhouse go 10 degrees higher with safety, because when the days are long the cooler mornings and evenings help to offset the heat of the day. And the plants can survive unusually hot spells of weather, which fortunately are of short duration.

Night temperatures are kept cooler, as close to 60° F. as possible, not lower than 55° F., because at lower temperatures respiration is cut down and less of the valuable food reserve is consumed. Here again, there would be no point in running the greenhouse at an even lower temperature, just to save food, because then growth would be slowed down. And the orchids (as do most plants) make their best growth at night.

There may be a time when the night temperature accidentally drops lower than the desired minimum, perhaps when the outdoor temperature suddenly falls below normal, or when something goes wrong with the heating system of the greenhouse. If it doesn't go too dangerously near freezing, the plants will probably come through unharmed. Such an experience as I had one year adds one more bit of proof to the evidence that orchids are tough. The gas pressure went down on one of the coldest nights of the winter (20° F. below zero) so that many furnaces in town went out. One of my greenhouse heaters went out, and the others burned so low that for several hours the temperature was 39° F. It frightened me considerably, for I thought surely the orchids would be injured. But not one plant, even among the tiny seedlings, showed any damage. It probably would harm them, however, if it happened very often.

In cloudy weather the plants cannot make as much food as on bright, sunny days, yet respiration continues in proportion to the temperature. It follows that a medium cool temperature, around 65° F., is better under such conditions. This allows the plant to make what food it can with the lessened amount of light, and keeps respiration down in proportion.

Temperature and Relative Humidity. Temperature and relative humidity are inseparable. With the same amount of water in the air, relative humidity goes down as the temperature goes up. Outdoors the relative humidity may be 35% at noon of a summer day, with the thermometer standing at 80°. When evening comes, and the temperature falls to 50° F., the relative humidity will rise to 100%. No water has been added to the air in the form of rain, yet in the cooler evening the air becomes saturated, and water vapor condenses out of the air as dew.

Most people think of an orchid house as dripping with water, but this is a false idea. Cattleyas like a lively, invigorating atmosphere and do not thrive when the air is kept too close and damp. Even in their native habitat, the daytime humidity is only 65% to 70% when the sun is shining, so growers aim at that percentage in their greenhouses. On warm, bright days the relative humidity in a greenhouse falls as the temperature rises, with a desiccating effect on the plants. It is necessary to add water to the air by wetting the walls and ground, or by using fine mist sprayers above or below the benches, to prevent too much loss of water from the plants. In the more humid regions of this country, this may not have to be done as frequently as in the drier West, but must be done often in any greenhouse that has dry winter heat.

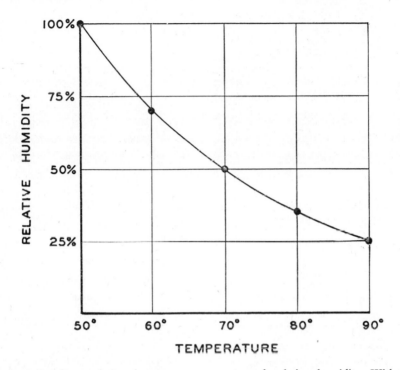

Diagram to show relation between temperature and relative humidity. With the actual amount of moisture in the air remaining constant, relative humidity falls as the temperature rises. Conversely, as the temperature becomes cooler, relative humidity becomes greater.

On cloudy days and at night, the humidity in the greenhouse will naturally rise, and the plants will lose little, if any, water.

Light. People are growing orchids in every part of the United States. Light conditions vary from one place to another, even from city to country in the same region. So the only way to tell whether your plants are receiving the right amount for their particular needs is to watch the plants themselves.

You can tell by looking at a Cattleya plant whether it has been grown with good light or under too much shade. The heavily shaded plant is tall and spindly, with slender pseudobulbs, leaves long and narrow and of a soft, succulent character, and deep green in color. In contrast to these, a plant grown in ample light is shorter, with thick, stocky pseudobulbs, and broad, tough leaves that are grass green in color. The growths of the spindly, shaded plant often come "blind," without sheaths, and consequently their flower

production is poor. The sturdy plant, in response to more light, produces more flowers, which incidentally have better keeping qualities. When a plant has had too much light, the leaves are yellow or bronze, and may have burned spots on them.

These signs will appear in your own plants. Change in leaf color appears rather rapidly under different light intensities and is a good indicator of their needs. The leaves of colored varieties are sometimes tinged with red normally, or produce the red pigment (anthocyanin) under conditions of bright light. Often when the leaves show no red-

Mist sprayers under the benches add moisture to the air without wetting the plants. Note natural gas heater at end of walk.

ness, the new growth and even the sheath may have red speckles. This is not a sign of too much light, but rather that the plant is receiving just about the optimum amount. As the growth matures the red speckles disappear. Pure white Cattleyas never produce any red pigment.

A greenhouse will require some form of shading from spring through summer and early fall. The usual white greenhouse shading compound (see Chapter XVIII for details) may be sprayed or painted on the glass, and is satisfactory. Roller blinds are prettier, and preferred by some, but are more expensive. They may be used alone, or in combination with a light coat of white shading. Roller blinds allow a moving pattern of sunlight to fall on the plants, which gives them full sun and shade intermittently, imitating the way the sun reaches them in nature. But as the white shading becomes flaked by the weather, it, too, has somewhat the same effect.

In the summer, Cattleyas can stand about 20% to 30% of outdoor sunlight. Roller blinds are designed to admit about this amount. If you use white shading, it should be applied to transmit 2000 to 3000 foot-candles, measured on a bright day. This can be measured with a photographic light meter, pointed up at the sun through the greenhouse roof. Readings may be taken of reflected light by pointing the meter at a sheet of white paper. The paper should be held toward the light. Measured this way, the light intensity should be between 200 and 300 foot-candles.

When you have applied the shading, watch your plants to see how they react. If the leaves start to turn yellow, apply a little more shading. A few plants may turn yellow, while the rest remain normal, so just these few may need heavier shading. Move them to the shadier end, or perhaps adjust the shading in one spot for them. When you find the right amount of light for a plant, its leaves will turn a good green again. The oldest leaf or two will eventually turn yellow and drop off, so watch the other leaves and judge the light by them.

Extremely intense light will quickly burn the leaves. A burn appears first as a scorched area that later becomes soft and turns brown or black. The burned part of the leaf dies, and of course cuts down the efficiency of the leaf. Some plants are more susceptible to burning than others, so that if burns appear on a

Burned spot caused by too intense light.

plant or two, these plants can be removed to another place. A patch of clear glass may let in too much light, or an imperfection in the glass may act as a lens and focus the light on one leaf, so look for such places. However, if there is much burning throughout the greenhouse, another coat of shading had better be applied.

You will never be able to bring all your plants to exactly the same shade of green, because of inherent differences in the plants themselves. So, when you have made all the adjustments that seem critical, let well enough alone. Over a period of a year or two, if your plants make good, stocky growth, and bear flowers, you can know that they have been well treated. Later, if some of them do not bloom, they may be worth individual experiments.

Adjustment of shading throughout the year follows the same principle of giving the plants all the light they can stand. In the winter the sun's rays travel obliquely through the atmosphere, and are not as strong when they reach the earth. Plants can therefore stand much more light. Most growers give them full sun from the first of November through February, which means 80% to 85% of outdoor intensity, since the glass cuts out some of the light. This can be a pretty general rule. There may be regions where the winter sun is too intense and a light shade is needed.

To prepare for winter, remove some of the shading as fall approaches and the days become shorter, or let the rain do it for you, always watching the plants for signals as to how much light you can let them have. The change to more light must be gradual to avoid the possibility of burning. When a plant that has been shaded is suddenly given full sun it becomes badly burned. But if the light is increased bit by bit over a period of time, the same plant can finally adjust itself to the greater amount of light. Brighter light in the winter is not only a necessity to the plants for making food, but helps to warm the greenhouse and keep it from becoming a damp, unhealthy place. As spring arrives, shading will have to be added gradually until the right amount is reached for summer.

Ventilation. Ventilation is as important to plants as it is to human beings. Similar factors make a close, musty basement unhealthy for people and a too damp, close greenhouse unhealthy for plants. Stagnant, moist air allows the growth of fungi, molds, etc., in either place. In the former, human beings pale for lack of oxygen, in the latter, plants starve for lack of carbon dioxide. Good air circulation would be necessary if only to keep the place clean and invigorating. But, just as important, air from outdoors brings plants their supply of precious carbon dioxide.

Ventilation for orchids begins with circulation of air around the pots themselves. The plants should be set on benches made of wire mesh (hardware cloth) or wood slats, so that air can get under and around the pots. If your greenhouse benches are solid, each plant should be set on an overturned pot or a wire holder. Orchids should never be allowed to stand in a puddle of water.

In the summertime the ventilators should be open most of the day, otherwise the heat will become intolerable. They may even be left open on a very warm night. Since orchids do not like drafts, only roof ventilators should be used, and they should always be raised on the lee side if it is windy, away from the direction of the wind. Then the air moves slowly, without being blown directly on the plants. Some orchid houses have ventilators set in the foundation under the benches, for extra ventilation.

In the winter the ventilators should be open just a crack whenever possible, and especially on bright days. Dark winter days do not allow the plants to make as much food, so the fact that the ventilators cannot be opened on such days is not as significant.

It is best not to let the greenhouse temperature change suddenly. If it should become too cold, let it warm up slowly, and, if it should get extremely hot, let it cool off slowly. Sudden change may do more damage than either extreme.

Chapter III

ADULT CATTLEYAS AND THEIR CARE

(CONTINUED)

Watering. Literature on growing almost any kind of plant is filled with warnings such as "Do not overwater," and "Keep damp but not wet." Roots in general like to be aerated, in fact, must be aerated in order to function efficiently. The warning is doubly important in the case of Cattleyas. It is surprising how nearly dry the mature plants like to be.

The very nature of osmunda fibre makes overwatering a temptation. It is difficult to realize that even when it is nearly dry, the fibres still contain a good bit of water. When the plant is watered, the roots and osmundine quickly absorb their quota, and the rest drains through. If the osmundine is watered again while still wet, it will hold too much water and the interstices become filled, to the exclusion of the much-needed air. Not only does the absence of air hinder the efficiency of the roots, but allows the accumulation of toxic substances and promotes the growth of harmful bacteria. If overwatering is continued, the fibre becomes soggy and sour. The sodden condition allows algae and mosses to cover the wet surface, contributing to a vicious circle of less and less aeration. A pot full of continuously wet, soggy osmundine is usually full of rotten roots. The growth of algae over the surface of the fibre and on the pots themselves is an indication of too much moisture. Mosses often appear and, if kept under control, are not injurious. However, the moss itself may conceal the condition of the fibre. It is also an attraction to, and a hiding place for, slugs and insects.

Orchids in nature receive almost a daily rain, so it may seem odd that when they are in pots they are watered infrequently. However in nature only a few of the roots are imbedded in the substratum, while the rest hang out in the air. The substratum is only a shallow collection of decaying bark and leaves. Hence the orchids are subjected to rapid drying between rains. Your orchids have most of their roots in the osmundine, which, since it is enclosed by the pot, dries out slowly. The difference is comparable to that between the drying rate of a shirt hung on the line and one left crumpled in the laundry basket. The former dries in a few hours, the latter may stay damp for days. The roots in the pot receive a good wetting when watered, and then for some time replenish their supply from contact with the damp osmundine.

Since orchids resist dryness better than continued wetness, it is better to water with a light hand, err on the dry side if necessary, at first. The plants in nature are constantly threatened with drying and have, therefore, been equipped to withstand it. It will take you only a short time to learn how to water them, and that short period of scanty water will not work any hardship on them. In fact, they will be much healthier than if you give them too much water for the same period.

Never use icy water on the plants. The water should be close to the air temperature, somewhere between 50° and 60° F.

Always examine the fibre before watering. It is best not to let the fibre become bone dry between waterings, but to water it just before it dries, while there is still enough moisture in it to make it readily absorbent. Press it between your fingers. If your fingers come away wet, then it is not ready to be watered. If they come away dry, but with a feeling of damp coolness, then it is time for watering. Eventually you will learn how to tell the condition of the osmundine by the weight of the pot. A nearly dry pot is light, and one that is more moist is noticeably heavier.

There can be no regular rule as to how frequently to water. A large pot dries more slowly than a small one. The pots will dry more rapidly in warm, bright weather than in cool, cloudy weather. In the winter you may have to water the large plants only once a week, or once every two weeks, and the smaller ones perhaps twice a week. In the summer, with the ventilators open most of the time and with greater air circulation, the plants will have to be watered more often. Different types of osmundine dry with different rates. The fine, soft kind holds water longer than the coarser fibre. The black, wiry kind, which incidentally is not as good as the brown, dries out rather rapidly. The job of watering can be made easier if you can organize the plants into groups that are in about the same size pots, and dry in about the same length of time. Then, by examining two or three of the group, you can tell whether the whole group is ready for a drink.

Watering should be done in the forenoon, or at least not long after noon, to allow excess water to dry off before the humidity rises at night. If in your examination of the plants you find that they need watering, but the day is cool and rainy, or dark, withhold water until the next day.

Your community water supply will be all right for orchids. Most large growers use it. Some have systems to catch rain water, which is considered ideal, but the slight advantages are hardly worth the trouble and expense. People sometimes doubt that alkaline water is good for orchids. Experiments have been carried out that show that Cattleyas can be grown with water up to a *p*H of 8, which is probably as alkaline as would be found in most city water systems, but do better at *p*H 6.4. From my own experience, I know that they do well with water of *p*H 7.4, which has a mineral content beneficial to the plants. Perhaps also, the alkalinity helps to offset the tendency of the fibre to become acid. Many growers suggest adding bits of charcoal to the pots for this very purpose.

Potting. Mature Cattleyas should be repotted every two years, as this is as long as the fibre remains in good condition. After two years, it rapidly deteriorates, and plants suffer if left longer in it. The ideal time to repot is after flowering, before the new roots make their appearance, or just as they begin growth. If potting is put off until the roots grow long, there is danger of damaging them. You will notice that some plants habitually produce their new roots before or during flowering. With these plants, be particularly careful not to disturb the fibre around the new roots.

Ordinary flower pots may be used, with the drainage hole enlarged to provide better aeration. Pots with slits in the base, "azalea pots," are often used.

Orchids are fitted pretty carefully as to size of pot. Since the fibre is good for two years, a size is chosen that will allow two new growths to be made, with the last one coming close to the rim. It is a waste of osmundine to put a plant in too large a pot, because the plant will have to be repotted before it has been able to make use of all the fibre. More serious is the danger, if a small plant is put in a big pot, of overwatering it at first, since the central part of a large pot takes longer to dry out. To help decide what size of pot a plant will require, measure the distance between the last growth and the one that preceded it. A plant in a 4-inch pot will usually go into a 6-inch, but if the growths are very close together, a 5-inch size may carry it along. By the time a plant is old enough to fill a 7-inch pot, it may have some shriveled pseudobulbs at the back which can be cut off to allow the plant to go back in that size again.

The softer pieces of osmundine might be saved for young seedlings if you have them, and the coarser pieces used for larger plants. Osmundine comes in chunks, just as it has been collected. To prepare it for use, select several pieces, soak them in a bucket of water, rinse a time or two, and squeeze out as much water as you can. Let them drain so that they are just damp when

COLOR PLATE 2. Cattleya Bow Bells.

you are ready to use them. Cut these up into pieces a little smaller than your fist.

The pots should be soaked if new, or washed thoroughly in plain water if they have been used before. If they are the ordinary kind, turn them upside down and with a hammer break in the edges of the hole to make it larger. Broken crock to be used for drainage should also be clean. The pieces should be large for large pots, small for smaller ones, and should fill one-third of the pot. You can lay an arched piece over the hole and drop in the other pieces, or, better, put all pieces vertically. The latter method insures good drainage, and also good air circulation into the bottom of the pot.

The plant to be repotted should be soaking all this time in a pail of water to loosen roots adhering to the pot. Otherwise these roots will stick to the pot and be broken when the plant is knocked out.

Potting equipment consists of a potting stick, a strong stick whittled wedge-shaped at one end, scissors for trimming the plant, cotton string and a metal stake for tying, a cup of nicotine insecticide (Black Leaf 40, or some other) made up according to directions, a soft old toothbrush, and the pot and osmundine prepared as above.

Knock the plant out of the pot, and, beginning at the older end, gently remove the old fibre, particularly the central core which will be more decayed than the outer part. Be careful not to break the brittle roots as you remove the fibre from around them. It is good to leave some of the fibre around the newer roots so as not to disturb them more than necessary. Cut off roots that are soft or decayed, and sever any of the old pseudobulbs that are completely dried or rotten, and the rhizome to which they are attached.

Examine the plant for scale (an insect that lives on the plant and covers itself with a hard shell-like material) which is likely to be found on the rhizome or bulbs. It particularly likes to cluster under the tissue like skin clinging to old bulbs and rhizomes. It is well to remove this skin from the older parts of the plant, but leave it intact on the newer growths. Dip the toothbrush in the insecticide, and gently wash off the tissue and the scale. Be careful not to scrub too hard, lest you injure a dormant bud that might later develop. The leaves can also be washed with the insecticide. (See Chapter XVII for use of DDT.)

Now hold the plant in the pot, with the rhizome at a level just below the rim, and the old end touching the pot at the back. Pack chunks of osmundine around and under the plant, letting the roots be placed naturally between the chunks. Roots that have hung over the edge may possibly be put inside, but if their length or shape is such that you would have to break them, you might

A plant badly in need of repotting.

Enlarge the hole in the new pot by knocking in the edges with a hammer.

Add pieces of broken pot to one-third the depth.

Chop the damp osmundine into chunks a little smaller than your fist.

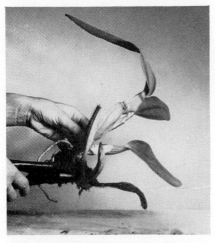

Remove all fibre possible, trim off dead roots, cut off useless back-bulbs. If scale is present, clean it off at this time.

Hold plant in pot with oldest bulb at one edge. Stuff fibre under and around plant.

With a potting stick force fibre down at edge and toward the center. If more fibre is needed, add chunks at the rim and again force toward the center.

The finished product, tied and labeled. Note room in front of lead growth, and rhizome just at fibre level. Pseudobulbs that have been removed will be potted separately.

as well cut them off to begin with. Keep the rhizome on the surface of the fibre. Since it is a stem structure, it must not be buried. Its under surface may rest in a groove, but the upper surface must be uncovered so as to prevent rotting, and so that the buds which break from it will not have to struggle through the fibre to get to the surface. When the plant is well arranged in the fibre, stuff osmundine between the sides of the pot and that which is already in place, forcing it in with the potting stick. Always push it toward the center, as you would push the books together in a bookcase to make room for one more at the end of the row. And hold the rhizome down on the fibre so that it will not hump up out of the pot. The fibre should be firm, with the solid feeling of sod, when you are finished, and about one-half to one-third of an inch below the rim. If you can stick your fingers between the fibre and the pot, it is not firm enough. Pack in some more.

When the plant is firmly potted, drive a wire stake into the fibre and tie each bulb separately to it. Make one wind of string around the stake, then pass it around the bulb and back, and make the tie at the stake. Never wind the string around the bulb for fear of squeezing it. You may think you will never forget what this plant is, but after you have potted several it is easy to mix them. So before you put the plant back on the bench, make sure you have replaced its label. A label stuck in the side of the pot is in danger of being lost. A better way is to tie it to a pseudobulb, or to the wire stake.

Care of Plants after Potting. Plants that have just been repotted need special care until they have become re-established. Their roots have been disturbed, and some may not survive the operation. They are therefore unable for a while to take up moisture from the osmundine. It is useless to pour water into the pots during this time, and not only useless but may be fatal, for the roots are more susceptible to rotting at this time than normally. The leaves will draw on the reservoirs to survive until the old roots are readjusted and new roots have formed, so the plant must be protected from losing too much water during this period.

Newly potted plants should be kept cosily warm and should have a little extra shade for several weeks. Two or three times a day the leaves should be syringed lightly, just enough to dampen them, and moisten the surface of the osmundine. In three or four weeks new roots will appear. When you can see them coming from the new lead, or can see the little green tips showing through the osmundine where they are breaking from old roots, you can start watering in the pot, but be particularly careful not to let the fibre stay wet. Continue syringing for a couple of weeks longer, until the roots are long enough to supply the plant with the water it needs. You can estimate by the size of the roots near the surface when to remove the extra shade and discontinue their syringing. And from then on, treat the plant as established.

Care of Jungle Plants. Jungle plants (unless they have been potted and established by the importer) reach you in a dried condition, without any roots

Steps in reconditioning jungle plants. Left, a plant with new roots just starting. Right, a plant with new growth well along and pseudobulbs filling out. Center, pseudobulbs plump, new growths with sheaths.

at all. The leaves and bulbs are shriveled, the buds dormant. As soon as you unpack them, wash them with clean water, or soapy water followed by a good rinse, and cut away all dead or decayed parts of leaves and bulbs. It is best to pot them at once, but if you cannot get to it right away hang the plants upside down on strings in an airy, shady place in the greenhouse. To enable the bulbs and leaves to plump up, and the dormant buds to become active, syringe the plants lightly, several times a day in bright weather, once a day if it is cloudy. The plants will start their new roots in a few weeks, and the buds will break soon afterward. Some growers leave the plants hanging until these activities begin, but if you follow their example, you will have to be most careful to pot them before growth is too far along. New leads follow their nature and grow upward, which means that when the plants are righted the leads will point downward, straight into the osmundine. Potting at this stage damages the new leads and roots and sets the plants back.

If the plants are left lying on a bench, water from syringing will collect in the joints of the rhizome and around and under the leaves and bulbs, causing decay. When the plants are hanging, they drain perfectly, and air circulating around them prevents rotting.

Although it is good to have a safe method of keeping the plants if potting must be delayed, nothing quite takes the place of immediate potting. With the plants in pots, there is no doubt about their safety. When growth starts, the plants are in position for roots and buds to go in the right direction. And there is no danger, as there is if growth progresses too far while the plants are hanging, either of setting them back or of damaging the new growths.

The odd shapes and sizes of the jungle plants will tax your ingenuity when you try to pot them. Large clumps will have to be divided so as to leave a lead on each half. Plants that grew in humps or spirals, or that grew uphill causing their leaves and rhizome to be nearly parallel, will require some maneuvering to make them fit in pots.

Since the plants are rootless, there is little to do but fill the pots with fibre, packed hard, place the plant on the fibre, and then work in more to hold the rhizome firmly in a groove on the surface. Use a large wire staple to hold the rhizome in place, and tie each bulb to a wire stake. Large plants, or ones with an uneven shape, may need two stakes. Until a plant has rooted, the staple and stakes are all that hold it. If the plant wobbles whenever it is touched, the new roots will be damaged before they have a chance to grow well into the fibre.

Keep the newly potted plants in a shady place, and syringe them until they are well established. Since they are starting from scratch, and have not only to make growth but replace the water they have lost since they were taken off of their native trees, this process takes longer than for other plants. The surface of the osmundine may be kept just damp, to give the new roots a humid atmosphere, but here again, be careful not to let the fibre stay wet. When the bulbs and leaves are plump again, and the roots well developed, they may be treated like any established plants.

Some of these jungle plants will bloom the first season, probably the stronger, stockier ones of the lot. Plants are collected out of bloom, and some may have already started new growth. These tender, immature growths usually do not survive the trip to this country and the fumigation process, but occasionally one does. Then you have the fun of watching the maturation and blooming of a growth that had its beginning in the jungle.

The vigor of the jungle plants will amaze you. Often one plant will send out four or five new leads, and if its blooms are of good quality, will develop into a specimen plant bearing a dozen or more flowers at a time.

Propagation. Until a method was discovered for growing orchids from seed (see Chapter VI) the usual way of increasing the number of plants was propagation by division. It is still a valuable method, but because orchids grow so slowly, it does not net any tremendous increase in numbers of plants except over a long time. A large plant may be divided into several smaller ones, or a group of pseudobulbs may be removed from a large plant as it outgrows its pot. Large divisions become re-established rather quickly, and show no setback from having been separated from the parent plant. But it may take two or three years for a small group of back-bulbs to produce a blooming plant. The method is of particular value in increasing the stock of a choice variety, which might not be reproduced by a repetition of the original cross, since combinations of genes are purely accidental. It is also of value to growers who want more plants that can be counted on to bloom at a certain season. Its special appeal for amateurs is that every group of healthy pseudobulbs is a potential plant, which, for a little growing, costs nothing.

Until a plant is so large that it is outgrowing a 7-inch pot, there is no point in dividing it, as it will produce more flowers if left intact. A planned propagation should always consist of four or five bulbs to give vigor to the new growth.

There are several ways of making propagations. A large plant (one with eight or nine bulbs or more) has two more or less definite areas—the front part that is actively growing, and the back part (or "back-bulbs") that is on the decline. Such a plant may be divided between these two parts. You can cut it in half at potting time and repot each half separately, but a better method is to cut through the rhizome about a year before repotting, leaving the plant otherwise undisturbed. Cutting the rhizome may stimulate a bud to break on the older part, which then has the advantage of becoming established before the two halves are separated. When you finally separate the parts, both will go on growing without any marked setback from the division.

Often a large plant will have several leads, be growing in two or three

distinct "lines." Then a good place to make the division is where one of these
lines takes off from the main stem. Perhaps you can divide the plant into as
many parts as it has leads, provided each one is made up of four or five bulbs,
and you may still get a plant to grow from the back-bulbs, the older part of
the plant from which the leads branch off. Or you might leave the older part
attached to one of the younger lines, and sever it later on.

Even single pseudobulbs may produce good plants. These left-overs from jungle plants
are making new growths. It will take about three years for them to reach flowering size.

There is a nice little trick that can be practiced on plants that are to be
repotted as well as those to be divided. Often a plant will outgrow its pot
before the passing of the two years that would naturally bring it into another
pot. The lead may overlap the edge of the pot and its roots will grow down
over the side. Tie a chunk of osmundine under the lead so that the roots can
grow into it. Then, when you are ready to repot the plant, the roots are
already established in new fibre and can be potted just as they are with less
chance of being disturbed. If you are to divide the plant, this front part will
go on growing without any delay.

I mentioned above that a planned propagation should consist of at least
four or five bulbs. But there will be times when you may have to trim off
just a bulb or two to make a plant fit a pot of convenient size. Save all these
stray pseudobulbs. Put each in a small pot, or several in a large one, and see if

they make new growth. In two or three years, you may have some good plants from them. If a pseudobulb is accidentally broken off of a plant, pot it up and you may be able to save it.

Flowering Plants. Plants in flower should be moved to the cooler, shadier end of the greenhouse. The flowers will last longer if they are not directly in strong light. Having all the flowering plants in one spot is also a convenience, for it is easier to avoid syringing them when the rest of the greenhouse is being hosed. A canopy of cheesecloth makes good shading for flowering plants, with its sides raised when the sun is not directly on it.

Slugs are particularly fond of flower buds, and can wreak destruction in short order. A piece of absorbent cotton tied around the base of the pseudobulb or sheath will keep them away from the flower. The cotton should be removed when blooming is finished.

An orchid flower must be perfect. There are no extra petals that can be removed (as with a rose) to leave an apparently good flower. A few tiny blemishes show up most embarrassingly, so every care should be taken to prevent the slightest injury. Red spider and thrips are enemies to be controlled. Red spider injury consists of minute white spots where the cuticle has been chewed. Tiny, fast moving thrips cause colorless blotches. If they damage the bud, these areas do not develop, and the flowers are badly distorted.

Thrips are destroyed when DDT is used, but red spider is not. To control the latter, spray the plants with a rotenone insecticide. (For details on plant sprays, see Chapter XVII.)

If some sheaths fail to produce flower buds, just leave them alone. Occasionally buds will form when a later growth is ready to flower. But if buds develop in a sheath that is too dry to allow them to push up in it, you can help matters by carefully cutting off the top part of the sheath.

Chapter IV

THE CATTLEYA SPECIES

Many wonderful things have been discovered by accident, and it was an accident that introduced the first Cattleya plants to European botanists. The story goes that in 1818 a Mr. Swainson was collecting mosses and lichens in Brazil, and gathered some heavy, thick-leaved plants to tie around some of his collections for shipment to England. When this material arrived, William Cattley, an eminent horticulturalist, realized that the odd plants were something unusual and rescued them from oblivion. The first of these plants bloomed in 1824, and was studied by Dr. Lindley, a renowned botanist, who found it to be of a genus entirely new to science. Lindley described the plant and gave the new genus the name Cattleya, after its happy possessor. The founding specimen he named *Cattleya labiata autumnalis,* because of its beautiful lip and its habit of flowering in the autumn.

For many years these were the only *Cattleya labiata* in Europe, for no one could rediscover its native habitat. It seems odd that this was so, for many other Cattleyas were discovered in the following decades, *Cattleya Mossiae* in 1838, *Cattleya gigas* in 1848 or '49, *Cattleya Trianaei* in 1856, and so on. No great numbers were imported and many plants did not survive the long voyage. The Cattleyas were highly prized by horticulturalists and brought high prices from wealthy collectors, but their future in the commercial market was not realized until 1891. In that year a tremendous number of *Cattleya labiata* were found, and their purchase by two different companies, one English and one Belgian, caused quite a stir in orchid circles. There ensued a heated argument as to whether these were indeed the true *Cattleya labiata autumnalis,* each company hoping that it alone held the prize. Finally it was established that all of them were the real *labiata.* Possession of so many of the same species caused the price to drop from about $20 to about $1 per plant.

That was the beginning of the great demand for Cattleyas for the commercial market. Improved steamship travel sent a stream of collectors to South America who sent back hundreds of thousands of Cattleya plants to importers in their various countries. These were sold at auction to commercial growers, horticulturalists, and amateur growers.

THE LABIATA GROUP

The tremendous variety exhibited by the Cattleyas ranges from little green flowers speckled with brown or purple to the large "orchid" colored flowers so familiar to all of us. Amateur and commercial growers long ago chose the latter, or labiata type as the ideal Cattleya, and almost all of those grown

Cattleya labiata, the founding species of the genus.

today on a commercial scale are of this type. The labiata group is made up of a number of species so similar to *Cattleya labiata* in habit and appearance that they were once considered botanically to be merely varieties of that species. For convenience and brevity, it became customary to treat them as separate species, but *Cattleya Mossiae* was once *Cattleya labiata,* variety *Mossiae, Cattleya Trianaei* was once *Cattleya labiata,* variety *Trianaei,* and so on for *C. Dowiana, C. Gaskelliana, C. gigas, C. Lueddemanniana, C. Mendelii, C. Percivaliana, C. Schroederae,* and *C. Warneri.*

The labiata group are the most showy of the Cattleyas. All have a large lip, the two side lobes of which fold up to form a tube around the column. The lower part of the lip, called the middle lobe, is continuous with the side lobes. It spreads wide and is usually handsomely ruffled and richly colored. This brilliant lip stands out against a background of two wide, flaring petals and three evenly spaced sepals. Their shape is simple, dignified, and graceful, and, in combination with their lovely coloring, gives them perpetual charm. When you consider along with their beauty their quality of lasting a long time in perfection, it is easy to see why they have found favor as the most valuable of the Cattleyas.

Since these are the most frequently grown, it would be of value to consider for a moment how to select good specimens. The condition of the plant is important. It should be sturdy, clean, well rooted, and should (unless it is a recently made propagation) show evidence of having bloomed.

The quality of the flowers is judged on the basis of several features, of which the most important are size, shape, color, texture, and posture. In any species an individual is judged in comparison to the best that that species is capable of producing. Size varies from species to species, from the huge 8–9 inch spread of *C. gigas* to the modest 5 inches of *C. Percivaliana*. The species differ from each other in general coloring and marking, and in the shape and character of the flower parts.

A good bloom should be of generous size, with pure, fresh coloring. The petals should be broad and full, filling the space between the sepals, and sepals should stand out straight from the base and not bend back toward the stem. The lip in some species is more nearly tubular than in others, but in any case it is desirable that the lower part should open out wide. The whole flower should hold itself nicely on the stem, with its face straight toward you. The texture or substance of the flower should be firm and turgid, which gives it added beauty and better keeping quality.

In any species there will be some blooms that fall short of the best in one or more of these characteristics. Some may be well colored but too small, or large but poorly colored. Others may have excellent petals and sepals but a poorly shaped lip, and so on. Nothing could be prettier than some of the small, brilliantly colored *C. Trianaei* I have seen, and you might prefer them for your personal use, but they would bring very little on the market and would suffer by comparison with larger blooms in a flower show. Obviously, the choice ones are most in demand and the plants are more expensive. They are the pride of collectors and are selected for use in hybridization.

Outstanding color variations in a species are often distinguished by a name. If the variety occurs in considerable numbers in nature, it may be designated by a botanical term, as *Cattleya Percivaliana,* var. *grandiflora.*

Or if it is a particularly handsome individual its owner may name it himself.

It is natural to have personal favorites among these Cattleyas, but each is lovely in its own way. I should like to translate for you a bit from an old book, "Les Cattleya" by Léon Duval, a French orchid grower, 1907. "It is no more just to establish comparisons or classes of beauty among certain Cattleya than it would be to compare certain works of art; let us leave to beautiful plants their own special qualities, which command our admiration for these same qualities, and not establish a royalty among the Cattleya. . . ."

Selection of species for a beginning collection will be discussed later, but a few species from the labiata group should be present in any collection, chosen to give a sequence of flowers throughout the year.

OTHER CATTLEYAS

While emphasis is laid on the handful of species that are best known and in greatest demand, the other members of the genus have a definite appeal, particularly for the amateur grower who wants variety in his collection. Many of them are distinctive and attractive, quite different from the labiata type. Some have been used in hybridization. As time goes on, I believe that these little known species will become more popular for the sake of their unusual characteristics. Among them are found little flowers of green, yellow, and bronze, as well as purple and rose, some of them daintily or boldly speckled with contrasting colors. They are smaller than those of the labiata group, but often make up for it by producing ten to twenty blossoms on a stem.

SEASONAL HABITS OF THE CATTLEYAS

A glance at the flowering times of Cattleyas might raise the question, why do the species bloom at such different times when they come from regions where the climate is so uniform throughout the year? What is it that sets the pattern of one species to flower in January, another in October, and another in May?

The tropical rain-forests, where most of the Cattleyas grow, do not have distinct wet and dry seasons, nor cold and warm seasons. There are, instead, seasons of more moisture or less moisture (seasons when it rains and seasons when it pours) in a constantly humid climate. During the period of less moisture there are still frequent rains. The ground vegetation is never dry at any time of the year. But in the upper levels of the rain-forests, the tree branches holding epiphytic plants are subject at all times of the year to a drier atmosphere than that which prevails on the ground.

It is generally supposed that the vegetation in the tropical rain-forests is constantly in growth, that there are no periods of dormancy or rest such as we are familiar with in the temperate zone, where seasonal changes are more marked. This impression is given by the constantly green appearance of the forest. But closer study reveals that the plants in the forest have their own cycles of growth, flowering, and rest, just as do those in the temperate zone. Trees lose their leaves and form new foliage. Evergreen plants and trees have periods of rest. But the cycle of one kind of plant does not coincide with the cycles of its neighbors, so that at all times there are plants in flower, plants at rest, and plants making new growth. In some the branches become independent of each other, and on the same tree some may be flowering while others are losing their foliage.

Dr. A. W. F. Schimper, one of the great botanists of the end of the nineteenth century and the man who opened up the field of ecology (the study of living things in their natural environment), studied vegetation in all parts of the world. His masterpiece "Plant Geography" includes fascinating descriptions of plant life in the rain-forests, and his observations and theories have been substantiated many times by modern botanists. Of the periodic phenomena of plant life Schimper says, "The less marked the periodicity of the climate is, the less dependent on its influence is the periodicity of the plant. Internal causes are mainly or solely responsible for the alternation of rest and of activity in a nearly uniform climate. Such a rhythmic change is however never abandoned, for it arises from the nature of living organisms and not from external conditions; its connection with external conditions is a secondary feature—an adaptation."

Thus, under externally identical conditions, plants establish their own cycle of behavior in response to their inherent internal make-up, so that side by side different plants exhibit different phases of their cycle. This accounts for the fact that each species of Cattleya has its own pattern of growth, bloom, and rest, and that even within one limited region, each species maintains its own habit. Within the general cycle of a species, individual plants follow their own inherent patterns. For instance, the species *C. gigas* usually flowers from May to July, yet there are individual plants that always flower in May, others that always flower in June, and still others that always flower in July. Some few plants will bloom in August or September.

The term "rest" applied to plants is a bit deceiving. It does not mean complete inactivity, even in regions where plants seem dormant in the winter.

As explained by Schimper, ". . . There are no periods of rest for the vital processes, but only resting periods for certain functions. A plant during its hibernation is by no means inactive." When an orchid plant is not producing flowers or new vegetative growth, we say that it is in a period of rest. Yet during this time the plant is making, using, and storing food, and invisible changes are going on, which when they have reached a certain point, cause the buds to begin growth, new roots to form, and the plant to enter a new period of growth.

The development of flower buds is also affected by conditions within the plant. The tissues which will produce flowers are already determined when the new lead is about 4 to 6 inches long, so that flowering depends on the condition of the plant long before the sheath emerges. In some species as soon as the sheath is formed, the flower buds grow up in it and flowering follows immediately on the period of growth. In other species, after the leaf and sheath are formed the flower buds wait for several months before they develop.

Day length does not vary appreciably from season to season near the equator, but in this country orchids are subjected to alternately longer and shorter days. It has been found that many other types of plants are sensitive to length of day, that some flower only when the days are short, others only when days are long. Still others are day-neutral, and their flowering seems not to depend on day length. Exploratory research has shown that some orchids are sensitive to length of day. For instance fall flowering Cattleya species and hybrids make their growth in the summer but do not develop buds in the sheath until the days become short. It has been found that if the days are kept long by artificial means, by turning on lights in the greenhouse at sundown, their flowering can be delayed at will until winter or spring. For practical purposes this is done by spacing 100 watt bulbs ten feet apart in the greenhouse, and keeping them on for four hours every evening, or all night on alternate nights. Artificial lighting is started well before buds develop in the sheath, perhaps as early as July, and is continued until two months before flowers are desired. When the extra light is discontinued, the flower buds start to develop.

It is not unreasonable to expect that the time of flowering may be controllable for species and hybrids that habitually flower in the winter, spring, or summer. The exploration of possible relationships between day length and temperature may prove fruitful. Future research will give more data from time to time, on the control not only of flowering of Cattleyas but of other kinds of orchids as well.

It has been seen that there are no dry seasons in the native habitats of Cattleyas, and that even during the seasons of heaviest rainfall they are subject to some drying between rains. There follows the natural conclusion that there is no reason to treat Cattleyas differently when at rest than when they are in growth. And this is true, at least to the point that Cattleyas do not need an enforced drying-out as do some other types of plant. However, it is well to remember always that orchids in a greenhouse are not in their native forests. We must always take particular care to give the plants only what water they need. Activity on a large scale is lessened when the plants are at rest, and they do not use as much water as when they are actively growing. In order to avoid oversaturation of the roots in their less active state, watering should be less frequent. It is difficult to give a rigid schedule, since so much depends on the weather, size of pots, and type of fibre. A method that you can try, and vary judiciously according to daily conditions, is to double the interval between watering, starting a month after flowering, and continuing until the first signs of new growth appear.

However, orchids are not machines. There are always a few plants that do not go according to the rule. Some plants may start to make new growth instead of observing a period of rest. There is nothing to worry about in such cases. Just continue to treat them as actively growing plants. *C. Mossiae* often does this. After it flowers in the spring, it regularly makes new growth, and then rests through the winter with its sheaths formed, to flower the following spring. But sometimes a plant will start a second new growth in the fall, which will proceed to grow all winter and will flower along with the first growth in the spring.

THE SPECIES

The species are about evenly divided in numbers between those in which the pseudobulbs bear a single leaf and those in which the pseudobulbs bear two or three leaves.

GROUP I. ONE-LEAVED SPECIES

This group includes all of the "labiata" group, and a few others less well known but which have similar characters. The one species distinctly different from the rest is the last one of the group.

Cattleya Dowiana. A beautiful nankeen yellow with a large purple lip lined with gold. Once considered a variety of labiata. It is not grown commercially now as the flowers do not keep well, but has contributed its yellow color to many hybrids. The flowers are 6–7 inches across, occurring 2–6 in a cluster. Discovered in Costa Rica in 1848 by a Polish gardener, Warscewicz. However, the specimens that he sent to Europe arrived in poor condition, and it was not until 1864 that good specimens were obtained by Mr. Arce and purchased by Messrs. Veitch and Sons, English horticulturalists, who flowered it for the first time. The species was named for Captain Dow, whose ship carried many an orchid hunter and many a cargo of orchid plants. It is the most celebrated of Costa Rican orchids, but is quite rare now, having been nearly cleared out by collectors.

Cattleya Dowiana, variety *aurea.* Occurs in Colombia, entirely separated from the *C. Dowiana* of Costa Rica. The flowers are a deeper yellow and the lip is more copiously marked with gold. It is a large plant, similar in every way to *Cattleya Dowiana.* Its period of vegetative growth is from May to September, and flowering follows immediately in September and October. It rests during the winter.

Cattleya Eldorado. Pale rosy-lilac with slender petals, and lip of the same color but marked with a central orange blotch surrounded by white and purple. A variety of labiata, but not grown commercially. Discovered in Brazil in 1866. Flowers in late summer and fall.

Cattleya Gaskelliana. Large, fragrant, handsome flowers, 6–7 inches across. The sepals and petals are usually purple-violet, suffused with white, occasionally marked with a median band of white. The lip is generous in proportions, the tube the same color as the petals. The front lobe of the lip is deep violet with a pale border, the throat streaked with yellow and marked on each side by a spot of yellowish white. French growers used to call this species *"Cattleya chou"* (Cattleya cabbage) because it is so easy to grow. It is a variety of labiata and is popular commercially, though not as extensively grown as some others. Vegetative growth starts in about April and flowering follows immediately, from July to September, after which it rests during the winter. Occurs in Venezuela and Brazil, where it grows on rocks at elevations from 500 to 3000 feet. Introduced into England from Venezuela in 1884 or '85. It was named for a Mr. Gaskell of Woolton. There is a white variety, alba, and one that has white petals and sepals with the front lobe of the lip crimson.

Cattleya gigas. This species should be correctly called *Cattleya Warscewiczii,* but the name gigas is commonly used and will be found in lists and catalogues. It was discovered in 1848 or '49 in Colombia by the same man who found *Cattleya Dowiana.* This is the largest flowered of all the Cattleyas, the blooms being 7–9 inches in diameter, and is the most showy. The petals and sepals are rosy-lilac, and the huge, rich red-violet lip is marked with two brilliant yellow eyes. The edge of the lip is ruffled and has a pale border. *C. gigas* is one of the most popular of the labiata group, both with amateurs and commercial growers. It needs especially good light, with care not to burn or yellow the leaves, and likes a warm, airy position. The species flowers from late May to September. The earlier blooming plants start their new growth in January, while those that will bloom later on wait to begin new growth until about March. Flowering follows as soon as the growth is formed. The resting period is from October to January. Its white variety, alba, is the rarest of all Cattleyas.

Cattleya labiata. Beautifully proportioned flowers, of wonderful texture, and a rich, vibrant rose, almost luminous in quality. The dainty lip is modest in size, with the throat more open than tube-like. The front lobe of the lip is ruffled, deep red-violet with darker lines which run through two orange spots into the yellow throat. The flowers keep a long time. This species is very popular commercially, and is one of the most uniform, having a low percentage of plants that give poor blooms. *Cattleya labiata* starts its growth in March or April, and flowers without pause in the fall, from October through November. The flower buds are produced in a double sheath, one sheath within the other. The period of rest, except for those that might have started new growth in the fall, is from December to March. Among the many color variations are a white form, var. *alba,* and one which has white petals and sepals with a crimson lip, var. *Cooksoniae.* A native of Brazil, discovered in 1818.

Cattleya Lawrenceana. A small flowered species, not grown commercially, with reddish-brown pseudobulbs. The flowers are 4–5 inches across, 5–8 in a cluster. The petals are rather slender, and the lip small and tube-like. The color varies from pale rosy-purple to white, and the front lobe of the lip is purple with a maroon blotch. Occurs in British Guiana, where it was discovered about 1882. It grows actively during the summer and remains through the winter with the sheaths formed, to flower in the spring.

Cattleya Lueddemanniana, also called *Cattleya speciosissima.* Closely resembles *Cattleya labiata,* and was once considered a variety of that species. The flowers are rose-purple, suffused with white, the front lobe of the lip is amethyst-purple, and lines of this color extend into the throat between two yellow blotches. Since it is one of the few whose handling is rather tricky, it is not grown commercially. The clue to its behavior is probably that it grows natively under such a variety of conditions that the plants show more individual differences than found in most species. It grows actively from spring to fall, and can flower anywhere from April to September. Its period of lessened activity is November to February. Occurs in Venezuela, where it was discovered in 1850. It was named by Professor Reichenbach for Mr. Lueddeman, for many years his chief gardener and a well-known horticulturalist. There is a white form, var. *alba*.

Cattleya luteola. Charming little yellow flowers, only 2 inches across, with petals about the same width as the sepals, and a small tubular lip that is yellow or whitish, often streaked with purple. The pseudobulbs are 2–3 inches tall and leaves 3–4 inches long. Occurs in Brazil, where it was discovered in 1853.

Cattleya maxima. The flowers, though large and nicely colored, have slender parts and lack compactness. Sepals and petals are lilac or pale rose, the front lobe of the lip is ruffled, pale rose or a deeper shade, with a central stripe of yellow from which radiate darker lines, and a pale border. Not grown much now, though it was once very popular. Occurs in Ecuador and Peru. Flowers in the fall.

Cattleya Mendelii. One of the most distinct of the labiata group, with large delicately colored flowers, 7–8

Cattleya Mendelii, a jungle plant flowering a few months after arriving in this country.

inches across. The sepals and petals are whitish or pale rose, and the lip is generous in size with the outer lobe very much ruffled and marked with a clean-cut patch of purple. The throat is yellow, more or less streaked with crimson. Easy to grow, and much loved by amateurs. It is also grown commercially, though not to as great an extent as some others. Its native habitat is Colombia, where it was discovered in 1870, and named for Samuel Mendel, an English orchid lover. In habit it is similar to *Cattleya Mossiae* (below), grows from June through September, and waits through the winter after the sheaths are formed to bloom in April and May.

Cattleya Mossiae. Sometimes called the Queen of the Orchids. A beautiful species, rivaling *Cattleya gigas* in richness of coloring, whose spring flowering season gives it great value for Easter and Mother's Day. It is rosy-lilac in color, with wide, beautifully ruffled petals. The lip is as wide as or wider than the petals, the broad front lobe frilled, mottled with violet-purple, with a pale border. The throat is yellow, striped with purple. It was discovered in 1836 in Venezuela, where it grows in large quantities, and flowered for the first time in the collection of a Mr. Moss, after whose wife it was named. It has been collected in such a ruthless way that it is threatened with extinction, and the Venezuelan government has had to place a temporary embargo on its export to give it a chance to reproduce. There is wide variation in coloring in this species including some that are rather pale and not too desirable. But there are many magnificent named varieties, among them several whites of which the best known is var. *Wageneri,* white with a yellow spot on the lip. The species grows during the summer and early fall, and waits through the winter with its sheaths formed to flower in April and May. Some individuals flower as late as August.

Cattleya Percivaliana. One of the smaller flowered of the labiata group, but a lovely orchid. The richly colored flowers are 4–5 inches across, varying from light to deep rose, and are nicely proportioned. The dainty, rather short lip has a pale, exquisitely frilled border surrounding a deep maroon center. The throat is orange, variegated with deep violet. Flowers at Christmas time, which gives it commercial value, though it does not bring as much on the market as *Cattleya Trianaei.* Occurs in Venezuela, and introduced in 1882 to England by Sander. Named after Mr. R. Percival, an English orchid grower. There is great variation in the species from good to poor quality. Growth may start in January, without any rest after flowering, or it may wait to begin new growth in April or May. Sheaths are formed by the end of the summer, but the flower buds wait until October to begin development. Flowers in December.

Cattleya Rex. Large cream white to pale yellow flowers, attractive but seldom grown. The lip is of good size, the throat yellow veined with purple, the front lobe crimson lightly veined, with a white, ruffled border. Occurs in the Peruvian Andes. Growth starts in April, and the plants flower in September, after which they rest during the winter.

Cattleya Schroederae. Lovely fragrant flowers, entirely pale rose faintly suffused with white, except that the lip has yellow or deep rose in the throat. It was originally designated a variety of *Cattleya Trianaei,* and therefore belongs in the labiata group. However, it is much more ruffled than *Cattleya Trianaei* and has a later blooming season, rivaling *Cattleya Mossiae* for the Easter trade. Another of the handsome Colombian orchids, discovered in 1885 or '86, and named for Baroness Schroeder, wife of a famous orchid grower. It grows from May through September, and then, like *C. Mossiae,* waits through the winter with the sheaths formed. The flower buds start to develop about the first of January, and open from March to May. The flowers mature more slowly than some other species, and should not be cut until they have been open four or five days. There are many named varieties, a white form and several near-white.

Cattleya Trianaei. The flowers of this species are a little more plain, the petals and lip a little less ruffled than others of the labiata group, but they are still lovely, and a handsome specimen ranks with the best of the Cattleyas. The sepals and petals are pale pinkish-lavender. The lip is a little narrower than the petals, but sometimes equal their width. The front lobe is usually purple, but is often a brilliant crimson hardly rivaled among the Cattleyas. The pale border of the lip varies in width, being fairly wide in some and hardly discernible in others. The throat is yellow, faintly streaked with deeper yellow. The average size of the flowers is about 6 inches, with a range from 3 to 7 inches. It is a species in which there is a great variation in coloring, and also a species that pro-

Cattleya Trianaei growing in a Florida garden. This beautiful species produces its mid-winter blooms from Christmas to Valentine's Day. (Courtesy of H. F. Loomis)

duces a high percentage of poor flowers. Because of its mid-winter blooming season, it has been in great demand among commercial growers for many years, and collectors have been pressed to find enough wild plants to fill their orders. The number of poor specimens of *Trianaei* arriving in this country today is a reflection of this situation. Collectors have evidently cleared out the best types of plants and are now going into regions that produce less desirable flowers. *Cattleya Trianaei* is a native of Colombia, where it was discovered in 1856 by the celebrated traveler, J. Linden. The species was named for José Triana, a well-known botanist of Bogota, who died in Paris. The blooming season extends from late December through March, with the largest number flowering in January. New growth starts a short time after flowering, about in March or April, and continues until August, at which time the sheaths are completely formed. The flower buds wait until October to begin developing. Among the varieties is a white form.

Cattleya Warneri. A lovely member of the labiata group, similar to

Cattleya labiata, but with larger flowers. The sepals and petals are rose-lilac, the front lobe of the lip is heavily ruffled and bright purple. The throat is yellow-orange, streaked with white or pale violet. Growth starts in February and the flowers develop as soon as the sheaths are formed, opening during May and June. Its period of lessened activity is during the winter. Occurs in South Brazil and discovered in 1859. There is a lovely white form, var. *alba,* that has a yellow throat.

Cattleya Walkeriana, welcome to any collection for its fragrance and its pretty shape and coloring. (Courtesy of H. F. Loomis)

Cattleya Walkeriana. A dwarf species with a flower quite distinct from the labiata type, but classed with this group because its stocky little pseudobulbs bear single leaves. The flowers are 3–5 inches in diameter, delightfully fragrant, rose-lilac in color, with a jaunty little fleshy lip. The lobes of the lip, instead of being continuous as in the labiata type, are cut in at the sides. The front lobe is triangular, spreading out from under the tip of the column, yellow and purple, veined with a brighter shade of purple. The pink side lobes turn up around the column like flaring wings of a collar, leaving the column exposed. This species produces its flowers on a stem that arises from the base of the pseudobulb instead of at its top. It is a native of western Brazil, where there are definite wet and dry seasons. Discovered in 1839, and brought to Europe for the first time in 1848. Its flowering season is irregular, extending from fall to spring, and the flowers last for six weeks. The plants require much less water during their period of rest.

GROUP II

These are the species whose pseudobulbs bear two or three leaves. There is great variety in this group, both in size and character of the plants, and in the coloring of the flowers, some of which are quite startlingly marked with brown or black-purple.

Cattleya Aclandiae. Greenish-yellow flowers, barred and spotted with chocolate brown, with a bright rose-purple lip. The short side lobes curve up over the column, and the middle lobe is fleshy in the center, fiddle-shaped.

The plants are small, and the flowers 4 inches across. Discovered in Brazil in 1839. Blooms in June and July.

Cattleya amethystoglossa. Daintily colored, attractive flowers, 3½–5 inches across, 5–8 in a cluster. Sepals and petals are white suffused with rose-purple, and spotted with amethyst. The lip has small, erect side lobes, and a broad, rounded middle lobe that is violet-purple marked with radiating ridges of papillae. The plants are very tall, with pseudobulbs reaching 3 feet, and bearing two leaves 6–12 inches long. Discovered in Brazil in 1862. Flowers in mid-summer.

Cattleya bicolor. A remarkable flower, olive-green tinged with copperish brown, with a bright crimson tongue-like lip that has no side lobes and leaves the column completely exposed. The pseudobulbs are tall and jointed, 1–3 feet high, bearing two leaves 4–6 inches long. This species has been used in hybridization with Cattleyas of the labiata group. Discovered in Brazil in 1837. It blooms during spring and early summer, producing 8–10 flowers on a stem which last a long time.

Cattleya Bowringiana. A strong growing plant that produces sometimes as many as 20 flowers on a stem and is often used in hybridization with members of the labiata group. The flowers are small, less than 3 inches across, the sepals and petals rose-purple. The lip is similar to the labiata type, deep purple with white in the throat. It grows on rocks and rubble near streams in British Honduras, and needs a little more water than most Cattleyas. Grows during the spring and summer, flowers in October and November, and has a short mid-winter rest. Discovered in 1884.

Cattleya citrina. An attractive and unusual plant that has the habit of growing with its head hanging down. The flowers are spicily fragrant, yellow except for the white border of the tubular lip, and the sepals and petals enfold the lip giving the flower the appearance of an upside down tulip. The bloom lasts a long time in perfection. The pseudobulbs are egg-shaped and bear 2 or 3 greyish leaves 4–7 inches long. The plant should be grown in a basket suspended in a tilted position to allow the growths to hang over the edge. Discovered in Mexico in the 17th century by the Jesuit, Hernandez, but it was not until 1859 that any large number of plants reached Europe. Flowers in late spring and early summer.

Cattleya dolosa. Rose-magenta flowers with the front lobe of the lip amethyst-purple marked with yellow. The little side lobes of the lip are erect. Resembles *Cattleya Walkeriana,* of which it was once called a variety, but produces its flowers from the top of the pseudobulb. Occurs in Brazil.

Cattleya Forbesii. Pale yellow-green flowers, 3–4 inches across. The lip is small and yellow, the side lobes forming a tube, the inside of which is streaked with red, while the roundish front lobe has a bright yellow center marked with purple. Discovered in South Brazil in 1823. Flowers in mid-summer, rests during the winter.

Cattleya granulosa. Well worth growing because of its striking flowers, olive-green, sometimes yellowish brown, spotted with crimson-purple or red, occurring 5–9 in a cluster. The white side lobes of the lip form a tube that is yellow or rose inside, while the pale middle lobe is marked with crimson papillae. Occurs in Guatemala and Brazil, and discovered in the latter country in 1840. Flowers in late summer, and the flowers last a long time.

Cattleya guttata. Beautiful yellow-green flowers spotted with deep purple. The lip has small white side lobes, and a spreading middle lobe that is amethyst-purple marked with papillae. The pseudobulbs reach 30 inches in height, and bear two leaves 5–9 inches long. The flowers are 3–4 inches across, 5–10 in a cluster. Discovered in South Brazil in 1827. Flowering season is from summer to fall.

Cattleya Harrisoniana. A popularly grown and attractive species. The flowers are bright rose-lilac, 4–4½ inches across, 2–5 in a cluster. The tube of the lip is the same color as the flower, while the ruffled middle lobe is a deeper shade marked with a large orange spot. The blooming season is August to October and the flowers last a long time. Occurs in Brazil.

Cattleya intermedia. A charming species, with flowers 4–5 inches across of delicate rose or white with a bright rose-purple lip. The sepals and petals are of about equal size. The lip is small, with the side lobes rounded and the middle lobe ruffled. Occurs in South Brazil, discovered in 1824. Flowers through the summer.

Cattleya Leopoldii. Lovely clusters of 10–25 fragrant flowers, each 3–4 inches across. The sepals and wavy petals are brown, spotted with purple. The small side lobes of the lip are pointed, the middle lobe is spreading and wavy, bright amethyst-purple, and covered with lines of papillae and small fleshy spots. Occurs in South Brazil. Flowers in early fall.

Cattleya Loddigesii. One of the most common orchids of Brazil. Sepals and petals are rose-lilac. The lip has rounded side lobes and a nearly round middle lobe quite ruffled at the outer edge, pale amethyst with yellow at the base. The flowers are 3–4½ inches across, 2–5 in a cluster. Blooms in late summer and the flowers last three or four weeks.

Cattleya nobilior. This species produces its flowering growth from the base of the pseudobulb (as does *Cattleya Walkeriana*). The purple-lilac flowers are very fragrant, 3–4½ inches across, but only one or two on a stem. The lip is fleshy, the side lobes folding up over the column, the middle lobe broad and yellow. Occurs in Brazil.

Cattleya Schilleriana. Rather large, striking flowers, 4–5 inches across, olive-green tinted with brown and spotted with black-purple. The side lobes of the lip are white externally, marked with purple inside, while the middle lobe is kidney-shaped, crimson, with a white margin and streaks of white. Discovered in Brazil in 1857. Flowers from June to September.

Cattleya Skinneri. Called the "Flower of San Sebastian" in its native Costa Rica and used by the natives to decorate their altars and the roofs of their houses. The flowers are 3½–5 inches across, entirely rose-purple except for white in the throat, and grow 5–10 on a stem. The lip is similar in character to the labiata type, but slightly more tubular. This is a popular species and widely grown. Also grows in Guatemala, where it was discovered in 1836. Flowers in late spring.

Cattleya Victoria Regina. Grows with *Cattleya labiata* and *Cattleya Leopoldii* and may be a natural hybrid between the two. Its pseudobulbs bear sometimes one, sometimes two leaves, and this may be proof of its hybrid nature. The flowers are very attractive, intermediate between *labiata* and *Leopoldii* in size. Sepals are purple tinged with yellow, the petals are purple tinged with violet, and both are striated with darker purple. The lip has small, blunt side lobes, and a broad, ruffled, kidney-shaped front lobe, rose-violet and yellow. Discovered in Pernambuco in 1891. Its flowering time is variable.

Cattleya violacea. Very lovely fragrant, bright rose-purple flowers 4–5 inches across. The lip is fleshy, deep purple-violet, with triangular side lobes that expose the column, and a rounded, ruffled front lobe marked with a patch of yellow streaked with purple. Occurs at rather low altitudes in the northern part of South America, where the temperature is quite hot. Can be adapted to the usual Cattleya temperatures but needs a warm place in the greenhouse and rather more water. Flowers through the summer.

Chapter V

HYBRIDS

In 1852 orchids were still new to Europeans. People were busy just learning to know them and grow them. The possibilities of hybridization were apparently unthought of until a surgeon saw how it could be done and suggested it to an orchid grower. The surgeon was a Dr. Harris of Exeter, and the grower, Mr. J. Dominy, foreman of the firm of Veitch and Sons. In 1852 with Dr. Harris' help, Mr. Dominy performed the first hand pollination, and in 1856 the first hybrid orchid flowered, *Calanthe Dominii* (*Calanthe Masuca* × *Calanthe furcata*). Mr. Dominy worked for twenty years, and produced about 25 hybrids, among them, in 1863, the first bi-generic hybrid, *Laeliocattleya Exoniensis* (*Cattleya Mossiae* × *Laelia crispa*).

The exciting note injected into orchid growing by Dr. Harris had a powerful reaction. The best of the newly produced hybrids created a sensation at exhibitions. Old orchid books are full of glowing accounts of the new marvels, and predict wonderful things to come. Mr. Dominy worked alone in the field for most of the twenty years, for it was not until 1871 that a hybrid was produced by someone else. No one at that time could have foreseen the future extent of hybridization during the next seventy-five years. In 1890 there were 200 crosses registered. Now there are thousands upon thousands, and the number grows each year.

A large proportion of the best hybrids have been made by experienced growers, but amateurs have had a hand in hybridization, too. Success on both sides was largely a matter of chance, and indeed still is. Curiosity plus the desire to create something unusual prompted nearly everyone to cross whatever orchids he had at hand, in the hope that he would achieve some striking result. Many of the crosses thus made have not been wise, and have only cluttered the lists. But it was that great desire to see what would come of odd matings that produced the first Sophrocattleya in 1886, the first Brassocattleya in 1889, the first Sophrolaelia in 1894, and the first tri-generic hybrid, *Brassolaeliocattleya Lawrencei,* in 1897.

The nature of orchids themselves, in being slow to mature and flower, necessitated accurate records, lest the parentage of seedlings be forgotten. The great interest in hybrids led to the registration of crosses, not only to insure credit to the first person to think of a cross, but to save others from repeating what had already been tried. The fortunate result of these factors has been the development of an orchid genealogy as accurate and complete as any family history in existence.

It early became the custom to give a hybrid a name of its own. At first this was done to honor the creator of a hybrid or someone who had achieved fame in the orchid world. The system gives us a handy way to identify the complicated hybrids that exist today. It would be impossible to call an orchid by the names of a dozen or more ancestors. It is even awkward to give the immediate parentage of a plant every time we want to speak of it. For instance, how much more simple it is to say *Cattleya Hardyana,* than to say *Cattleya Dowiana, aurea* by *Cattleya gigas.* Nowadays growers are pressed to find names that have not already been used. Hybrids are named after the gods of ancient mythology, the letters of the Greek alphabet, presidents, generals, opera stars, and the grower's own relatives and friends.

Once a name has been given to a cross, it stands for any repetition of that cross. For instance, *Cattleya Fabia* is *Cattleya Dowiana* × *Cattleya labiata,* and every time those two species are mated the offspring must be called *Cattleya Fabia. Cattleya Fabia* × *Cattleya Hardyana* produced *Cattleya Princess Royal,* while the mating of the white forms produced *Cattleya Princess Royal, alba.* Knowing the name of any hybrid enables you to look up its complete ancestry. For this purpose, Sander's *Complete List of Orchid Hybrids,* complete to January 1, 1946, 1947 edition ($25, obtainable through the American Orchid Society, Inc.), is indispensable. It is the complete record of registered hybrids, of all genera, from the time of Mr. Dominy's work to the present day.

Primary crosses, crosses between two species, are likely to yield plants that are intermediate between the parents, and more or less uniform. But crosses between two hybrids are more complicated and show great variety among the offspring. A hybrid is made up of factors inherited from each of its parents and, when two hybrids are mated, these factors recombine in many ways. The offspring will show various combinations of the characteristics of the parent plants, as well as reversions to many of the types found in their ancestry. The same thing happens when a hybrid is self-pollinated, for its inherited characteristics also recombine to give a number of different kinds of offspring. The only way to reproduce a specific hybrid is to repeat the cross that made it originally, or to increase the plant itself by propagation.

The fascination of achieving new combinations of characters keeps people interested in hybridization, yet there is ever present the problem of what to do with poor plants that crop up in many (if not most) crosses. A hybrid is made in order to combine the good qualities of one flower with the good qualities of another. However, the looked-for combination may occur in only a few of the offspring, while the rest may be an odd assortment of types. Among the assortment may be some perfectly acceptable things, but also

Laeliocattleya Princess Margaret, a colored hybrid that illustrates the qualities sought for in making hybrids. Sepals broad and straight, petals full and round, lip broad, generously ruffled, and brightly marked. (Courtesy H. Patterson and Sons)

Cattleya Marion Davies, a pure white hybrid that embodies the desirable characteristics of broad sepals, broad, straight petals, and full lip. If self-pollinated, this white will give all white offspring. (Courtesy of H. Patterson and Sons)

some entirely undesirable. While the latter are a disappointment, the grower of hybrids must take them as they come. The poor ones as well as the good ones all travel under the name given to the cross, which explains why two plants of the same name may be priced at $5 and $100, respectively.

Careful growers have cut down the percentage of poor hybrids by breeding parent plants with great care. In the first place they select only the best for cross-pollination. When the offspring mature, they study the percentage of good and poor plants among them. If the percentage of poor plants is high, it shows that those particular parents do not have the ability to pass on their own good qualities. So, no matter how lovely they may be in themselves, they are not used again for breeding. On the other hand, parent plants that do show the ability to pass on their good qualities, as proved by a high percentage of good offspring, may be used again and again, in different combinations. Even in such carefully made crosses there is likely to be a percentage of poor progeny.

Vigor, floriferousness, and desirable growth habits also enter into the choice of parent plants, in order to avoid making hybrids that are weak, slow growing, or that give few flowers.

GENERA USED IN HYBRIDIZATION WITH CATTLEYAS

LAELIA, BRASSAVOLA, AND SOPHRONITIS

Three genera of orchids are closely related to Cattleyas. Few are grown for cut flower purposes, but many are charming additions to collections. Each genus has some member or members whose striking characteristics lend charm to hybrids made by combining them with Cattleyas. The mating of two genera produces what is called a bi-generic hybrid, and that of three genera a tri-generic hybrid.

LAELIA. Laelias are the most nearly like Cattleyas in appearance, differing from them in structure by having eight pollinia, while the latter have four. Their similarity has given rise to some disagreement among botanists as to whether certain of them should be classed as Cattleyas or as Laelias. Their special contribution to hybrids is their brilliant coloring, which includes yellow, coppery-bronze, scarlet, and red-orange, as well as deep tones of violet. Their flower parts are slender, and with a few exceptions, the flowers are small. The object in hybridization is to combine the Laelia coloring with the better Cattleya shape.

The genus consists of about 30 species occurring in Mexico and Guatemala, and South Brazil, and none of the species is common to both regions. They are found on rocks and trees, often at quite high altitudes. Their culture is the same as for Cattleyas, with care to shift plants that do not thrive to warmer or cooler spots until the right conditions are found. Some may do well suspended from the roof of the greenhouse.

There is great variety among the species as to height of plants, shape of pseudobulbs, and other characteristics. They are usually divided into four groups. There are a few with the labiata type of lip, but most of them have a markedly 3-lobed lip. Some bear one leaf to a pseudobulb and some vary in the number of leaves. The more useful ones have been chosen for description.

Group I. Pseudobulbs rounded or egg-shaped

Laelia albida. Small, fragrant flowers, 2 inches in diameter, pure white except for a yellow streak down the lip and crimson dots at its base. The lip has small, erect side lobes and a rounded middle lobe. Occurs in Mexico, and flowers through the fall and winter. Popular in collections.

Laelia anceps. The species most commonly grown. Two to four showy, rose-purple flowers, 4 inches in diameter, are borne on a long jointed stem, 1 to 1½ feet high. Sepals and petals have a green line on the back. The side

Laelia anceps, one of the most popular of the genus. (Courtesy of H. D. Sawyer)

lobes of the lip fold up over the column. The front lobe curves downward and is deep purple, with a thickened yellow keel down the center terminating in three ridges. Occurs in Mexico, flowers in December and January. Popular in collections, grown somewhat commercially, and occasionally used in hybridization.

Laelia autumnalis. Similar to *L. anceps,* but lacking the green line on the sepals and petals. Five to six flowers are borne on a stem 1½–2 feet long. Occurs in Mexico, flowers in the fall. Quite popular in collections.

Laelia flava. Bright, pure yellow flowers, 2–2½ inches in diameter, borne in groups of 4–8 on a stem a foot high. The lip has blunt side lobes and a ruffled middle lobe with four elevated ridges down the center. Occurs in Brazil, flowers in the fall. Valuable in hybridization.

Group II. Pseudobulbs short and stem-like, consisting of several internodes

Laelia pumila. A pretty, dwarf species that has several lovely varieties. The single, large, drooping flower is rose-purple. The lip has squarish side lobes and a short, curling, ruffled middle lobe, yellow in the throat and deep purple at the edge. Occurs in Brazil, flowering time variable. Used somewhat in hybridization.

Group III. Pseudobulbs similar to those of Cattleya. Includes those species with the largest and most showy flowers

Laelia crispa. A popular, summer-flowering species. The flowers are large, fragrant, white, except for yellow and purple in the lip. The petals and lip are attractively ruffled. Five or six flowers are produced on a rather long stem. Occurs in Brazil. Used somewhat in hybridization, popular in collec tions.

Laelia purpurata. The largest of the Laelias, with flowers as much as 8 inches in diameter. The petals are white, suffused with light rose, and the handsome, bell-shaped lip is a rich velvety purple. Occurs in Brazil, flowers in the spring. Used more than any other Laelia in hybridization because of its large size and beautiful lip.

Laelia Sawyeri. A newly discovered species that will soon be sought after for collections because of its deep red-violet color and its wealth of flowers. Found by H. D. Sawyer in 1942 in the mountains west of Acuitlapan, and named after him. While the sprays hold usually 10 to 20 flowers, plants with 80 to a spray have been found.

Laelia superbiens. A large plant, with pseudobulbs a foot long, from which arise flower scapes 5–6 feet long. Ten to twenty flowers are borne in a roundish cluster. The flowers are about 6 inches across, lilac-purple. The lip has yellow side lobes with margins and stripes of purple. The front lobe is ruffled, yellow, with deep crimson margins and several toothed crests. Occurs in Guatemala, flowering time variable. Handsome but not much grown.

Laelia tenebrosa. Sometimes given as a variety of *Laelia grandis*. The flowers are a little better shaped than many of the Laelias, and range from coppery-bronze to citron-yellow. The lip is trumpet-shaped, deep purple with a border of white, marked with darker veins. A very striking and unusual flower, parent of many hybrids. Occurs in Brazil, flowers in the spring.

Group IV. Pseudobulbs slender, reed-like, sheathed with scales and swollen at the base

Laelia monophylla. Interesting because of its unique habit, but not much grown. The rhizome is a matted mass, from which arise tufts of stems each bearing a short thick leaf. The single flowers are 1–2 inches across, vivid orange-scarlet, with a tiny, three-lobed lip. Occurs in the mountains of Jamaica, the only species that grows outside of the Mexico-Guatemala and Brazil regions.

Laelia cinnebarina. An attractive, reddish-orange flower, about 3 inches across, borne 4–5 on a stem 15–20 inches high. Sepals and petals are slender. The lip has short, pointed side lobes, and a rather large, oval, ruffled middle lobe. Valuable in hybridization. Occurs in Brazil, flowers in the summer.

Brassavola Digbyana, whose large fringed lip is its stunning contribution to hybrids. (Courtesy of H. D. Sawyer)

BRASSAVOLA. *Brassavola Digbyana* is the only species of this genus that is much used in hybridization, the rest (about 20) being of botanical interest only. *Brassavola Digbyana* has a huge, marvelously fringed lip, often 4 inches across, which is the characteristic it bestows upon hybrids. The sepals and petals are small and plain, pale green tinted with pinkish lavender. The lip is white or cream color, and remains wide where it folds up over the column, carrying the fringe around to meet at the top of the tube. It is slow growing and not very floriferous. *Brassavola Digbyana* has also been classified as *Laelia Digbyana* and may be found in some lists under that name. Like Laelia, it has eight pollinia. Occurs in Honduras, flowers in July and August.

SOPHRONITIS. Here again is a genus (of about 6 species) of which one species, *Sophronitis grandiflora,* is frequently used in hybridization for the sake of its red color. All are dwarf plants, with brilliantly colored flowers that bear 8 pollinia.

COLOR PLATE 3. Laeliocattleya Clint McDade.

Sophronitis grandiflora. A beautiful little plant, compact, with short, egg-shaped pseudobulbs and oval leaves, of a total height of 3–4 inches. The single flowers are bright scarlet, sometimes red-orange, 1½–4 inches across, very plain and neat. The sepals are spatula-shaped, the petals more rounded, and the narrow, orange lip folds over the column. Occurs in the Organ Mountains, Brazil, flowers through the winter.

Sophronitis cernua. Very small plants. The flowers are colored like *Sophronitis grandiflora,* but are smaller and borne in clusters of 4–8. Occurs near Rio de Janeiro, flowers in the winter.

Sophronitis violacea. One of the smallest of cultivated orchids, with pseudobulbs 1 inch long and leaves 2–3 inches. The tiny flowers are only an inch across, bright rose color. Occurs in the Organ Mountains, Brazil, flowers in the winter.

INHERITANCE IN ORCHIDS

The foundation of the individual, in all species of living things both plant and animal, lies in its genetic make-up. Every cell in a plant, whether of roots, leaves, or flowers, contains in its nucleus a set of microscopic structures called chromosomes. On each chromosome there are still smaller structures called genes, so tiny that they cannot be seen with the microscope. The genes (derived from genetics, which in turn comes from genesis, the beginning) control every single characteristic of the individual. Try to list all the observable traits of an orchid plant, from the most obvious to the most minute, including such things as the following: pseudobulbs, tall or short, thick or thin; leaves, long or short, wide or narrow; sheath, single or double; lip, bordered or plain, "eyes" present or absent; throat, open or tubular; texture of flower, waxy or thin, and so on. You would soon have quite a list. The internal structure of the plant, if you could discern it, should be added to your list, as should its growth and flowering habits and the keeping quality of the flowers. Every one of these items is controlled by genes, and it probably takes several thousand, working together in a most complicated way, to produce the plant under scrutiny.

Environment cannot be overlooked in the making of a plant. Without the necessary growing conditions, a plant cannot develop properly. But proper growing conditions only give the genes a chance to express themselves. A plant that gives poor flowers under the best of care will never give good ones. It does not have the genetic make-up for good flowers. Such characteristics as petals that fold back too far, blotched coloring, or misshapen flower parts, are genetic faults. (However, if a plant that has consistently produced good flowers suddenly gives defective ones, you might look for insect injury, or some other environmental cause.)

Every species has its own standard number of chromosomes. In man there are 48. In the fruit fly there are 8. The garden pea, used by Mendel in the experiments which gave the world the fundamentals of genetics, has 14.

Chromosomes exist in pairs, but the members of each pair actually stand side by side only during reduction division (see below). The two members of each pair of chromosomes are identical in shape and size, but not necessarily in gene content. Genes also occur in pairs, one member of a pair on each of the matched chromosomes. Each pair of chromosomes is different from every other pair in the cell. Fig. 1 shows a cell that has two pairs of chromosomes, which have been made black and white to distinguish the individual members of each pair. The shape and size of the chromosomes, as well as the total number, are standard for the species. Of the 40 chromosomes in *C. Trianaei,* there are twenty distinct kinds, two of each, and every cell in the plant, except the reproductive cells, contains the full complement.

Fig. 1. Diagram of a cell containing two pair of chromosomes.

Certain tissues of a plant are set aside for the formation of reproductive cells. In these tissues the cells divide in a special way, called reduction division. The chromosomes come together in pairs. Then the members of each

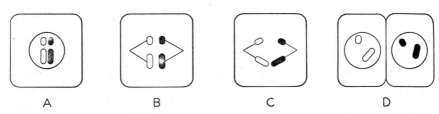

A   B   C   D

Fig. 2. Reduction division, formation of the sex cells. A, the chromosomes come together in pairs. B, one member of each pair is drawn to each pole. C, separation of the chromosomes carried further. D, division into two cells, each with half of the original number of chromosomes. These cells with the reduced number develop into reproductive, or sex, cells.

pair of chromosomes separate, and travel to opposite ends of the cell, which then divides in half to form two new cells. Fig. 2 shows this process. Each of the new cells now contains one member of each pair of chromosomes, or half of the original number. This is called the "haploid" number. The haploid cells later develop into sperm and egg cells. When fertilization takes place,

see Fig. 3, and a sperm and egg come together, the full number of chromosomes, the "diploid" number, is again present. The new individual that
develops from the fertilized egg thus receives half of its chromosomes from
one parent, half from the other. The chromosomes never fuse, but remain
separate and distinct from each other. Each chromo-
some carries with it its own gene content, and when
it goes into the making of a new individual it takes
its genes along with it to that new individual. It makes
no difference genetically which of two plants is the
male (pollen) parent and which is the female (pod)
parent.

Fig. 3. Fertilization is
the fusion of male and
female sex cells, each
of which contributes
one set of chromo-
somes.

During the development of reproductive cells, it is
pure chance which member of a pair of chromosomes
will go into a resulting sperm or egg cell. We can
think of the chromosomes as pairing with one to the
right of the other, but just as often, the position is
reversed. If the members of each pair are identical in gene content, it does not
matter how they separate, for the resulting reproductive cells will be identical.
But where the members of a pair differ from each other, if by only one gene,

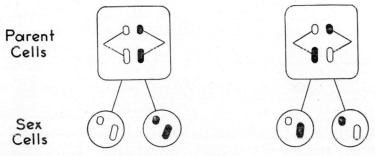

Fig. 4. Chance orientation of two pair of unlike chromosomes will give rise to four
different types of reproductive cells.

it makes a great deal of difference. Fig. 4 shows the possible combinations of
genes in the reproductive cells arising from one that has two pair of unlike
chromosomes. Where only one pair of unlike chromosomes is involved, there
are two types of reproductive cells, or 2 to the first power, 2^1. Where two
pair are concerned, there are four types, or 2^2, and where there are three
pair of unlike chromosomes, there will be eight different types of reproductive cells, or 2^3. The figures become almost astronomical for cells
that contain a large number of chromosomes. For instance, where there are

20 pair, if each member of every pair is unlike the other, the possible types of reproductive cells is 2^{20}, or 1,048,576 different kinds.

Such a figure gives some idea of the problems confronting geneticists who try to make a complete analysis of a plant or an animal. The genetic make-up of an individual cannot be known from its appearance. The only way to find out what genes it contains is to breed it and see what comes out in the offspring. This reveals why geneticists usually choose subjects that have a short life cycle. In contrast to orchids, the fruit fly produces a new generation

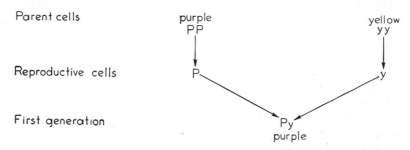

Fig. 5. A cross between *Cattleya gigas*, in which purple is dominant, and *Cattleya Dowiana*, in which yellow is recessive, produces all purple flowers in the offspring.

every few days, and wheat and corn in a matter of months. A planned study of orchid genetics started now would take several lifetimes to complete. We do have quite a body of facts, however, collected by careful observers, that show how certain factors in orchids behave, and their pattern follows the same general behavior seen in plants that have been studied in more detail.

Genes are of two general types, "dominant" and "recessive." Dominant genes have the power to induce the appearance of the characteristic they govern whenever they are present. Recessive genes can manifest themselves only in the absence of the dominant. For instance, in Cattleyas purple is dominant over yellow. A cross between *Cattleya gigas* (purple) and *Cattleya Dowiana* (yellow) gives all purple offspring. In Fig. 5, the dominant gene for purple is indicated by P, and the recessive gene for yellow by y.* *Cattleya gigas,* the parent plant, has the pair of genes PP, and gives one to each reproductive cell. *Cattleya Dowiana,* similarly, has the pair yy, so that each reproductive cell contains one y. Each individual among the offspring inherits a gene for purple P and a gene for yellow y, and, since purple is dominant over yellow, the offspring have purple flowers. On the other hand, the

* The system of symbols used here has been devised for the sake of simplicity.

yellow of Laelia is dominant over the purple of Cattleya, so that a mating between *Laelia flava* and *Cattleya gigas* would give all yellow flowers. This is shown in Fig. 6, where Y now stands for dominant yellow and p for recessive purple.

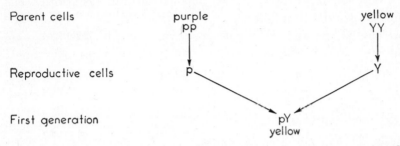

Fig. 6. A cross between *Cattleya gigas,* in which purple is recessive, and *Laelia flava,* in which yellow is dominant, produces all yellow flowers in the offspring.

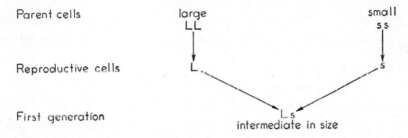

Fig. 7. Incomplete dominance is shown when the dominant gene, L, for large size is coupled with the recessive gene, s, for small size. The resulting offspring are intermediate in size.

There are cases where the dominant gene can manifest itself fully only when present in a double dose, that is, when two dominants are present for the same characteristic, instead of one dominant and one recessive. This seems to be true of flower size; see Fig. 7, where L stands for large size and s for small size. If a large Cattleya, LL, is crossed with a small one, ss, each of the offspring will inherit one gene for large size and one for small, Ls. The size of the resulting flowers will be intermediate between the two parents. The gene for large size, when present in a single dose, is dominant to the extent that it can make the flowers of the new generation larger than the smaller parent, but it is not able to bring them up to the size of the larger parent. This is called "incomplete dominance."

Plants that have identical genes for any one character are said to be homozygous (pure) for that character. For instance, a plant that contains two genes for large size, LL, will give every one of its sperm and egg cells one of those genes, and when used as a parent, will transmit this gene to every individual among the offspring. The same is true of a plant that has identical recessive genes, such as one with two genes for small size, ss, which is said to be homozygous for this character.

A plant that contains unlike genes for any character is called heterozygous (impure, or mixed). If it is heterozygous for size, it means that it contains one dominant gene for large, and one recessive gene for small, Ls. The offspring of the two yellow-purple crosses described above are heterozygous for color, those of the Cattleya cross being Py, and those of the *Laelia* × *Cattleya,* pY. When used as parents, heterozygous plants give half of their offspring the dominant gene and half the recessive.

The species tend to be homozygous. However, there are various types within a species, and these types pass their characteristics on to their progeny. There are, for example, good *Cattleya Trianaei,* and poor ones. If the types are well separated geographically, the chances are that the good and the poor are respectively homozygous. But if there has been interbreeding among them, they may be heterozygous. The only way to tell whether a flower is homozygous is to pollinate it with its own pollen (self-pollinate it). If all the offspring are identical to the parent, you may know that the parent is homozygous. But if the progeny differ markedly from each other in any way, you will know that the parent is a mixture. A plant that is homozygous for all of its good qualities can be used as a "stud" plant. One that proves to be heterozygous is not a "stud" plant.

Whether you intend to enter into a serious breeding program or just cross two orchids for the fun of it, it makes the work more interesting and insures a greater measure of success if you follow some plan based on genetic principles. If what you want is merely a large number of good flowers, perhaps to make your hobby profitable, you will be saved from making crosses that would produce a large number of poor flowers. Or if you want to obtain a unique combination of characteristics from two individuals, you will be spared much pain in knowing ahead of time that the type you want may be only one out of a wide assortment of types in the offspring.

TYPES OF CATTLEYA HYBRIDS

Enough has been said about hybrids in general to explain the purpose of the straight Cattleya hybrids, the improvement of the flower, the added vigor and floriferousness of the plant. One item has not been mentioned, and that is the influence of the blooming seasons of the parents. *Cattleya Trianaei* is often used in crosses in the hope of setting the blooming season of the hybrid at mid-winter, or another species may be chosen to set the season at some other desired time of the year. It works for some members of the offspring, just as any other inherited characteristic. Often, however, the offspring show a wide variation in blooming time. Hybrids frequently start new growth while flowering, or immediately afterward, and bloom as soon as the new growth develops, so that over a period of time they will have flowered at all seasons of the year.

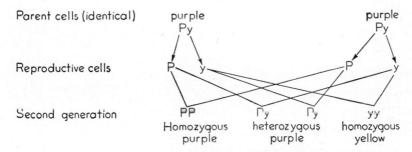

Fig. 8. The F_2 generation obtained by crossing members of the F_1 will be three-fourths purple and one-fourth yellow.

It is interesting to go a little further into the inheritance of yellow in Cattleyas. The purple *Cattleya gigas* crossed with the yellow *Cattleya Dowiana, aurea* gives a first generation (F_1 to geneticists) that is all purple, *Cattleya Hardyana*. Suppose *Cattleya Hardyana* is self-pollinated, and a second generation (F_2) of seedlings is raised. A person who did not know the inheritance of *Cattleya Hardyana* would be astonished to get some yellow flowers in this second generation. But those who knew its genetic make-up would have expected just that. Fig. 8 shows how this happens. *Cattleya Hardyana* is heterozygous. Its color genes are Py. In the formation of reproductive cells these genes segregate so that half of them contain P and half of them y. The second generation will recombine these genes in three ways, PP, Py, and yy. One-fourth of the plants will be homozygous purple, one-half of them will be heterozygous purple, and the remaining one-fourth will be homozygous yellow.

Again, someone who did not know genetics might think he could increase the "potency" of that homozygous yellow by crossing it back to the yellow *Cattleya Dowiana, aurea*. It is true that he would get all yellow flowers, but the yellow always remains a recessive gene. If he is looking for a plant to use for breeding yellows when crossed with purple, he will not get it this way. Fig. 9 shows why. The only way to get a yellow that will always be dominant over purple is to use a yellow Laelia as a parent, as described below under Laeliocattleyas.

Breeding white orchids has its own special problem genetically, as well as its own special appeal esthetically. The genetic problem has been pretty well worked out, so that you will not have the troubles experienced by some of the early growers. You will not have the sorrow of crossing two pure white flowers only to raise from them a batch of all purple offspring. White orchids

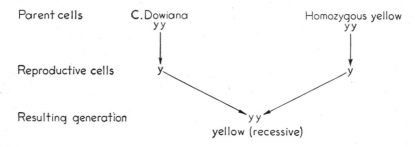

Fig. 9. The back cross of the homozygous yellow F$_2$ hybrid to *Cattleya Dowiana, aurea* simply produces another homozygous recessive yellow.

are now produced in fairly large quantities commercially, so that there are plenty to satisfy the demand. Every collection, however, should have a few whites in it.

Before we discuss their genetics, we must first define what is a pure white orchid, odd though it may seem to have to define "white." From the point of view of its appearance, a pure white orchid is one in which there is not the slightest trace of purple pigment, either in the plant or in the flower. Plants that give purple flowers show purple pigmentation in the plant, in the new growths, sheaths, or leaves, even though their flowers may be extremely pale. Plants that give pure white flowers are all pure, bright green. Nor is there any trace of purple in the flowers. Green and yellow plastids are present, and the white flower may have yellow markings in the throat, indeed it is desirable that it should. But the rest of the flower must be a chaste paper-white, not tinged with color in any way.

The necessity for this definition arises from the carelessness of people who call any very pale flower white, even one that has the veins or the tips of the petals and sepals obviously tinged with color. These tinged whites are nothing but dilute color forms. It is not so significant when the tinged whites are sold by the florist for pure white, because the recipient of the corsage probably does not mind the slight tinting of the flower, may even prefer it that way. But a tinged white cannot be crossed with a pure white without giving colored offspring, at best a mixture of colored and white. Pure whites must be used if you want all pure white progeny. Or, if you are buying seedlings with the intention of having all pure white flowers, be sure that the parents are pure, and not "almost white" or "nearly white."

As if purposely to confuse the matter and make the breeding of whites more difficult than colored orchids, white Cattleyas (and other genera, too) divide themselves into two groups genetically. It is simple when understood, but it puzzled early growers to find that combinations of the albino forms of some species gave all purple flowers, while different combinations of the same parents would give all white.

The mystery was solved by Charles C. Hurst, an English geneticist, who published his interpretation in *Experiments in Genetics* in 1925. He figured out the probable genetic make-up of white orchids from the way they behave in breeding. His deduction is briefly this. Manifestation of color in orchids depends on at least two types of genes working together, and the absence of one or the other (really the presence of the recessive form) in a flower causes it to be colorless. In order that a specific color may appear, there must be a gene, which Hurst calls R, to govern what color it is to be. And in order for that color to manifest itself, there must be another gene that allows color as such to be formed, which he calls C. In a colored orchid these two types are both present in their dominant form. However, if only the recessive form of the first type is present, no color may be made in the flower, even though the gene for color as such, C, is present. Or, if the situation is reversed and the plant contains only the recessive form of the second type, c, no color will show, even though the gene for specific color, R, is present. The two types of albinos are therefore, according to Hurst, ccRR and CCrr.

Any pure white when self-pollinated will give all white offspring, and any two of the same type when crossed will produce all white. You can see at a glance, however, that if ccRR and CCrr are crossed, the offspring will inherit c and R from its ccRR parent, and C and r from the CCrr parent, so that both types of genes will be present in the dominant form. The offspring will have the genetic make-up CcRr, and the resulting flowers will all be colored.

Hurst figured out to which of the groups, ccRR or CCrr, the various albino forms of the species belonged, according to the way they behaved when intercrossed. The Cattleya species from his list are given below, with the addition of other species that have shown their make-up by their behavior.

Group I, ccRR	Group II, CCrr
*C. Mossiae, Wageneri**	*C. Harrisoniana, alba**
*C. Gaskelliana, alba**	*C. Mendelii, alba**
*C. intermedia, alba**	*C. Schroederae, alba**
*C. labiata, alba**	*C. gigas*, var. *Firmin Lambeau***
*C. Trianaei, alba****	*C. Trianaei, alba****
C. speciosissima, alba	
C. Skinneri, alba	
C. Loddigesii, alba	

* Hurst's original list. All others have been added.

** Pure white *C. gigas* are very rare. The var. *Firmin Lambeau* by its behavior seems to fit in this group, but there is no data on other white *C. gigas*.

*** *C. Trianaei, alba* seems to include both genetic types. Only breeding with other whites can prove to which group a particular plant belongs.

Any of the members of Group I when intercrossed will give all white offspring, and any of the hybrids made from these species may be crossed to produce all white. For example, *C. Mossiae, Wageneri* × *C. labiata, alba* = pure white; *C. Trianaei, alba* × *C. Gaskelliana, alba* = pure white, and the offspring of each when crossed will also give pure white. Similarly, any members of Group II and the hybrids derived from them will give all white offspring.

A word should be said about inheritance in flowers that are white with purple lip. It is characteristic of Cattleyas that lip color is inherited separately from color in the rest of the flower, evidently governed by an independent set of genes. In white with purple lip, the same rule for purity applies to the whiteness of the sepals and petals as for the whole flower of a pure white, and no faintest trace of color should appear. Purple pigment is present in the plants that produce white with colored lip, but the flower bud when it breaks the sheath is as pure green as the bud of a pure white flower. A white with colored lip bred to a pure white will give white with colored lip in the offspring. The fact that the lip is colored in no way influences the whiteness of the sepals and petals.

LAELIOCATTLEYAS. Laelias are used in crosses with Cattleyas to lend their unusual coloring to the resulting hybrids. *L. cinnabarina*, a bright orange-red, can produce Laeliocattleyas of the same color. *Laelia tenebrosa*, which is reddish brown with coppery suffusion and a darker lip, when crossed with

Cattleyas produces bronze flowers with deep purple lip, in which the bronze ranges from yellow-bronze to purple-bronze. *L. purpurata* has perhaps been used more than any other in hybrids with Cattleyas, partly because of the deep velvety purple of its lip, and partly because it is itself a large flower and the resulting hybrids are of good size from the beginning. Hybrids that have small Laelias for parents have to be crossed again with Cattleyas to bring the size up to the desired dimensions.

In the discussion of yellow-purple crosses above you will remember that the yellow of Laelias is dominant over the purple of Cattleyas. The great value of this type of cross is that it is possible to breed a stud plant that is

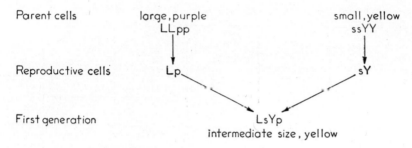

Fig. 10. The F₁ generation obtained by crossing a purple Cattleya with yellow *Laelia flava* gives all yellow flowers, which are heterozygous for both size and color.

homozygous for yellow (that carries the double dose) and in which the yellow is dominant. Such a stud plant should also be homozygous for large size, in other words, it should be a yellow Laeliocattleya that has the desirable Cattleya shape. Two steps are necessary to achieve this.

Suppose we choose the all-yellow *Laelia flava* and cross it with any Cattleya. Here we will be dealing with two characters, size and color. Fig. 10 shows the primary cross between these two, giving the first (F₁) generation. The Cattleya is LLpp, where L represents the gene for large size, and p the gene for purple, which in this cross is recessive. *Laelia flava* is ssYY, where s stands for the gene for small size, and Y for yellow, which is dominant. The reproductive cells from the Cattleya are all the same, Lp, and from the Laelia similarly are sY. The offspring combining these genes are therefore identical, LsYp. They are of a size intermediate between the two parents, and all yellow, though the yellow is not quite as clear and pure as where the double dose of Y is present.

The plant we want to make in the next step is one that will be homozygous for both large size and yellow color, LLYY. Off hand, you might think that the way to get it would be to cross a member of the F_1 generation back to the Laelia parent. The Laelia parent gives only one type of reproductive cell, sY. The plant from the F_1 generation gives four types, LY, Lp, sY, and sp. Combine sY with each of these and you get LsYY, LsYp, ssYY, and ssYp. These come out in equal proportions as to the numbers of plants

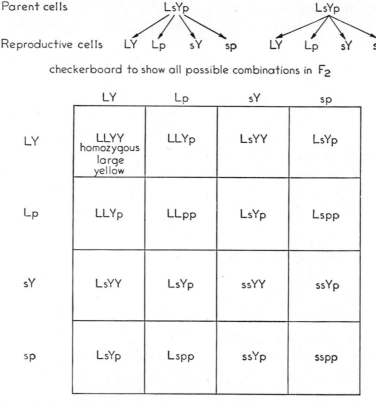

Fig. 11.   Inheritance in the F_2 when members of the F_1 from Fig. 10 are crossed.

of each type. There are two types that are homozygous for yellow, LsYY and ssYY, but of these one is intermediate in size and the other is small. Nowhere can you find the plant you want, the LLYY type. The back cross to the Cattleya would not give it either, for here you would get Lp combined with the four types of germ cells from the F_1, and the results would be LLYp, LLpp, LsYp, and Lspp. Two would be homozygous for large size, but none for yellow. So we have to go at it another way.

Look at the four types of reproductive cells that arise from a member of the F_1 generation, LY, Lp, sY, and sp. The homozygous large yellow plant we want would have to come from the fertilization of an LY egg cell by an LY sperm cell, and we can get this by self-pollinating a member of the F_1, or by mating one F_1 plant with another. Fig. 11 shows all of the possible combinations, in checkerboard style. The four types of reproductive cells are written horizontally and vertically, and each line contains the combination of the genes at the left with each group on the top. The proportions of types in the second generation, F_2, are given in sixteenths. In the checkerboard the type LLYY occurs only once, so that this type will be $\frac{1}{16}$ of the total number of offspring. Perhaps you will think it is hardly worth the trouble of making the cross to get only one out of sixteen. A plant breeder would consider it very worthwhile, for this LLYY plant when self-pollinated will give a whole generation of large yellow flowers, and when bred to any large Cattleya will carry its dominant yellow to every member of the offspring. Among the other types on the checkerboard, some will give good

A primary Brassocattleya, the hybrid Mrs. J. H. Leeman, *Cattleya Dowiana* × *Brassavola Digbyana*. The huge fringed lip is its beautiful feature.

flowers of large and intermediate size, both yellow and purple, plants that will be an addition to your collection, though not useful in breeding.

BRASSOCATTLEYAS. *Brassavola Digbyana* has been combined with Cattleyas for the sake of its marvelously fringed lip. In a primary cross with a Cattleya, the offspring are all intermediate between the two parents. The petals and sepals are somewhat reduced from the ideal Cattleya size, due to the influence of the smaller *B. Digbyana* flower parts, but the lip has the added charm of the Brassavola shape and fringe (see the accompanying photographs of *Brassavola Digbyana* and *Brassocattleya Mrs. H. J. Leeman,* a hybrid between *B. Digbyana* and *Cattleya Dowiana*). The colors of the primary crosses are diluted with green, which makes them very delicate and beautiful. Some prefer this subtle coloring to the stronger tones acquired when the first generation Brassocattleya is crossed back to a Cattleya, or with another Brassocattleya. But there is no question that the brilliant secondary hybrids are among the most handsome of orchids. In a secondary cross, segregation of the genes causes both lip types to show up, so that there are Brassocattleyas with the Cattleya lip as well as those with the Brassavola lip. The size of the sepals and petals is improved in the secondary cross, a desirable feature.

BRASSOLAELIOCATTLEYAS. Brassocattleyas crossed with Laeliocattleyas produce another wonderful set of hybrids, the tri-generic Brassolaeliocattleyas. Imagine an already beautiful Laeliocattleya with its brilliant lip increased in size and enhanced with fringe. If you should want to make this kind of a hybrid, starting from the species, time may be saved by making simultaneous crosses, on the one hand the *Brassavola Digbyana* × *Cattleya,* and on the other hand the *Laelia* × *Cattleya.* When the first generation (F₁) of each has matured, you would cross a member of one with a member of the other. There would be a tremendous variety in this second generation. Half of them will have the fringed lip, and of this half about three-quarters will be large or intermediate in size and the rest small. The other half of the plants will have the plain lip, and again three-quarters of these will be large or intermediate in size. You could carry each line a step further and make the second generation (F₂) before crossing the two kinds. This would be done by self-pollinating the best member of each F₁ generation. Out of each second generation you would get some plants that are homozygous, which, when crossed, would give all large flowers, all with the fringed lip.

SOPHROLAELIOCATTLEYA. *Sophronitis grandiflora,* a gem of a flower in itself, has been made to contribute its redness to the large Cattleya and Laeliocattleya hybrids. The primary cross of *Sophronitis grandiflora* with a Cattleya necessarily gives quite small flowers, and even smaller and less well-shaped with a Laelia. But when either of these is recombined with a Cattleya or a Laeliocattleya, large flowers of various deep rosy or red-violet hues appear. The gene for red in Sophronitis is dominant, and where it is present in a double dose it gives a beautiful clear red. Where it appears in combination with the gene for purple, the red is modified somewhat and the resulting color is a blend between red and purple. When, however, the single dose of red is combined with the brilliant coloring of a Laeliocattleya, the hue is intensified in all respects. This is probably the reason why Sophrolaeliocattleyas are preferred to the straight Sophrocattleyas. The blended tones of any of the crosses are, however, very rich and lovely.

Since most of the Cattleya hybrids are variations of violet, a few clear reds add much to a collection or to the florist's showcase. The pure red may be obtained in a number of ways, of which the most simple is to self-pollinate a member of the first generation Sophrocattleya. The homozygous large red flower will appear in one-sixteenth of the second generation.

POTINARA is the name given to the quadri-generic cross, Brassosophrolaeliocattleya. It can easily be imagined that a combination of all the desirable qualities of the four genera would be an outstandingly handsome thing. However, plants in which all the desired qualities show up occur in only a small proportion of the offspring, and the percentage of plants homozygous for all qualities even less often. A rather extensive breeding program would be necessary to achieve the ideal results. Many lovely combinations do occur in Potinara crosses, although relatively few have been made.

COLCHICINE

The chemical, colchicine, a poisonous drug, is used in plant breeding for two purposes, to create giant sized plants and flowers, and to make otherwise sterile hybrids able to produce viable seed. (Few Cattleya hybrids are sterile, so the latter is not particularly applicable here, but it may be useful in breeding Cypripediums.) Both results come from the same function of the chemical, which is to double the number of chromosomes in the cells.

Plants containing more than the usual number of chromosomes for the species (polyploid) occur in nature. They are larger, stockier, bear larger flowers, and are often more resistant to environmental vicissitudes. Horticulturalists, always seeking larger and more showy flowers, have produced a few by applying methods discovered by scientists to double the number of chromosomes. Colchicine has been used for this purpose with some success, but its use in orchid culture is relatively new. Orchids present special problems in the application of the chemical, and since very little has been accomplished in this line, anything you may try will be in the nature of an experiment.

Colchicine upsets the normal process of cell division. During the normal division of vegetative cells (mitosis), the chromosomes split lengthwise, in preparation for the formation of two new cells which will each contain the full number of chromosomes, see Fig. 12. For instance, in *Cattleya Trianaei* while the cell is getting ready to divide, each of the 40 chromosomes splits in two, so that for a brief interval of time there are 80 chromosomes. As division goes to completion, 40 of these migrate to one end of the cell, and 40 to the other end, and the two groups are cut off from each other by a partition (the new cell wall) that grows in between them. Thus two new cells, each with 40 chromosomes, are formed. The peculiar action of colchi-

cine is to interfere with the division process just at the point where the
chromosomes have split, when there are 80 present. The cell is made to
cease its activities and return to a resting condition, carrying still the 80

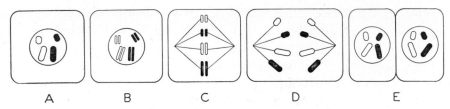

Fig. 12. Mitosis, the division of vegetative cells. A, the resting cell. B, each chromosome splits. C, the chromosomes gather in a plane through the center of the cell. D,
opposite halves of each chromosome are drawn to opposite poles. E, the new cell wall
comes between the newly separated sets of chromosomes, and two cells, each with the
full complement of chromosomes, are formed.

chromosomes. When the effects of colchicine wear off, the cell returns to the
process of division, and the chromosomes split again. At this point there are
160, half of which migrate to each end of the dividing cell. When division
is complete, the two new cells each contain 80 chromosomes, instead of the original 40. Typical action of colchicine is shown in Fig. 13.

Cells containing the normal number of chromosomes are said to be diploid, whereas those in which the number has been doubled are tetraploid. (Cells containing just one extra set of chromosomes are triploid.) The action of colchicine is not always perfectly regular. Sometimes an odd number of extra chromosomes is produced. Occasionally the doubling action is repeated, giving rise to cells that have four or eight times the normal chromosome content. Often not all cells are affected, so that the resulting plant may have some tetraploid parts mixed with normal parts.

Photomicrograph of chromosomes in *Paphiopedilum hirsutissimum*. Mitosis is approaching completion. One set of chromosomes is going to one pole, and the other set to the opposite pole. (Courtesy of Clarelen Orchids; Photo by A. Owczarzak)

COLOR PLATE 4. Laeliocattleya Snowdrift.

Many tetraploids, while they may produce huge flowers, are less floriferous than normal plants. While these huge flowers may be desirable from the point of view of an exhibitor, they are not as profitable for a grower. Many also are partially sterile, but there may be some that produce a good quantity of viable seed. These latter can be chosen for use in breeding.

In order to produce a plant that is entirely tetraploid, all cells must be affected evenly. This would mean treating the young seedling so that its growing stem becomes tetraploid throughout. A method suggested is to

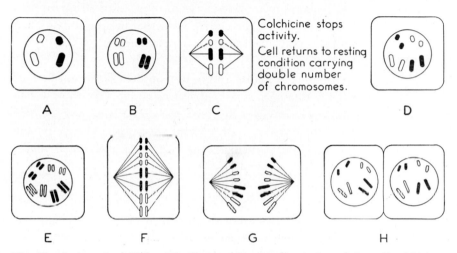

Colchicine stops activity.

Cell returns to resting condition carrying double number of chromosomes.

A   B   C   D

E   F   G   H

Fig. 13. Action of colchicine. Mitosis proceeds normally, A, B, and C, until colchicine is applied. Colchicine prevents the migration of the chromosomes to the poles, C, and returns the cell to resting condition, D. When mitosis again resumes, after the influence of colchicine has worn off, the chromosomes split again, E. The process goes to completion, F, G, and H, producing new cells with double the original number of chromosomes.

take a few large flask or community pot seedlings, wrap their roots in wet cotton, and immerse the leaves and stem in the colchicine solution. Colchicine is injurious to roots, so great care must be taken in handling the small seedlings. Concentrations must be very weak (see below), and the exposure to the solution should be varied with different groups of seedlings, in an attempt to find a period of time that is effective.

The community pot seedlings may be treated in another manner. A wad of cotton wet with colchicine solution may be laid in the axil of a leaf. A drop or two of solution would be added from time to time to keep the cotton wet for the desired period. In this case, the colchicine would penetrate the stem and affect new buds from which future growths are to come.

Instead of treating seedlings, it might be desirable to treat new growths on older plants, for the purpose of producing tetraploid flowers. Application of the colchicine to the tough outer coverings of the developing eye might not be effective. It would be better to inject the solution into the growth so as to reach the cells that are going to produce flowers. Treatment would have to be given before the flower parts start to differentiate, or before the lead reaches a length of 1 inch. The growing tip of the lead is way down inside. A hypodermic syringe may be employed to place the solution in contact with the deep cells. Another method might be to draw a fine string through the growth near its base, and let the end be immersed in a dish of solution to act as a wick. The string would be removed at the end of the desired period of time.

Colchicine is poisonous to plants and to human beings. It must be used on plants in very weak dilutions, measured very carefully. Too strong a concentration may kill the plants, yet the dose, to be effective, must be very near the lethal strength. Workers are cautioned not to let colchicine remain in contact with the skin, and particularly not to get it in the eyes. It should be kept out of the reach of children.

Suggested concentrations to start with are between 0.05% and 0.20%. Not all plants respond to the same concentration or duration of exposure. Since there are little data on its use with orchids, your trials will be purely experimental, and should in fact be set up as an experiment.

You might make up (or have your druggist do this for you) three concentrations, 0.05%, 0.10%, and 0.20% colchicine in tap water. Each concentration would be applied to separate plants for three different intervals of time, 4, 6, and 24 hours. For your experiment, you would pick out nine plants, certainly not valuable ones. To the first you would apply 0.05% solution for 4 hours, to the second 0.05% solution for 6 hours, and to the third 0.05% solution for 24 hours. To the next group of three plants you would apply 0.10% solution in the same manner, and to the third group the 0.20% solution. Somewhere out of the nine plants there might be one for which the treatment proved just right. A record of the treatment given each plant would be kept, so that conditions that prove favorable can be repeated. If none of the treatments is effective, the concentration might be increased, but probably should not be made stronger than 0.30%. Perhaps it would be better to use the weaker dilutions for longer periods.

Changes caused by colchicine may not be apparent for some time. The first reaction is a slowing down in the growth rate. Then, as growth is resumed, the tetraploid tissue grows larger than the normal tissue. If the effect of colchicine has not been even in all cells, one side of the growth may be larger than the other. The leaves on one side of the stem may be large, while those on the other side remain small. If only the flower-forming cells were affected, no changes would be apparent until the plant came into bloom. And even supposing that this particular plant produced larger flowers than it had previously, the aid of a microscope would be necessary to ascertain whether it was tetraploid or not.

From all this you can readily see that you cannot expect simply to apply colchicine to a plant and come out with magnificent giant flowers. In its present stage of development, where orchids are concerned, the use of colchicine is a novelty. Whether it ever becomes a tool for general use remains to be seen.

Chapter VI

SEEDLINGS FROM FLASK TO COMMUNITY POT

One of the main cares of Nature, after assuring the nourishment and growth of a plant, is to insure its reproduction and the continuation of the species. Various ways have been devised for scattering the seed, for moving it away from the parent plant to more open ground.

The diversity of such mechanisms is a fascinating study in itself. There are plants that have ways of forcibly ejecting the seed from the pod or capsule, such as the Siberian pea and Oxalis. Others offer fruits tender and tasty, brightly colored, which attract birds and animals that carry away their seed. The cockleburs make a nuisance of themselves by their method of forcing their seed upon whatever agent happens their way. The exquisite forms of wind-borne seed are well known for their delicate umbrellas and parachutes.

But not every seed that is produced finds conditions suited to its germination. Only those fortunate enough to land in just the right spot can grow to maturity. Hence plants in even the best of circumstances must produce more seed than will ever grow.

Epiphytic orchids face a special problem in seed dispersal. The chances are slim that a seed will find some obscure crevice in the bark of a tree where it can germinate, or that it will have there the necessary conditions of air and light, moisture, and mineral nutrients. If only one seed from each plant should germinate and survive to maturity the continuation of the species would be well assured. But in order to guarantee this against such odds, each plant produces hundreds of thousands of seeds every year.

The formation of so many seeds by rather small plants means that the seeds must be very tiny, which is true of all epiphytic orchids. The seed of Cattleyas is as fine as powder, and uncountable numbers are formed in one capsule. Its small size allows it to be carried by the gentle air currents in the jungle which are not strong enough to lift heavy particles to great heights. As the seed capsule ripens and splits open, the drift of pale yellow powder is picked up by the moving air and dusted from branch to branch. Some of the seed is blown away by stronger winds that meet the upward air currents above the jungle. Much of the seed, of course, drifts down to the ground where it has no chance to grow.

Because of its small size, the seed contains little, if any, food to nourish the embryo during germination. It must find a ready supply where it falls. In a pocket of decaying vegetable matter, there will be available minerals and sugars released by the decomposing action of fungi and bacteria. And as will be seen in a moment, the presence of sugars is all-important to bring about the germination of the seed.

Even after successful germination, the seedling still faces hazards of destruction, overgrowth of fungi, burning by the sun if it has not enough shade, or even desiccation if it does not receive frequent enough rain.

The first growers who tried to germinate orchid seed ran into problems that plagued them and their followers for three quarters of a century. As late as 1922 no one had had any consistent luck. Those who were successful in one attempt might fail in the next. A man felt himself fortunate sometimes to raise half a dozen seedlings from a cross that could have produced thousands. The urge to grow hybrids had two purposes behind it: the desire for greater variety, and the need to increase the domestic supply of orchids without having to depend on repeated importation.

Various methods were tried to induce germination. The seed was sown on leaf mold, decaying bark, sphagnum moss, etc. More often than not, if the recalcitrant seed did germinate, much of it was killed by invading bacteria and fungi. When these attempts failed, growers set to work on the theory that germination might be induced by contact of the seed with some fungus found in association with adult orchid plants. The experiments that followed were intricate, and consisted of infecting the seed with isolated strains of fungi. Enough success came from this work to carry the fungus method on for many years. But it was a technique that could be used only by experts, and even in their hands there followed frequent destruction of the seed by the fungi.

It remained for Dr. Lewis Knudson of Cornell University, in 1922, to find a completely controlled, standardized, simple method for germinating orchid seed. He had done previous work which showed that sugars had a favorable influence on plant growth, which suggested to him that orchid seed might require the presence of sugar in order to germinate. He interpreted the success with fungi, not to its effect on the seed itself, but to digestion by the fungi of some of the carbohydrates and nitrogenous substances present in the growing medium. Sugars would be among the materials released in this process.

This proved to be true. Dr. Knudson found that the seed germinated readily without the presence of fungi when sown on an agar jelly to which had been added the necessary mineral nutrients plus sugar. Patiently he worked to find out what was the best sugar to use, and in what concentration. He also had to adjust the proportions of the mineral nutrients. The flasks containing the agar-nutrient mixture were sterilized, and the seed was disinfected to kill foreign organisms that might enter the flasks with it. The flasks were stoppered after being sown, and left untouched until the seedlings were developed some eight months to a year later. The flasks were perfect little glass houses, protecting the tiny plants from insects and contamination, and providing them with a constantly moist atmosphere until they were well developed.

Dr. Knudson's method revolutionized orchid growing. He removed the guesswork, the confusion and the hazards, and gave growers a technique that was easy to use and certain of success. It is simple enough to measure out the ingredients for making the agar-nutrient jelly (for details see Chapter VIII), and now it is even possible to buy the mixture all prepared except for the addition of water.

In the jungle, only an occasional seed of the tremendous numbers produced has a chance to germinate. Now, in the hands of man, nearly every seed may become a plant. Growers who once zealously guarded every hybrid seedling, now hardly know what to do with the countless thousands they produce. One grower estimates that he has 80,000 seedlings in flasks at present. This has put orchids on a par with other greenhouse crops, and made orchid plants available to all who would buy.

Needless to say, Dr. Knudson's flask method has given a tremendous impetus to orchid growing, not only by increasing the numbers of plants grown commercially, but by making it possible for amateurs to grow their own.

Buying Flasks

Flasks are offered for sale when the seedlings are fully developed, at prices varying from $20 to $50. The value of a flask depends on how many seedlings it is estimated to contain, which may vary from 100 to 250 (or rarely 400 to 500), and on the type of parent plants used in the cross. A hybrid of average commercial quality will not be as expensive as one made from the grower's prize plants and expected to give show quality blooms. You make your choice from a list that gives the names of the parents, with usually a description of their size, coloring, and flowering season. Often the grower adds helpful information as to what may be expected from the cross.

The flasks are packed in boxes or baskets and sent by railway or air express. Sometimes they arrive in perfectly undisturbed condition, depending on the care with which they are handled and the distance they travel. Occasionally the soft jelly is jumbled and the little plants are clustered in tangled masses, which does not seem to harm them. If the flasks arrive in the latter condition, it is necessary to transplant them at once, but undisturbed flasks may be kept for a time.

If you have not seen flask seedlings before, nothing I can say will prepare you for their sheer beauty, the delicacy of their little shiny green leaves, and their tiny translucent roots. The plants are so small and fragile that you will handle them with tender awe, wondering that it has taken a year for them to grow to this size. There will be a few larger seedlings, perhaps an inch and a quarter from tip to tip, with several leaves and three or four roots. Most of them will have leaves and roots a quarter of an inch long, and in some the leaves and roots will be mere pin points just starting to form. Also, you will see some that are no farther than the spherule stage (see drawing, p. 115), the little round green ball stage that precedes leaf formation.

Preparation of Pots and Removing Seedlings from Flasks

Before removing the seedlings from the flask, prepare a number of pots to receive them, a dozen 3-inch ones, or seven or eight 5-inch pots. The 3-inch size is usually recommended, but the 5-inch is more easily cared for as it holds moisture longer.

The usual care to use clean pots is especially important here. Fill the pots half full of broken pieces of pot for good drainage, and put a little shredded osmunda fibre over this. Then cut (with scissors or an axe) slices about an inch thick from good soft brown fibre that has been rinsed and allowed to drain until all the excess water is removed. Do not use coarse or wiry fibre. Arrange the slices in the pot side by side, with the fibres running vertically, pressing them together until the whole is flat and evenly firm (not hard) to the touch. The surface of the fibre should be about ¼ inch below the level of the rim. The vertical fibres can be easily spread apart for the insertion of a little plant, and when released they close together to hold the roots of the seedling.

Removing the seedlings from the flask is simple, although I must confess that my first experience baffled me. After considering the problem for some time, the only way seemed to be to wrap the flask in a towel and smash it with a hammer. The result was that I spent some time separating the seedlings from bits of broken glass. Then I shook the towel in the garbage can to dispose of remaining glass splinters, and saw to my horror that I had also shaken out several dozen seedlings. These I carefully rescued from the trash. Not a very auspicious beginning for the tender little plants! Nor was their potting carried out with any great skill. The stiff, black fibre I had to use (because I didn't know there were differences in osmundine when I ordered it) was difficult to manage, and nowhere had I read how to put it in the pots. The tedious job of potting was not completed until midnight, at which time whenever I closed my eyes I saw little orchid plants swimming about, pointing their roots at me like antennae. I tell you all this to encourage you, for from this first flask 450 seedlings survived to grow into big, vigorous plants.

The next few flasks taught me simple methods that made the job much less tedious. Most of the seedlings may be removed from the flask by repeating several times the procedure of pouring half a cup of water (just cool, about 65° F.) into the flask, swirling it gently, and pouring out seedlings and water into a shallow pan. A few seedlings may remain, either between the glass and the agar, or embedded in the jelly. You can reach into the flask with a dinner knife and cut out the pieces of agar containing such seedlings.

Some people prefer to pour the seedlings onto a turkish towel instead of into a pan. But I find that sometimes the roots adhere to the fibres of the towel and are difficult to pick up. One grower recommends allowing the seedlings to dry for a few hours laid out on paper, and states that he prevents "damping off" by this method and so loses fewer seedlings. My losses from damping off have been practically nil, so I continue to remove them to a pan of water and pot them immediately.

POTTING THE SEEDLINGS

It is well to put plants of the same size in each pot, so, as you go along, try to select either all large or all small seedlings for one pot. It helps if you first sort the seedlings into separate pans according to size.

With a pointed stick separate the fibres of the osmundine, and with a pair of tweezers gently lift a seedling out of the water and set it in the space you are holding ready. If the roots are short, there is no problem in making them fit the space. Seedlings with longer roots, or roots that grow at odd angles, may require a bit of maneuvering. The seedling should be settled in place

Potting flask seedlings. The fibre in the prepared pot is spread apart with a pointed instrument and the seedling inserted in the space. Then the fibre is pressed together about its roots. The seedlings in the dish to the right have been sorted according to size.

with its base just within the surface of the fibre, and the fibre then pressed back in place around it.

The seedlings should be evenly spaced, the smaller ones about ½ inch apart, larger ones 1 inch apart, and the number per pot related to their size. In a 3-inch pot it is possible to put 40 or more small plants or 20 larger ones. Arrange them in concentric circles, working around the outer ring first.

When a pot is finished, give it a light syringing to moisten the leaves of the seedlings.

Care of Community Pots

Newly potted flask seedlings need a close, moist (not saturated) atmosphere to imitate the natural conditions they would find in a protected pocket of leaf mold in a tree crotch. They need more shade than do older plants and must not be allowed to get dry. They can survive an accidental drying, if not too prolonged, but repeated drying only stunts their growth. Success with seedlings depends on keeping them growing constantly, and under the right conditions they will develop rapidly into sturdy plants.

A wooden box about 8 inches deep makes a good case for community pots. Holes bored in the sides allow for ventilation, or the upper half of the front part may be knocked out. A sheet of glass makes the lid, covered with a thin skim of white paint for shading, or covered with layers of cheesecloth. The amount of shading should be adjusted to allow about 500 foot-candles

Seedlings in community pots thrive in a damp, close atmosphere. The cover of the box shown here has been removed. Note a part of the front of the box has been knocked out to give some ventilation.

of (direct) light to enter. If you have a great number of community pots, they may be kept on the bench, the sides of which are built up, and may be covered with a hinged sash.

The leaves of the seedlings should be a bright green. Their color responds very quickly to changes of light intensity. I might draw again on my own first experiences to illustrate the effects of light. I kept my first community pots in the house for some time before I acquired a greenhouse. Shortly after they were transferred to the greenhouse, the leaves of the seedlings turned almost white. Shading had been put on the greenhouse glass in what seemed sufficient quantity, so it did not at first occur to me that there was still too much light for the seedlings. Instead I thought of all sorts of things, that the water was too alkaline, or that the plants were suffering from some mineral deficiency. I organized the plants into groups for experiments, and gave some water that had been acidified to *p*H5, others a complete nutrient solution, and still others solutions of various minerals. Nothing had any effect. As a last resort, I tried covering the glass lid of the seedling bench with a piece of sheet. Within a few weeks the leaves had regained their nice green color.

The temperature of the Cattleya house will suit the seedlings, 70°–72° F. in the daytime, 60° F. at night. However, if there is a spot in your greenhouse that runs to 65° F. at night, this slightly higher temperature would be better.

The glass lid of the box should be left closed all of the time. The seedlings have received a shock in being transferred from their tightly closed flasks to open pots, and the change in amount of ventilation should not be too sudden. The holes in the side of the box will give enough air circulation. If the seedlings are on the bench and the cover fits very tightly, it should be raised a few inches part of every day to keep the air within from being constantly saturated.

Syringing with a fine spray once or twice a day may be nearly all the watering necessary. The spray will wet the box and the pots, and so help to maintain a humid atmosphere. But watch the fibre closely. It must be kept soft and moist, and water should be given in the pots when needed. Young seedlings require more water than do mature plants, yet they must not be allowed to stay sopping wet. The greatest care must be given to this detail.

A community pot of seedlings is just a good sized meal for a slug. One slug can mow down twenty or thirty little plants in an evening. Even if you have not seen a slug in your greenhouse, keep close watch over the seedlings. Slugs can come up from the soil under the benches, where their presence is not suspected. It would be well to put some slug bait here and there in the case or on the bench, and examine the pots from time to time. During the day the slugs hide just under the rim, on the sides, or on the bottom of the pots.

Thrips often cause considerable damage to young seedlings, but these can be controlled with a nicotine or DDT spray. (See Chapter XVII.)

Seedlings stay in these first community pots for about six months, or perhaps a little longer, which brings them to the age of one and a half years (from the time the seed was sown).

Second Community Pots

Mature plants seem to resent being repotted more often than once in two years. But seedlings benefit by frequent changes of fibre. It may be that the accumulation of toxins in the seedling pots is more rapid under their condition of greater moisture, or that the small plants may be more sensitive to the increased acidity of the fibre. At any rate, they level off growth after they have been in the fibre for longer than six months, and make a sudden spurt forward as soon as they are put in fresh fibre. Attention to repotting is part of the secret of keeping the seedlings constantly moving and may mean having many of them bloom a year or two ahead of the accepted average time.

The temptation at this time is to put the larger seedlings in separate 1½- or 1¾-inch pots. There may be a few exceptionally large seedlings that would merit this treatment, but most of them are better kept in communities for a while longer. The smaller pots dry out much more rapidly, and it takes older plants to resist drying for a part of each day. The young seedlings may only be retarded if put in single pots. The larger amount of fibre in the community pots gives the more constant moisture condition they require at this age.

A community pot ready for transplanting. One or two are ready for individual pots. The smaller ones will be put back in a community pot.

Transplanting

This is a good time to check up on the success of your first potting. Fibre that was too loose to begin with will by now be light and spongy. So make a mental note as to how firm you should make the fibre in this next operation.

To remove the seedlings from the pots, first soak the pot in a pan of water to loosen roots adhering to the sides, and then either knock out the contents of the pot or insert a flat instrument at the side and lift up fibre and plants. Tenderly separate the plants, taking care as much as possible not to break the roots, and leaving some fibre around each seedling. The plants may be set in a shallow dish with a little water in the bottom to prevent drying.

Again, they should be sorted as to size, so that each pot will hold plants of about equal vigor.

The pots are prepared with crock to one-half their depth, topped by a layer of fibre. Cut up soft brown fibre that has been first rinsed and drained into small chunks and slices. The seedlings have now developed a larger root system which must be protected in potting. It is especially necessary to avoid injuring roots that are just making their growth. Since each plant will need more space in which to grow, only five to fifteen can be put in one pot.

Take up a plant and place a piece of fibre on each side of it, so that the base of the plant is about ⅛ inch deeper in the fibre than previously. Then set the little bundle in the pot. Arrange other plants in the same way, and set them side by side in the pot. As you add more plants, press those already in the pot gently together. It is important not to let a plant stand up on a pedestal, with its base higher than the level of the fibre. Each one should be firmly held in the fibre. When the pot is full, check the consistency of the fibre, and if not quite firm enough, add pieces of fibre at the sides, pressing it down and toward the center with a small potting stick. The level of the fibre in the finished pot should be ¼ inch from the top of the rim, and flat across its surface.

Care of Second Community Pots

Transplanting is always a shock to plants, and for a time the roots are not very active. These second community pots may be put back in covered boxes and must be shaded carefully. For the first few weeks, until the roots have regained their activity, the amount of shade should be about equal to that which they received before, about 500 foot-candles of light. After this period the shade may be gradually lessened until the light equals about 800 foot candles. Light intensity is of course always measured on a bright day. Individual shading for groups of community pots may be arranged according to your own ingenuity. My method is to build railings on the sides of the bench and stretch wires across to support a cheesecloth cover. The cheesecloth is nailed to one side of the bench and the free side is fastened to a stick on which it may be rolled up. The covers may be rolled back on dull days. Their thickness can be regulated according to the amount of light required by the seedlings.

Keep the fibre moist, not wet. For the first few weeks the seedlings should be given a light syringing two or three times a day, just enough to moisten their leaves and the merest surface of the fibre. Later on, syringing should be

given with judgment on bright days, but omitted on dull days. Water in the
pot when necessary to keep the moisture even.

At the end of a year in community pots many of the plants should be ready
for single pots (see Chapter VII). However, you will find striking differences in size between individual plants, and between seedlings of different
parentage. Many will grow less rapidly, and when others are put in single
pots, these may need to be put back in community pots with fresh fibre, to
stay a few more months. The slower growing ones are certainly worth
carrying on as long as you have space for them, for, although they will take
longer to mature, they will eventually be fine plants.

Chapter VII

SEEDLINGS FROM COMMUNITY POT TO FIRST BLOOM

By the time seedlings in community pots are ready to be moved into single pots, they have become fairly sturdy little plants. They have passed the most crucial phase of their lives, the first year out of the flasks. During this year the weaker plants have been weeded out, and those that have thrived offer good promise of growing to maturity. At this age, two to two and a half years from seed, they are a wonderful buy for amateurs. Their price is low enough to make it possible to buy quite a few. At present, five to ten seedlings in a community pot are $1 to $1.50 per plant. For a few dollars here and there you can have all the color variety imaginable, white, white with purple lip, yellow, and all the shades from pale pink to deep red-violet. You can have samples of the various bi- and tri-generic crosses. And you can have a continuation of fine blooms throughout the year.

While a flask of seedlings is a thrill that everyone should have at some time, the owner of a small greenhouse does not want to buy too many flasks. If your space is limited, you will acquire a collection of far wider variety if you buy only a few each of many different hybrids. The flask seedlings do not take up much room at first, but as they grow larger their very numbers may prevent the addition of other plants to your collection.

TRANSPLANTING TO FIRST SINGLE POTS

Seedlings from community pots usually go into 1¾- or 2-inch pots. You may use either size for the whole group of plants, or put smaller seedlings in the smaller size and larger ones in the larger pots. The latter are cared for a bit more easily. Put two or three small pieces of crock in the 1¾-inch and a few more in the 2-inch, and place a layer of fibre over the crock.

The seedlings are removed from the community pot just as before, by first soaking the pot, then knocking out or lifting up the whole mass of fibre containing the plants. Separate the seedlings from each other, leaving as much fibre around the roots as possible. It may be difficult to untangle the roots, as some of them grow to considerable length and wind through the

89

Seedlings ready for individual pots. Remove seedlings from the community pot, leaving a ball of fibre around each one. Set the seedling in its ball between two chunks of fibre, estimated to be enough to fill the new, small pot.

Place the whole bundle in the pot. Add more fibre at the sides, and work it all in together with a small potting stick, to give a good firm consistency.

Potting of the seedling completed. The surface of the fibre should be left rough.

fibre and around each other. Even with patience it is not always possible to keep from breaking the longer roots, so concentrate on saving the younger, newly growing ones.

Again, soft brown fibre is used. It should be rinsed and thoroughly drained, so that it remains just moist, and cut into chunks of various sizes.

Put a generous piece on each side of the plant, having the base of the plant securely held between them and not sticking up above the fibre. Set this bundle directly in the pot. Add more fibre at the sides, between the bundle and the pot, and work it all in together with a small potting stick. The fibre should be firm to the touch, still not as hard as for mature plants, and level across the top. The surface should be left rough, not trimmed down with scissors after potting. This allows the surface to dry out faster than the underneath part, and gives the new roots good growing conditions.

Put a label in each pot. This should be part of the potting routine, not only because it is more interesting to know what each plant is, but because a plant without a label is technically an "unknown" for the rest of its life.

CARE OF THE SEEDLINGS

It will take the newly potted seedlings several weeks to become active again after the shock of potting. Until the roots are again able to take up water from the fibre, the plants should be well shaded and lightly syringed two or three times a day. The purpose of the syringing is to reduce loss of water from the plant until the roots can again supply its needs. Do not syringe heavily, or the fibre will become saturated and the roots will be harmed. Soon you will see new roots growing through the surface of the fibre, and when these have reached a good length the number of syringings can be cut down. The fibre in the pots should be kept soft and moist. Pots of this size dry out rather rapidly, so they should be watered more frequently than larger ones, always being careful not to let the fibre stay too wet.

The extra shade required during the first few weeks can be supplied by stretching cheesecloth over the plants, thick enough to limit the amount of light to 500 foot-candles. At the end of this period, remove the shading gradually until in about two months the amount of light is increased to not more than 1000 foot-candles. This amount of light is about the standard until they reach flowering size. Watch the plants carefully, for they burn easily or turn yellow with too much light. If your greenhouse is devoted entirely to seedlings, the shading on the outside glass can be regulated to admit 1000 foot-candles of light, and individual groups be given additional shading as required. If you grow mature plants along with the seedlings, then the amount of light admitted must be greater, and all of the seedlings should be shaded in some way.

The atmosphere for seedlings should be warm and moist, but not saturated. Relative humidity should be about 70% in the daytime and 90% at night, and the seedlings should have a light syringing on bright days. Seedlings do not need as free ventilation as mature plants and should not be subjected to drafts. The ventilators should be opened with caution as to the outside temperature and wind direction. As with community pots, a slightly higher night temperature (65° F.) is beneficial, but not necessary.

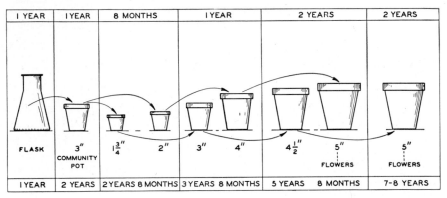

I YEAR	I YEAR	8 MONTHS	I YEAR	2 YEARS		2 YEARS
FLASK	3″ COMMUNITY POT	1¾″ 2″	3″ 4″	4½″ 5″ FLOWERS		5″ FLOWERS
I YEAR	2 YEARS	2 YEARS 8 MONTHS	3 YEARS 8 MONTHS	5 YEARS 8 MONTHS		7-8 YEARS

Diagram of potting schedule from flask to flower, showing size of pots required at certain ages, and the length of time spent in each.

The seedlings stay in these first individual pots for about eight months, after which they should be repotted. They will now be two and a half to three years old (from seed).

Seedlings Out of 1¾- and 2-Inch Pots

The difference in individual vigor of the seedlings shows up quite strikingly at this time. Some will be almost twice the size of others, and will probably flower a year or two earlier. Two more shifts to larger pots will bring the more vigorous ones to flowering size, but the others may have to be repotted a third time before they bloom. The diagram shown above illustrates the way the plants are moved into pots of suitable size and gives the approximate length of time in each. Each time, the faster growing plants move into pots of larger size than required by those that grow more slowly.

At each repotting, examine the roots of the seedling as you remove it from its pot. If they are in good condition and have made good growth, you may know that your treatment was right. Rotten roots are an indication of overwatering, whereas thin, emaciated roots show that the plant has been kept too dry.

The average size plant in this group will go into a 3-inch pot, while the smaller ones will need only a 2½-inch. Very large plants may go into 3½-inch pots, or even 4-inch ones if their growth merits it.

Stages of seedling growth. Center, a flask of seedlings six months from sowing. Left, growth is slow as the plants move from the flask to community pots, and then to the first individual pot. Right, each year's growth is larger as the seedlings become three, four, and five years old. The sheath on the largest indicates that it is attaining flowering size.

This time, after the pot has been soaked and the plant knocked out, there is a good ball of fibre around the roots. It is well to remove a little of this fibre, portions that do not contain roots, but leave the bulk of it undisturbed. Never remove fibre from around newly growing roots.

Set the plant in its ball of fibre into the new pot. Then with your fingers push pieces of fibre into the pot, around the plant, so that the fibre sticks up

Seedling in a 3-inch pot ready for a 4-inch. Soak the pot in water to loosen roots and then tap it gently on the edge of a table to remove the plant.

Remove some of old fibre, and trim off dead roots. Leave a good bit of fibre around new roots.

Place small chunks of fibre between roots to build up a compact ball.

Place the plant in its ball of fibre in prepared pot, centering it according to the direction of growth.

Work in more fibre with the potting stick. The fibre should be hard for a plant of this age.

above the rim. Now work it all in, shoving the potting stick down at the outer edge of the pot. This will tie the fibre together as one mass, giving it uniform substance and allowing for good drainage. The fibre should be firm, as before. It is poor technique to build up layers of fibre in the pot, which results when you poke pieces into the bottom and add piece after piece on top of these.

Care after potting is the same as for 1¾- and 2-inch pots, extra shade, light syringings, and care to keep the fibre from getting too wet.

When the seedlings have been in these pots for about a year, they will again be ready for repotting, and will be approaching four years of age.

Seedlings Out of 2½- to 4-Inch Pots

This time the plants have to be divided into two groups, the smaller ones that will go into 3- and 4-inch pots, and the larger ones that require 5-inch pots. The former, those that come out of 2½- and 3-inch pots, should be treated in exactly the same way as before. Those that have not made much progress should be given fresh fibre and kept in 3-inch pots for another year. The better plants may be moved into 4-inch pots, also to stay for a year.

The second group, those out of 3½- and 4-inch pots, are approaching flowering size, and the most vigorous ones may bloom in another year. These will stay in their new pots for about two years. The potting should be hard this time, as for adult plants.

Seedlings from 3½- and 4-inch pots should be put into 5-inch pots. An exceptionally large plant with many leads may need to be shifted into a 6-inch pot to give room for two years' growth. The plants should be staked, and each large growth tied to the stake, to avoid having the growths become sprawling. This not only makes neater looking plants but makes their handling safer. It is easy to break off a bulb that grows out of line and leans on the plant next to it.

To encourage the development of strong new roots, the care after potting includes what I call keeping them "on the dry side." The larger pots do not dry out as rapidly as the previous small sizes, and even when the surface of the pot seems dry, there is still quite a bit of moisture in the center. Watering should be much less frequent, therefore, and the fibre allowed to get really dry between times. If it is hard to resist watering the plants as frequently as you are accustomed to, just watch the fat, clean, new roots grow longer each day, and you will be rewarded for your abstinence. This should be continued until the roots are of good length and are penetrating the fibre to some depth, or until the surface roots reach the edge of the pot. Normal watering is then resumed. During the time the plants are kept "on the dry side," the usual light syringings prevent too much loss of water.

The leads that form at about five years of age often produce sheaths, which may or may not flower. The sheath is an indication that the plant is nearly ready to bloom, and the next growth will probably do so. A word should be said about repotting seedlings in sheath. If no flower buds form, and the seedling needs to be moved into a larger pot, do not hesitate to repot it. However, if buds are already forming in the sheath, wait until flowering is finished before repotting.

Vigorous five-year-old seedlings may be given gradually more light, but go slowly with this and watch the plants carefully for the usual signals.

First Flowering of the Seedlings

This is the long awaited reward for all your care of the seedlings. Not that watching their development from year to year has been without its own rewards, for it is a joy and a satisfaction to see them grow from tiny little things into large, stocky plants. An array of healthy seedlings is a sight almost as lovely as an array of flowers, and an achievement of which to be proud. But part of your pleasure in the seedlings is the knowledge that they hold a mystery in their being which will be unveiled only when they bloom.

At their first blooming the seedlings often produce only a single flower and become more floriferous later on. Stronger plants may give two or three flowers to a lead.

Before the seedlings flower their monetary value ranges between $15 and $25. As soon as they flower, their permanent value is set according to the quality of their flowers. One that gives choice blooms, of handsome shape and size, perfect texture, and rich coloring, may suddenly be worth $50 to $100. Another, equally good as a plant until now, may give poor blooms that suddenly lower its value. The percentage of fine flowers to be had from a group of seedlings is greater than the percentage from a group of imported species. And even poor hybrids are better than poor species.

The care of seedlings flowering for the first time is the same as the care of mature plants. The first flowers should not be left too long on a plant, unless it is quite vigorous. It is often thought that first flowers do not keep as well as those that come on mature plants. I have not found this to be true, but suspect that those who have had this experience may have watered the plant too heavily during flowering.

Conditions That Cause Flowering

Why do some plants flower at five years, others at six, and still others at the end of longer periods? What is it that takes the seedling out of its purely vegetative phase and makes it produce flowers?

The plant must have a sufficiently large leaf area to make the food necessary for the construction of flowers. This is, of course, related to the size, and consequently to the age of the plant. The length of time it takes a plant to reach such a size is fundamentally determined by its inheritance, and modified somewhat by environment. Since some Cattleyas flower at the age of five years, we might assume that that is the approximate age at which the genetic pattern allows flowering, provided that the plant is large enough. Also entering the picture here is the inherited blooming season.

But this is not the whole answer, and, in fact, the whole answer is not yet known. Although there is not much variation in length of day in the native habitats of Cattleyas, the slight differences may be influential. Certainly in this country the greater differences affect flowering seasons. Night temperature is a critical factor. There is evidence pointing to the existence of a hormone that causes flowering. Under favorable conditions a diffusible substance seems to be manufactured that initiates the formation of flowers. Indication of this has been shown in many experiments, of which the following is an example. If a branch of a seedling apple tree (which would not flower for some years) is grafted on an old tree, the seedling branch will flower when the tree flowers. Evidently it receives the flowering hormone from the old tree. The study of plant hormones is one of the growing fields of research in plant physiology.

There is, however, a very important factor in both growth and flowering which is well known. That is the balance between carbohydrates and nitrogen compounds within the plant. Both of these must be present in sufficient amounts in order to have good growth and satisfactory flowering. But the preponderance of one over the other at certain periods determines whether a plant will make purely vegetative growth or will set flower buds. Most of us are familiar with this in its practical application. Farmers use fertilizers on their crops to encourage rapid growth, but cease when they want the crop to initiate flowers. Growers of house plants shift them into fresh soil until they reach the desired size, and then let them become "pot bound" to induce them to flower. Vigorous vegetative growth depends on the accumulation of nitrogen compounds in some greater amount than carbohydrates. Flowering depends on the reverse situation.

Orchid seedlings moved frequently into fresh fibre grow rapidly because of the accumulation of an abundance of nitrogen. Nearly mature seedlings are left in the same pot for a longer time, which lessens the proportional amount of nitrogen available to them. During this time, the plants are given more light, the leaves manufacture greater amounts of carbohydrates, and the balance swings in favor of the latter. Thus, when the age and size of the plant and its inherited blooming season are right, and when the balance between carbohydrates and nitrogen compounds reaches the right proportions, flowering results.

Chapter VIII

GROWING AND SOWING YOUR OWN SEED

A simple maneuver with the forceps starts a seed pod on its way in your greenhouse. The human hand can perform in an instant the function of pollination, which in nature requires the most elaborate preparation and clever groundwork. Few orchids are capable of self-pollination. In fact, most orchids are constructed so that self-pollination in nature is impossible. It almost looks as if, in the long struggle for survival, those orchids which were perpetuated by cross-fertilization were the more vigorous, and lived to maintain their kind.

Orchids are equipped with fascinatingly ingenious mechanisms by means of which insects are practically forced to carry the pollen from one flower to another. Each mechanism is so well designed as to be almost foolproof, but an individual orchid lives under a perpetual handicap. Its mechanism will work only if an insect of just the right size and shape enters the portals so attractively spread for its reception. A tiny orchid, just ¼ inch in diameter, requires a very small insect, while another, whose nectar tube is in the form of a spur 10 inches long, needs the services of a species of moth with a 10-inch proboscis. A flower may be visited by scores of insects, yet may wither and die before the kind comes along that can serve as bearer of its pollen. However, when the right one does visit the flower, the insect is not allowed to leave without carrying with it a parcel of pollen glued to its anatomy.

The pollen grains are fastened together in rather large waxy masses called pollinia, so that if even only one insect visits the flower, it bears away with it enough pollen to fertilize another flower satisfactorily. Cleverly enough, in order to insure cross-pollination, orchids fasten the pollen masses to the insect as it leaves the flower.

Figs. 1A and 1B show in detail the reproductive parts of the Cattleya. The column is shown from its under side in A, and cut in half lengthwise in B. The anther (*a*), the cap that covers the pollinia, is fastened by a tiny hinge (*h*) to the end of the column. Protruding slightly from under the anther are the tips of the four caudicles (*c*) attached to the pollinia (*p*). The rostel-

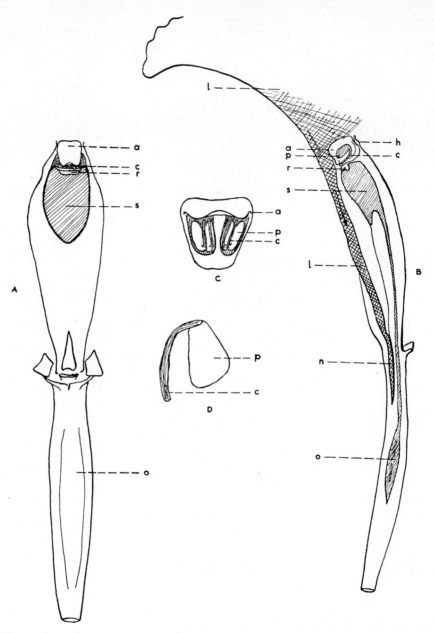

Fig. 1.   Reproductive parts of Cattleya. A shows the column from its under side, with the flower parts removed. B is a view of the column cut in half. It is seen from these drawings that what appears to be the stem of the flower is actually the ovary. (*a*) anther, (*h*) hinge that holds the anther in place, (*p*) pollinium, (*c*) caudicle, tail of the pollinium, (*r*) rostellum, (*s*) stigma, (*l*) lip, (*n*) nectary, (*o*) ovary. C is a view of the anther from its under side, showing the pollinia. D is a single pollinium with its caudicle.

lum (*r*), the partition between the anther chambers and the stigma, has on its under side a gland that secretes a sticky fluid. The stigma, which is really two stigmas grown together through the processes of evolution, is indicated by (*s*). The lip (*l*) presses up close under the column, forming a narrow passageway down which an insect must travel to reach the nectary (*n*) at its base. Fig. 1C shows the pollinia as they are situated in the anther chambers, after the anther has been raised, and Fig. 1D shows a single pollinium with attached caudicle.

The flower is pollinated by any rather large bee. When the bee lights on the lip its weight depresses the lip somewhat, and it then passes down the tube to get nectar. As it backs out of the tube, it pushes against the rostellum (*r*), ruptures the gland and becomes smeared with its sticky secretion. The force of the bee against the rostellum tips up the anther cap, touching off the spring. The anther flies back, rotating the pollinia so that the caudicles are exposed. As the bee backs farther out, the caudicles are caught in the sticky fluid on its back, and the pollinia are pulled out.

When the bee visits the next Cattleya, the pollinia on its back are forced into the stigmatic cavity. The stigmatic fluid is so sticky that it grips the pollen masses and tears them from the caudicles. After its feast of nectar, the bee leaves the flower with only the stumps of the caudicles attached, but in the process it will take with it the pollinia from this flower (if they have not already been removed) and bestow them on the next one it visits. You can imitate this by using a cotton swab for a bee. Push it down between the column and the lip, and as you pull it out watch the pollinia come with it. Then push it back into the flower and watch the pollinia stick to the stigma.

HAND POLLINATION

The simple sleight of hand that human beings can substitute for the natural process is to remove the pollinia from one orchid and place them directly on the stigma of another. But there is a difference between your responsibility and that of the flower where pollination is concerned. The flower makes elaborate preparations to insure pollination and the production of a huge number of seeds, from which possibly only one or two seedlings will grow. Your preparation consists of giving great care to the choice of parent plants so that the innumerable seeds you germinate will be worth your energy to raise.

If the flowers you wish to cross are of about the same size, and the plants are equally strong, it does not matter which one bears the pod. However, if one flower is much smaller than the other, it is better to put the pollen from the larger one on the stigma of the smaller. The reason is of a purely mechanical nature. The pollen from the small flower may give rise to pollen tubes too short to reach into the ovary of the larger flower, or at best they may reach only as far as the apex of the ovary. The cross might then produce little or no viable seed (seed containing an embryo).

A seedling blooming for the first time, or a propagation having only two or three bulbs, should not be allowed to bear a seed pod. The production of seed would take more food than it can afford and still be able to make good growth. Such a plant should donate the pollen and the larger, stronger plant should grow the seed. A very large, heavy plant may carry two or three pods at the same time or may bear pods in successive years. If you wish to cross the same plant with two or three different others, use a separate flower for each kind of pollen. Never put two kinds of pollen on one flower.

A flower must be allowed to reach its prime before it is pollinated, that is, it must have been open for several days. Remove its own pollinia before placing on its stigma the pollen with which you desire to cross it. If you have a particularly handsome flower with nothing else at the moment to match it in quality, it is possible to keep its pollen for use in the future (see below under storing seed and pollen).

It is not necessary to use all four pollinia in the pollination of one flower. Actually, nature has provided enough pollen in one pollen mass to produce a pod full of seed. The other three might be called a safety factor. However, it is customary to use two pollinia, one on the left lobe and one on the right lobe of the stigma.

To obtain the pollinia, hold a clean piece of paper under the tip of the column and gently tip up the anther cap with a clean toothpick or other pointed instrument. The anther chambers (actually the whole tip of the column) will come loose and fall onto the paper. Push the pollinia out of their chambers with the same instrument, being careful not to touch them with your fingers. An easy way to transfer a pollinium to the other flower is to touch the stigma with your instrument and then touch the pollen mass. The pollinium will stick to the viscid drop on the instrument. Pollination is performed simply by pressing the pollinia well into the stigmatic fluid, one on each side. Once covered by the sticky substance, they will not fall off.

The first reaction of the flower after pollination is to wilt, sometimes within a few hours, certainly after two days. After the flower parts have wilted they should be cut off at their base to prevent decay and possible infection of the column. The column is, of course, left intact during formation of the seed pod.

Hold a clean piece of paper under the tip of the column, then tip up the anther gently until it comes off.

The column is prepared by removing its own pollinia. Then the pollinia from the other parent flower are removed from their anther case. To pick up a pollinium, first touch the stigma with a pointed instrument and then touch the sticky point to the caudicle of a pollinium. Press the pollinium onto the stigma. In the photograph, one pollinium has been placed on the stigma, and the second, on the pencil point, will be put on the other side.

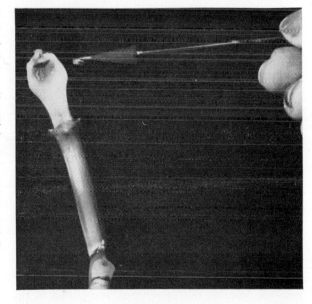

Development of the Seed Pod

Within a week after pollination, the tip of the column becomes swollen
and the pollinia seem to have been drawn deeply into the cavity. At about

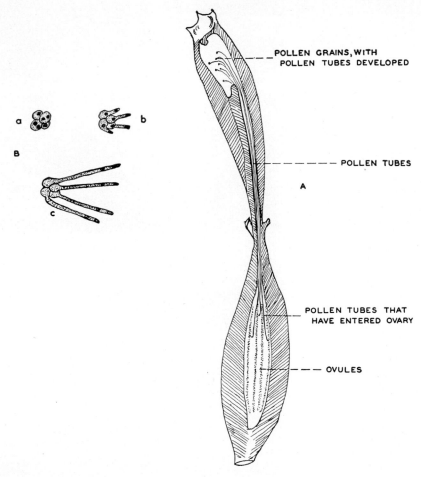

Fig. 2. A is the column and ovary 60 days after pollination. The pollen tubes have
reached the ovary, which by this time is definitely enlarged. B shows pollen grains at
various stages: a, as they originate, usually in groups of four; b, with tubes just
starting; c, tubes elongating, and the nuclei carried along near the tip.

the same time, the ovary begins to enlarge. These reactions are merely the
first responses to the presence of the pollen in the stigma. They are not a
sign that fertilization of the eggs has taken place.

Each pollen grain, stimulated by the action of the stigmatic fluid, sends out a long slender tube. The pollen tubes grow down through the channel of the column, along the walls of the ovary, and eventually each tube penetrates an ovule. Fig. 2A shows this process, and Fig. 2B pictures sprouted pollen grains. During the growth of the pollen tube, two sperm cells are formed within it, one of which unites with the egg nucleus in the ovule. (The other sperm cell unites with other nuclei in the ovule to form the endosperm, tissue used as food by the developing embryo.) It takes 60 to 90 days for the pollen tubes to complete their growth and penetrate the ovules.

Every viable seed formed is the result of the penetration of an ovule by a pollen tube. Production of 500,000 seeds means that 500,000 pollen tubes were able to find their mark. How the 500,000th tube manages to find a still unfertilized ovule is something to puzzle over. That many pollen tubes are not successful is attested by the fact that often the greatest concentration of viable seed is found near the top of the ovary.

Incompatibility between the pollen and the flower on which it is placed often occurs. Sometimes it shows up within a few days by the shriveling of the column. The same pollen used on another flower might, however, have effected a successful mating. Sometimes a seed pod that seems to be progressing will turn yellow and drop off after two or three months. The ovules are immature at the time of pollination. Their maturation proceeds and the ovary enlarges while the pollen tubes are growing the necessary length. If for some reason the pollen tubes finally fail to effect fertilization, growth of the seed pod ceases.

If the cross is compatible, the ovary enlarges steadily. During its development it becomes marked with three deep flutings, corresponding to the three faint linear depressions visible on the ovary before pollination. The seed pod is completely hollow, containing three broad bands (placentae) to which the ovules are attached.

At six months the seed pod is about the size of a lemon and it does not enlarge much after this time. It ripens at about 9–10 months, occasionally later, and cracks open down the center of the flutings. The time to remove the pod is just when the cracks begin to show, before they have opened wide enough to allow the seed to spill out. To prevent losing any seed, it is a good idea to tie tissue paper over the seed pod a few weeks beforehand, and examine it from day to day. When the time comes for its removal, cut the stem that holds it to the pseudobulb, and place the pod in a clean glass jar to dry. Set the jar in a dry place, leaving it uncovered. Do not leave it in the greenhouse. If your climate is damp, the seed pod should be wrapped lightly in tissue paper and dried in a desiccator containing calcium chloride. When the pod is dried and split completely open, the seed can be shaken out into a clean container. It is ready to be sowed at this time, if you desire, but excess seed should be properly stored.

A Cattleya seed pod, five months after pollination.

STORING SEED AND POLLEN

A desiccator is a glass container having two chambers, one holding calcium chloride which absorbs water vapor and the other containing the stored material. They can be purchased, but are rather expensive. A makeshift one will do as well. Use a wide-mouthed jar, and put two tablespoons of calcium chloride in the bottom. Make a shelf, out of hardware cloth or screen, that will rest in the center and divide the jar into two compartments, separating the calcium chloride from the upper part. A layer of paper over the screen will afford additional protection, yet still allow free circulation of air. Put the material to be stored in the top section, and screw on tightly a vacuum sealing lid. While drying the seed pod in the desiccator, let it remain at room temperature, as it will dry more rapidly this way than under refrigeration.

After the seed is removed from the pod, it should be kept under refrigeration. Cut pieces of writing paper (not wax paper) about 4 inches square, and in the center of each write the names of the parent plants so that the label

COLOR PLATE 5. Laeliocattleya Gold Gleam.

will be visible after the seed is wrapped. Then put a small amount of seed in each paper, and fold carefully, as the druggist wraps powders, fastening the ends with a paper clip. Place the packages in the desiccator, screw on the lid, and put in the refrigerator.

Seed retains its viability for a long time when stored in this manner, sometimes as long as six years. The percentage of germination decreases gradually, however, so that it may give only 20–40% after a long period.

Pollen does not remain viable for as long as seed, but may be kept for at least six months. Its viability is highest during the first few weeks. To store pollen, place the pollinia in a tiny glass tube, cork it tightly, and dip the corked end in paraffin to seal it. Then keep the tube in a refrigerator. Some advise the addition of a few granules of calcium chloride to the tube (in which case the pollinia must be wrapped in tissue paper to prevent contact with the calcium chloride), or else that the pollinia be dried in a desiccator for two days before placing in the glass tube.

CHECKING VIABILITY OF SEED AND POLLEN

Crosses between closely related species usually produce viable seed and pollen. Sterility is more likely to occur in complicated hybrids, particularly those derived from extremely dissimilar flowers. Testing the viability of seed and pollen is a simple matter, though in nine cases out of ten it is not necessary for amateurs to bother with it. Commercial growers and those who are carrying on serious breeding programs find it a necessary procedure. Discovery ahead of time that a certain pollen is not viable enables the grower to choose some other pollen for use on a choice flower. Otherwise he may have to wait another year to mate that particular plant. The benefit of checking the viability of the seed before sowing a hundred or more flasks is obvious.

To test the pollen, place a little of it on a flower that you do not wish to save, a "cull." Pollen tubes commence to grow within 48 hours and can be seen under a microscope. Remove some of the stigmatic fluid on a pin point, mix it with a drop of water on a microscope slide, and cover with a cover glass. The sprouted pollen can be seen unstained, but if you wish to stain them add a drop of crystal violet solution to the water. Fig. 2B, mentioned above, shows the pollen grains with tubes in various stages of growth. If you do not have a spare flower for this process, the pollen may be tested in a 0.2-molar sucrose solution (about 1 teaspoon of sugar in 13 teaspoons of water) with agar added, kept at 72° F.

In any batch of seed there are some that do not contain embryos. Figs. 3A and 3B show a sample of Cattleya seed, with and without embryos, as seen under a microscope. To observe your own seed, mix a small amount with water, and place on a slide under a cover glass. Count the seed with and without embryos and estimate the relative percentage of good seed; 80 to 90% is good. If no seeds have embryos, the lot must be discarded. You will have to use your own judgment as to whether to use seed that shows only a low percentage with embryos. Perhaps it will pay to try it for the sake of obtaining a few seedlings from a most unusual cross.

A further check of seed viability, and the one of real significance, is to sow a flask or two and see how well it germinates. This necessitates waiting three or four weeks, or until the seed swells and turns green. It sometimes happens (though rarely) that seed that appears under the microscope to be good is actually not living. This check would be well worth your while for seed that has been stored an excessively long time or has not been kept under good conditions.

Preparation of the Flasks

The agar-nutrient medium for growing flask seedlings can be bought ready-mixed, so that beginners need not be awed by the list of chemicals involved. It is prepared by the Difco Company, Detroit 1, Michigan, under the name of "Bacto Orchid Agar." Complete directions (requiring only the addition of distilled water and warming) are given, and if followed carefully, results should be perfect. The mixture is already adjusted to the correct acidity, so that the beginner does not even have this to worry him.

Usually, 500 c.c. Ehrlenmeyer flasks are used, but almost any type of jar or bottle will serve as well—large medicine bottles with screw caps, whiskey bottles, or ½-pint milk bottles. The main qualifications are that they should be capable of sterilization, have a large enough area in the bottom (several square inches), and either have a screw cap or be adaptable for the cotton plug type of stopper. Containers should be thoroughly washed, rinsed several times, and boiled to be sure that they are free from any material that might deter plant growth.

If you are going to use cotton plugs, you had better practice making them beforehand. They can be used for any bottle that has a neck dimension of ½ to 1½ inches. New cotton should be used, and must be nonabsorbent (obtainable at the drugstore). The amount of cotton necessary for the stopper will vary according to the size of the mouth of the flask or bottle. For one with a 1-inch diameter, tear a strip of cotton about 1 foot long and 4 inches wide. Lay it on a table and fold the wispy edges in about half an inch on each side. Now turn up the lower end and, with your fingers always pressing in the center, roll the cotton as tightly as you can. The finished plug should be hard, slightly smaller in the center than at the ends, and should not come unrolled. The ends should be smooth. Now put it in the bottle, with a screwing motion. It should not be so thick that you might break the neck forcing it in, yet it should fit tightly enough so that you can pick up the bottle by the plug.

When the agar-nutrient mixture has been prepared, it is ready to be poured into the flasks or bottles. Use a long-necked funnel so that the end comes close to the bottom of the bottle. Otherwise the agar will splash on the sides. Be careful not to spill any on the neck, either on the inside or outside. This is essential both to prevent sticking of the cotton plugs and to avoid giving molds a place to grow. The agar should be about an inch and one-half deep.

Each bottle should be stoppered before sterilization. Cotton plugs should be inserted so that two-thirds of the length is in the neck, with the other third protruding. Screw caps should be tightened and then released one-quarter of a turn.

Laboratory workers will be able to sterilize their flasks in an autoclave, but home canning equipment does just as well, either a pressure cooker or a hot-water-bath kettle, preferably the former. In either case, you must be sure that no water enters the flasks or bottles. In a pressure cooker, 20 minutes at 15 pounds pressure is sufficient. If a canning kettle is used, adjust the water level to the level of the agar in the bottles to prevent their tipping while boiling. Cover the kettle and boil for one hour. After sterilization, remove the bottles while still hot (be sure the pressure in the pressure cooker has gone down), pour the water out of the kettle, then quickly put the bottles back in the kettle and cover with a clean cloth. This will allow them to cool, and the stoppers to dry out, without becoming contaminated. If possible, keep them thus protected until you are ready to use them.

Sowing the Seed

This process is so simple that the doing of it takes no longer than the telling. In fact, none of the procedures described thus far is difficult, and if the detailed descriptions make any part of them seem so, you have only to try it all, step by step, to realize that each is essentially easy. The second time you go through the process, you will wonder that you could ever have thought it complicated.

Sowing the seed consists of two main steps: (1) disinfecting the seed by soaking it in an antiseptic solution, and (2) putting a little of the suspended seed in each flask.

Cleanliness has been emphasized as an important factor in each step so far, and is even more important here. The air is filled with mold spores. You are going to have to open the sterile flasks briefly to insert the seed, and you must take every precaution against contamination of the flasks during that short time. Wait until the day's activities in the kitchen are over and the air has had a chance to settle before you begin to work. I like to spread damp dish towels on the work surface as an extra protection against dust.

Equipment you will need includes a ¼-ounce vial with a cork, a new medicine dropper, a glass or china cup, a graduated cylinder that holds 100 c.c., two empty bottles, filter paper, glass funnel, and an open flame (gas burner or alcohol lamp).

The seed may harbor mold spores acquired during handling and must therefore be disinfected. A solution of calcium hypochlorite* is standard for this purpose. Buy a bottle of it at the drugstore and keep it tightly stoppered in the refrigerator. To make up the solution put 10 grams of the solid calcium hypochlorite in one bottle and add 140 c.c. of distilled water. Shake thoroughly, and filter off the clear solution into the other bottle. This must be used at once. (Any amount left over must be thrown away, and fresh solution made up each time you prepare to sow flasks.)

Fill the little vial two-thirds with the calcium hypochlorite solution, and add a tiny bit of seed. The amount you can pick up on the tip of a paring knife will sow ten or a dozen flasks. (The knife, incidentally, should be sterilized by flaming and completely cooled before touching the seed.) Cork the vial tightly. The seed must be thoroughly wetted with the calcium hypochlorite solution, which requires that it be shaken vigorously and continuously for at least 20 minutes to break up the minute air bubbles that surround each seed.

While you are shaking the seed, put some of the remaining calcium hypochlorite solution in the cup and place the dropper in it to soak, being sure to fill the bulb as well as the glass part. You might also check on the arrangement of your equipment. Everything should be close together, the flasks, still in their covered container, the flame (for flaming the flasks), and the cup with the dropper. The enamel top of a table-type gas stove is an ideal work place, or a kitchen table if you are using an alcohol lamp.

*Note that calcium hypochlorite is an entirely different chemical from the calcium chloride used in the desiccator. Calcium hypochlorite may be purchased as chlorinated lime.

When the seed has been disinfected, you are ready to sow the flasks. The work will move more smoothly if you can have a helper at your first session, either to attend to the flasks or to drop the seed into them, but you can manage alone if you must. The following operations must be performed quickly so that the flask will be open to the air for as short a time as possible.

Take one flask at a time from the covered container and remove the stopper. (A screw cap may be put in a dish of the disinfecting solution while the flask is being sown. A cotton plug must not be put down on anything. It is necessary to hold it (by its top end) during the sowing process, which is where a helper comes in handy.) Rotate the open neck of the flask in the flame for a few seconds, to kill spores that may have settled on it.

The seed will by now either have risen to the surface of the solution in the vial or sunk to the bottom, and you do not want to remove all of it in one dropper full. It should be quickly stirred up by putting the end of the dropper down in the bottom of the vial and forcing the air out of it. The bubbles will swirl the fluid and the seed, and you can then take up a few drops to be transferred to the flask. Hold the dropper in the neck of the flask so that the drops will not run down the sides. Four drops is a good amount to put in each one, and if you move the dropper slightly in a circle you can put each drop in a different place on the agar. As soon as the seed is dropped in, flame the neck of the flask again, and replace the cap or plug. Screw caps are tightened firmly.

An additional technique in the use of cotton stoppers is to flame them before re-insertion after sowing the seed. Flaming the stopper is, of course, a protection against spores that may settle on it during the sowing process, but I should suggest that you either omit it from your first series or else practice well beforehand with extra stoppers. Touch the cotton plug to the flame, let the flame surround it, and then very gently blow out the flame, rotating it as you blow. A good hard plug will burn slowly and evenly, but a loose one will flame up high and be impossible to blow out. There is the disadvantage of stirring up the air with the blowing, and shreds of burned cotton may drop into the flask. If your flasks are kept covered after sterilization and are used soon after cooling, flaming the stoppers is not really necessary. It is important to do it, however, if the flasks have not been kept covered.

When all of the flasks are sown, pick up each one and gently tilt it back and forth to spread the seed over the surface of the agar. Cotton plugs must be covered, preferably with waterproof cellophane, or with wax paper, tied with string. Be sure that all flasks are labeled and dated.

One or two of the flasks may have become contaminated at the time of

Add carefully weighed amount of Difco Bacto Orchid Agar to one liter of distilled water in double boiler. Heat until thoroughly dissolved.

Pour melted agar-nutrient mixture into flasks, using a long-stemmed funnel. The flasks are then stoppered and sterilized in a pressure cooker.

Disinfecting the seed. Calcium hypochlorite solution from the flask at the left is put in a small vial, to which is added a bit of seed on the tip of a knife. The dropper to be used in the sowing process is put to soak at the same time in a cup containing solution.

Flasks are taken one at a time from the pressure cooker, in which they were sterilized and allowed to cool. The flamed stopper is removed, the neck of the flask revolved quickly in the flame, and a few drops of suspended seed inserted. The neck of the flask must be reflamed before replacing the plug.

sowing and they will show growth of molds on the agar within a few days. It is to be hoped that not all of them will be so affected, for there is nothing you can do but start over if that happens. Do not let it discourage you. With further trials your speed and dexterity will increase so that eventually you will be able to turn out 100% clean flasks.

CARE OF FLASKS

Cattleya seed germinates and grows best at temperatures between 70° and 75° F. The temperature may rise a little in warm weather. Ideally the temperature should be 70°–75° F. at night also, but if you cannot maintain this, let the night temperature drop to 65°. A fluctuation of more than 10 degrees either way is not good for the developing seedlings and will retard their growth. Flasks may be kept on a shaded shelf in the greenhouse, or in a glass case with added humidity in the house. The latter is necessary to keep the flasks from drying in the drier atmosphere of the house.

In extreme cases of drying, it is necessary to add a little sterile distilled water to the flask. This is a risky procedure, however, and unless done expertly may result in contamination. The screw cap and neck of a bottle or jar must be thoroughly swabbed before opening with a disinfecting solution (one part of Clorox to ten parts of water). Then lift the lid only high enough to admit the dropper (previously sterilized) and replace it quickly after the water is added. Flasks with cotton plugs must also be treated with the Clorox solution. Swab the neck and rim of the flask, and allow the solution to moisten the cotton plug where it comes in contact with the glass. Then inject the sterile distilled water by means of a hypodermic syringe, inserting the needle between the glass and the cotton. Cover the stopper with fresh cellophane afterward.

During the development of the seedlings, disturb the flasks as little as possible. Jostling the flasks sometimes allows mold spores that have settled on the neck or the stopper to drop into the agar and cause contamination.

DEVELOPMENT OF THE SEEDLINGS

About ten days or two weeks after the seed is sown it begins to swell. Within six weeks the seed turns green, showing the development of chlorophyll. Fig. 3 shows the stages of development of the seedling. The embryo continues to increase in size until it is a little green spherule, about $\frac{1}{16}$ inch in diameter, shaped like a top, with a depression in its upper surface. Absorbing hairs soon cover the surface. Between two and three months after the seed was sown, the first leaf point makes its appearance in the middle of

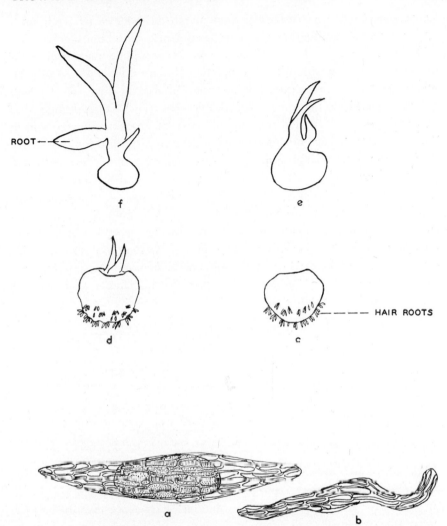

Fig. 3. Development of Cattleya seedlings. a, a seed with an embryo. b, a seed without an embryo. c, spherule stage; the embryo increases in size until it bursts the seed coat, and then enlarges into a spherule. Absorbing (hair) roots develop on its surface. d, the first leaves develop two to three months after sowing. e, elongation of the stem, with more leaves appearing. f, seedling at about nine months, showing first root growing from the stem below the second leaf.

the depression, and the spherule becomes larger and somewhat flattened. This disc-like structure is called the protocorm. Soon a second and third leaf appear, the stem elongates, and the first root grows down. By the sixth month the seedling is well developed. During the following months the leaves grow larger, and additional roots may form. Nine to twelve months after sowing, the seedlings are ready to transplant to community pots.

Differences in growth rate show up markedly among the seedlings in the flask. Some reach transplanting size in six months, while others are still spherules. If you remove the seedlings from the flask at this time, you will have fewer seedlings to grow on, for they do not survive transplanting unless they have gone well beyond the spherule stage. It is better to leave them in the flask the full time, until most of them have roots ¼ inch long. You will then have some very large seedlings among a quantity of average and small size. There are always some that do not develop beyond the spherule stage.

After you have grown seedlings with the Difco product, you may want to mix your own medium. You should start with a standard formula, and later, if you want to join the ranks of experimenters, you may want to try the addition of vitamins or other growth promoting substances to the media. It should be said here that, up to now, research has produced no better formulas than those of Dr. Knudson. Therefore his latest one, Knudson's "C," is given as the standard.

KNUDSON'S FORMULA "C"

Chemical	Symbol	Amount
Calcium Nitrate	$Ca(NO_3)_2 \cdot 4H_2O$	1.00 gram
Monobasic Potassium Phosphate . .	KH_2PO_4	0.25 gram
Magnesium Sulfate	$MgSO_4 \cdot 7H_2O$	0.25 gram
Ammonium Sulfate	$(NH_4)_2SO_4$	0.50 gram
Sucrose	$C_{12}H_{22}O_{11}$	20.00 grams
Ferrous Sulfate	$FeSO_4 \cdot 7H_2O$	0.025 gram
Manganese Sulfate	$MnSO_4 \cdot 4H_2O$	0.0075 gram

These chemicals must be weighed with extreme care, using a fine balance. Any discrepancy in the proportions of the chemicals, even of the sugar, may be disastrous to the seedlings. If you do not have access to a fine balance, or are unaccustomed to its use, you had better ask your druggist to do the weighing for you. (Incidentally, he will also assist you with the name of a chemical supply house where you can buy the ingredients, or will sell them to you himself.)

Add the above ingredients, one at a time, to one liter (1000 c.c.) of distilled water, and dissolve completely. Then add 15 grams of agar (Difco Bacto Agar*), and warm in a double boiler until all of the agar is dissolved.

After the medium is thus prepared, and before sterilization, it is necessary to check the *p*H (which means hydrogen ion concentration). The *p*H scale

* Plain agar containing no nutrients.

is based on units from 0–14, which indicate the degree of acidity or akalinity of a solution; 7 is neutral. Below 7 the solution is acid, and the lower the number the more acid it is. Above 7 it is alkaline. Cattleya seed (and that of most orchids) grows best in a solution that has a *p*H of 5.0–5.2. This degree of acidity is necessary to make the minerals available for the use of the seedlings. Too great an acidity often kills the seed, and a too alkaline condition impoverishes the seedlings by preventing the plants from obtaining the necessary minerals. Equipment to test *p*H can be bought from most supply houses, and ranges from the expensive electrode type to the cheaper color indicator kind. Full directions come with the equipment.

Checking the *p*H consists of removing a small amount of the agar-nutrient medium as soon as it is prepared (before sterilization), and testing it with whatever type of equipment you have. If it is found to be too alkaline, add a drop or two of 0.1 normal hydrochloric acid to the whole amount of medium, mix thoroughly, and then remove a small quantity again for checking. Continue until the *p*H reads between 5.0 and 5.2. If the medium as first mixed turns out to be too acid, add 0.1 normal potassium hydroxide solution, and proceed in the same manner.

Use of Wire Loop for Sowing Seed

Experts prefer a fine wire loop instead of a dropper for sowing seed. The loop is a bit difficult for beginners to use, so the dropper has been suggested to simplify things at first. The loop has the advantage of picking up the seed with very little of the sterilizing solution clinging to it, and in an expert hand the seed may be spread evenly on the agar. It is particularly useful in handling seed that sticks to the sides of the vial—Cymbidium seed, for instance.

The end of a fine platinum wire is made into a loop about $\frac{3}{16}$ inch in diameter, and attached by the other end to a long slender handle. When the loop is dipped into a suspension of orchid seed, it comes out with a thin film of fluid spread within the loop, holding a good number of seeds. For seed that floats, the loop is dipped only into the upper surface. Where the seed sinks, the sterilizing solution can be poured off first, leaving the collection of seed in the bottom of the vial.

The loop is sterilized by flaming, and completely cooled before touching the seed. To be sure that it is cool, you might dip it into another vial of the disinfecting solution you are using. To sow the seed, the loop is drawn lightly across the agar, not really touching the agar but merely the moisture that has exuded on its surface.

Clorox as a Disinfecting Solution

Preparation of the calcium hypochlorite solution for disinfecting the seed is really a simple matter, but a search has been going on to find some common household item that can be used satisfactorily in its stead. Clorox seems to fit the requirements, but must be used with caution. The dilution must be very weak, and the seed must not be allowed to stand in it for more than a certain length of time. Concentrations of clorox above a certain strength, or exposure beyond the time limit, are injurious to the seed and cut down the percentage of germination. The use of Clorox, therefore, depends on speed in the sowing process.

Experiments of our own and others indicate that a dilution of 1 c.c. of Clorox to 99 c.c. of distilled water (measured in a graduated cylinder) is strong enough to prevent infection of the flasks and not too strong to harm the seed. A dilution of 1 c.c. of Clorox to 54 c.c. of water is also suggested, but is the absolute limit of strength that is safe for the seed. Seed should be shaken in the Clorox solution for exactly 10 minutes (no longer), and sown at once, so that the total time in Clorox does not exceed 20 minutes, if possible.

Slanting Flasks or Bottles

Many growers prefer to have the agar on a slant in flask or bottle. This gives a little wider growing area, and with the flask held on a slant during the sowing process mold spores are less likely to enter the mouth. A simple rack can be built to keep the flasks tipped at the desired angle. The sterilized flasks are placed in the rack before the agar jells and covered to prevent contamination. After the flasks are sown they are kept in the rack.

Germinating Green Seed

Cattleya seed is easy to disinfect and germinates readily on the agar-nutrient medium. Some orchid seed, however, is both difficult to disinfect and slow to germinate. Research has been carried on with a view to finding some stage in its development when seed may be removed from an unripe pod and will germinate when thus planted green. One object of the research is to find a stage at which the obstinate Cypripedium seed may be planted and made to germinate more readily than it does when ripe. (See Chapter XII.)

In the course of this work it has been found that Cattleya ovules will germinate when removed six months after pollination. For most people this is merely a matter of interest, but the time it saves (three to five months of waiting for the pod to mature) may be used to good advantage by some.

To avoid having to sterilize the seed and run the risk of contaminated flasks, some workers like to open the nearly ripe pod just before it is ready to split open. This must be done under sterile conditions, of course, the seed pod swabbed or soaked with 1–10 Clorox and all instruments sterilized. The seed is removed with a loop and planted immediately.

Chapter IX

THE ORCHID TRIBES

When Nature drew the designs for the orchid family, she combined and recombined the basic flower pattern in every conceivable way and decorated her handiwork with all of the colors at her command. She created forms of beauty so serene, so pure, as to be almost sublime. She created other forms rich and showy, almost sensual. And then she turned or twisted, reduced or enlarged, shortened or lengthened each floral part to make thousands of new forms, lurid or beautiful, giant or pigmy, satanic or humorous. If a mathematician or a statistician were to try to compete with her, he would find that he could put together no new combinations that did not already have a counterpart in her work.

Man has been at work for more than a hundred years, naming and classifying the myriad orchids that have so far been discovered. Yet many are still hidden in jungle wilds or remote places, and each passing year brings to light some form new to his knowledge. It is characteristic of human beings that they must put a name to everything. And it is characteristic of scientists that the name must be so definite, so specific, that there can be no possible confusion of one object with another.

When a new orchid is found, even after it has bloomed and its major characteristics have been observed, it takes patient hours of dissection and study to determine with what group of orchids it belongs. Perhaps it does not fit with any established genus or tribe, and a new category must be made for it. Often the experts do not agree. One may feel that some slight difference is significant enough to warrant the creation of a new genus. Others may insist that it is only a variation of a kind already classified. When you look up almost any orchid in Bailey's "Standard Cyclopedia of Horticulture," you see evidence of past confusion in the chronology of names that have been given to a single species.

The major sorting process, which gives a starting point in the classification of the 15,000 species, is the division into tribes. Each tribe of orchids might be compared to a deck of cards, which you sort into a pack because of the distinctive design on the back of each one. As the deck is divided into suits, each with its outstanding mark, so the tribe is divided into genera, each with its own characteristic features. Every card in a suit differs from every other by the picture on it, or the number. Which brings us to the final division of the genus, the species. The species belonging to any one genus bear the hallmark of the genus, but each is different from the rest by some individual feature.

When you see the six of hearts, you have no doubt in what suit it belongs, or which card in the suit it is. But you cannot say just "six" or just "hearts." Similarly you cannot specify what member of the genus you mean by saying just "Cattleya," for there are many members of the genus Cattleya. Nor can you say just "labiata," for that name may refer to a member of another genus. As soon as you say *"Cattleya labiata"* you erase all confusion, for there is no other kind of orchid that goes by those two names together. For clarity and convenience, it is an established rule to give the name of the genus first, as *Cattleya,* and then the specific name, as *labiata.*

A species often has a number of color variations distinct enough to be given an additional descriptive, or varietal, name. For instance, *Cattleya labiata* has a white form that is called variety *alba,* a form that is white with a purple lip, called variety *Amesiana,* and one in which the coloring is much deeper than the type, called variety *superba.*

Most orchid tribes are so prolific that it would take a lifetime to collect a single specimen of all of the species included in just one tribe, to say nothing of the varieties of each species. Should you start on such a project, you might run into difficulties. Some tribes spread over a geographical area that includes all sorts of climatic conditions, so that its members may not be suited to the conditions of a single greenhouse. In any tribe, of course, there are some members more desirable for cultivation than others. Unless you have the urge to own every species in a tribe, you will select from many tribes those that have a special appeal for you. You may choose a plant for its graceful habit, its showy flowers, its intriguing shape, unusual coloring, delightful fragrance, or even for its size, for instance, a dwarf plant whose minuteness is a charm in itself.

Botanists are interested in all kinds of plants, however insignificant they may seem to most people. Because of this, orchids that are of no commercial value, or that are not widely known, are often called "botanicals." Many of the botanicals are every bit as lovely as those with which we have better acquaintance, and these may someday find a place alongside their more popular relatives. Many amateurs find their chief interest in orchids not usually seen in the florist shop or in general collections.

Genera are known which have as many as 1000 species. For others only two or three species are known, and the rest run somewhere between these extremes. Obviously nothing less than an encyclopedia could describe all of the species.

Certain genera have been acclaimed by the public as the most beautiful and the most useful. Others, not as valuable commercially, are loved by collectors. Instead of presenting them to you as disconnected genera, each will be introduced along with the other members of its tribe. Many lovely orchids exist in the less well-known genera. To learn to know them in their relation to the more famous ones is to acquire a better understanding of them.

The key to the tribes will be found in the Appendix and contains many more than can be included here. The nineteen tribes to be discussed will be given space in proportion to their current popularity and the actual value to orchid lovers of the genera they include.

THE AERIDES TRIBE

The genera belonging to this tribe number eighteen, and though many are attractive and well worth growing, two are particularly outstanding. These are Phalaenopsis and Vanda, whose lovely sprays of subtly tinted, sweetly rounded blooms are sublime among flowers.

The growth habit is distinct from that of Cattleyas. Instead of producing a new growth each year from the base of the preceding one, that is, from a continuous rhizome (sympodial), these have but a single stem which increases in height from year to year (monopodial). Each year the plant produces a new set of leaves from the tip of the stem, a new set of roots from between the recently matured leaves, and flower stems from the axils of the leaves.

The native habitats of the Aerides tribe are the hot, humid regions of the Asiatic tropics. They are found growing usually on trees, often on rocks. In general they are subject to abundant rain during their growing season, which is followed by a season of moderate dryness.

PHALAENOPSIS

The "moth orchid" (Greek, *phaluna* meaning moth, *-opsis* meaning resembling) receives its name from its similarity to some tropical moths. There are about fifty species. The beautiful flowers would be worth growing even if they lasted for only a few days, but the fact that they keep for weeks, and that one plant will produce successive sprays throughout a period of months, makes them all the more desirable.

The foliage is attractive. The long, broad leaves are leathery, often mottled

COLOR PLATE 6. Laeliocattleya Derna.

with gray, purple underneath, and usually drooping. The plants increase in height only slowly, and but two or three new leaves are produced each year. The roots appear from the stem between the mature leaves and grow down, sometimes into the fibre, but much more often attaching themselves to the pot or to anything with which they come into contact.

Phalaenopsis amabilis, popular among beginners, and one of the loveliest of the genus. Note that the stem just above the spray of flowers produced a second flower stem after the first was cut. (Courtesy of Jones and Scully, Inc.)

The growing season is from about March to October, after which the flower spikes make their appearance. The spikes are long and arching, sometimes branched, and carry a generous number of blooms. Part of the charm of the flower sprays is their habit of presenting every flower facing in the same direction. As your eye wanders the length and breadth of the spray, something stirs within you at beauty in such abundance.

The flowers divide themselves structurally into two groups. The first group, called Euphalaenopsis, is characterized by antennae-like appendages on the lip and by petals much broader than the sepals. The second group, Stauroglottis, has petals similar to the sepals, and a lip without appendages. In both groups, the variously shaped lip is united with the base of the column.

The plants are so generous with their blooms that they often produce a second and even a third spray after the first one is cut. The first spray is cut off just below the bottom flower, leaving several nodes from one of which

A house of Phalaenopsis, where breath-taking beauty abounds for months on end.
(Courtesy of Jones and Scully, Inc.)

the secondary flowering occurs. Each spray may last in blossom for as long as two months, so that flowers may be had on a single plant for five or six months. In order to keep a continuous show of Phalaenopsis, some growers delay the flowering of a few plants by pinching out the tips of the flowering spikes when they are about a foot long. The setback causes them to flower a few weeks later than usual. It also decreases the number of flowers, but this is offset by having them in blossom when the others have finished. Reducing the temperature by 5 degrees or so will delay the opening of flowers and is a method used to hold over the flowering of a plant for a special purpose. The white varieties flower over naturally longer periods than the pink ones.

Culture

Potting. Phalaenopsis requires rather small pots or baskets and need not be repotted frequently. Osmunda fibre, in a pot half full of drainage crock, is a good medium. It is something of a job to remove a plant from a pot to which the roots are clinging on all sides. So that, rather than repot every time, some growers replace the top fibre with fresh pieces. Also, as the plant grows taller bit by bit, pieces of fibre may be stuffed in between the newer roots. When complete repotting is necessary, take the plant from the pot and remove all decayed fibre from between the roots. Center the plant in its new pot, and stuff fresh fibre between the roots and around the base, which should be just below the surface. Push the fibre in with your fingers and potting stick, but do not pot as firmly as for Cattleyas. The best time to repot is just after flowering when the new roots are beginning to form.

After potting, give water sparingly until new roots are well formed. Keep the atmosphere well saturated, and spray overhead lightly on bright days.

Temperature. These plants from the hot, humid regions of Asia must be kept warm. The night temperature should not go below 60° F. at any time. During the winter, the night temperature may be maintained at 60° F., and raised to 65°–70° F. during the growing season from March to October. The day temperature should be 70° F., or higher with sun heat.

Water. The plants should be watered abundantly during their growing season. The atmosphere should be kept humid, largely by damping down and watering the benches between the plants. During the summer months the plants may be syringed lightly once or twice a day, but always early enough to allow them to dry off before night. Their growth tends to be succulent and is particularly liable to damage if kept wet. Toward fall, dispense with syringing, still keeping the atmosphere humid, in order to encourage the foliage to harden. Too succulent growth results in poor flowering. Water should be decreased somewhat as the flower spikes appear and for the flowering season, but the plants should not get dry. During the winter watch for drip from the roof, and move any plants that might catch the water.

Feeding. A dilute fertilizer or manure water is beneficial every two weeks during rapid growth.

Light. During the summer the plants should have diminished light, about 15% of outdoor light. This means somewhat heavier shade than required for Cattleyas. As autumn approaches, the amount of light may be increased to encourage flowering, and during the winter the degree of shading should be adjusted to local conditions. In many regions shading is necessary all year round.

Ventilation. It is not safe, even for the sake of maintaining humid conditions, to allow water to stand on the foliage or in the leaf axils. Air movement is absolutely necessary to Phalaenopsis, with protection against drafts. Careful ventilation is particularly necessary when the plants are in flower, as stagnant, humid air causes spotting of the flowers.

Propagation. Since the plants increase in height so slowly, they do not give much opportunity for propagation by pieces of stem, as do the Vandas. Vegetative shoots sometimes develop along the sides of the plant. These may be carefully removed, potted in sphagnum moss or soft osmunda fibre, and kept damp and covered. As the little plants reach a good size, they may be transferred to a regular pot. New plants also grow from dormant buds at the base of the flower stem. After the flowers are finished, the stem may be cut and inserted in a covered jar which has damp sphagnum moss or osmunda fibre in the bottom. When the new plant is well started, it may be trimmed away from the stem, put in a small pot, and kept in a close atmosphere as described for community pots of Cattleya seedlings.

Growers often remark on the temperamental nature of Phalaenopsis. When a plant finds a place in the greenhouse that it likes, there it should be allowed to stay. If a plant is not thriving, try it in another spot, perhaps hang it up if it was on the bench, or vice versa. Sometimes a move of only a few inches up or down, or from one end of the greenhouse to the other, will be just what the plant needs.

Growing Phalaenopsis from Seed. Pollination is carried out by hand, as for other genera. The seed pods mature quickly, about five to six months after pollination. When the pod reaches maturity it dries and splits open quite suddenly, so that it should be covered in advance to prevent loss of seed. The seed loses its viability soon after it ripens, so that it should be sowed within a short period of time.

The best method is to sow the seed directly from the pod, just when it begins to turn color. Use sterile technique. Soak the pod in Clorox, one part to ten of water, or flame the pod quickly. Slit it with a sterile knife, and pick up the seed on a sterile platinum loop. Sow directly in the flasks. If it is necessary to store the seed temporarily, you will have to risk the use of calcium hypochlorite solution for disinfecting, as directed for Cattleya seed. Allow the seed to remain in the calcium hypochlorite solution for 10 minutes, and work rapidly so as not to risk having the seed killed by being in the solution too long. The flask medium to use is prepared as for Cattleyas.

The seedlings grow rapidly and are ready to move out of the flask in six months or so. They may be transferred to flats of osmunda fibre or to 5-inch community pots filled with osmunda fibre. They should be kept covered with glass to give them a warm, close atmosphere. When they are ready for individual pots, put them in 3-inch pots. They reach flowering size in about three years, sometimes less.

The Species; Group I, Euphalaenopsis

The lip of this group bears antennae-like appendages called cirri. The petals are broader than the sepals and are contracted at the base into a slender stalk.

Phal. amabilis. One of the most popular of this lovely genus and a good one for beginners. The plants are vigorous and produce a wealth of flowers. The leaves are light green on top, purple underneath, 6 to 12 inches long. The long, arching stems carry many flowers, each from 3 to 5 inches in diameter. The pure white sepals and petals are set off by a lip which is tinted with yellow, spotted and streaked with red, and has yellow cirri. Secondary sprays will develop if several nodes are left on the stem when the flowers are cut. Occurs in Java, Borneo, Amboina, and the Philippine Islands. Flowers in the fall and early winter.

Phal. Aphrodite. Similar to the preceding species, but has smaller flowers borne in a drooping raceme. The flowers are white, with the lip tinted pink and yellow, and having two fine, twisted cirri. The leaves are brownish green, ribbed down the center, and about a foot long. Occurs in Java and the Philippines. Flowers in the spring and summer.

Phal. Lowii. The plants of this species are not as vigorous as some, and the flowers are small, 1½ to 2 inches in diameter. They make up for their size by their lovely coloring. The sepals and petals are white, flushed with amethyst toward the base. The middle lobe of the lip is deep violet-purple and is the exception in this group, being without cirri. The sprays may carry as many as twenty flowers. The species is deciduous in its native environment, Borneo and Burma. Flowers in the summer and requires a drier atmosphere to protect the blooms.

Phal. Schilleriana. The plants have long leaves, mottled with grayish white, and are characterized by flat, rough roots. The marvelous drooping flower sprays are branched and often cover an area 3 feet square, with nearly a hundred flowers. The flowers are 2½ to 3 inches across. The sepals and petals are rosy-lilac, a little paler at the edges, and spotted with dull red. The lip is similar in coloring, with larger spots. Instead of cirri, it has two divergent horns at its tip. Occurs in the Philippines. Flowers in the spring.

Phal. Stuartiana. An attractive species with small, oddly colored flowers. The leaves are mottled when young, gray-green with purple underneath when mature. The sepals are white, the lateral ones partly speckled with red. The petals are white, with purple dots toward the base. The golden-yellow lip is margined with white, spotted with red-purple, and has two long, curling cirri. The flowers have especially good keeping qualities and are borne generously on branching sprays. Occurs in the Philippines. Flowers in the winter.

Phal. intermedia. A natural hybrid between *Phal. Aphrodite* and *Phal. rosea* that has been repeated in cultivation. The leaves are generally green above, purple underneath. The flower stem is sometimes branched and bears flowers 2 inches in diameter. The sepals and petals are white, the petals speckled with rose at the base. The lip has violet side lobes dotted with crimson and a deep crimson middle lobe. The cirri are reduced to two short horns. Occurs in the Philippines. Flowers from March through October.

The Species; Group II, Stauroglottis

The lip of this group is without appendages, and the petals are more nearly the size of the sepals. This group is less widely grown. The plants are some-what smaller than in Group I, but the flowers are usually brightly colored, often strikingly barred or spotted.

Phal. amethystina. A small plant with leaves waved at the edges. The cream colored flowers have a lip of rich amethyst-purple, barred and mar-gined with white. Occurs in Java and Sumatra. Flowers in late fall.

Phal. cornu-cervi. Yellow-green flowers barred with brown and having a white lip are produced freely on a stem whose shape resembles a stag horn. The species is deciduous natively, but requires no rest period in a green-house. Occurs in Burma and Java. Flowers throughout the year.

Phal. Esmeralda. The smallest of the species, whose leaves are only 3 inches long. The attractive sprays have 15 to 20 one-inch flowers, which are deep purple to white, with a purple lip. This species is the exception in this group, for its lip has two slender appendages. Occurs in Burma and Cochin China. Flowers in the spring and summer.

Phal. Lueddemanniana. Another small species, with leaves 6 to 8 inches long and a flower spike of the same length. The flowers are few to the stem, but are most attractive. The sepals and petals are white, marked with bars that are purple toward the base and brown toward the tips. The lip is violet with yellow blotches. The flowers keep well. An odd characteristic is that the flowers turn green when pollinated. The plants are easily propagated by young plantlets on the old flower spikes. Occurs in the Philippines. Flowers variably.

Phal. rosea. A floriferous species, often producing a dozen flower spikes that continue in bloom for months. The small flowers are white, stained with rose, and the lip is marked with violet in the center. Occurs in the Philippines. Flowers variably.

Many lovely hybrids are being made among the species of this genus. But still the species are great favorites, for culture both in greenhouses and out-of-doors in the summer or where it is warm all year round.

VANDA

The Vandas are a genus of sun-loving, monopodial plants. Their fragrant flowers are beautifully shaped and exhibit wondrous blending of colors. They are of excellent texture, keep well, and are adaptable to many uses. According to the habit of the species, from three to eighty blooms may occur on one spray.

Their name is the Sanskrit word, Vanda, which was applied in ancient India to the Vanda of Bengal and related orchids.

The twenty-five or more species of Vanda range natively through a variety of climates in tropical Asia. If the native habitat of each kind had to be reproduced, it would require a great deal of ingenuity and make their culture quite difficult. Fortunately the plants can all be fairly well adapted to the same warm greenhouse conditions, with the exception of those that come from the highest altitudes, such as *Vanda caerulea.*

The majority of the species have strap-shaped leaves, a few have leaves that are fleshy, more or less cylindrical. The latter are called the terete species, terete, meaning round, referring to the character of the leaves. Greenhouse culture is the same for both types. Large, fleshy roots are produced at the base of the leaves, which cling to the pots, or to the posts often used to support the almost climbing plants.

The flower sprays arise from the axils of the leaves on the newly matured part of the plant. The sepals and petals are usually similar in shape and size, though in some species the lateral sepals are somewhat larger. They are narrowed toward the base, rounded toward the apex, and usually flat and spreading. The lip is attached to the column and spurred at its base, with the middle lobe spreading. The colors exhibited by this genus include white, yellow, rose, purple, blue, and brown.

Culture

Potting. Vanda requires a larger amount of growing medium than does Phalaenopsis. The potting medium may be osmunda fibre, to which may be added one-fourth leaf mold and a small amount of cow manure. The pots should be ample, but as for all orchids, not too large, and have good drainage. Potting is done just as new growth starts. The plant is centered in the pot, and coarse fibre worked in around the roots. Newly potted plants should be kept a little on the·dry side until new root action starts.

Vandas increase rapidly in height. Some will grow to 6 or 7 feet. This is not always an advantage, for often the flowering is less abundant when the plants become straggly. Rather than allow them to become so tall, it is better to cut off the top half of the plant and pot it in fresh material. The bottom half should also be repotted and will soon make a new, compact plant. The stock can be rapidly increased by this method. New plants may also be obtained by a method called marcottage. A cut is made part way through the stem between the leaves, a few inches from the tip of the plant. Damp osmunda fibre or sphagnum moss is bound to the wound. Soon roots appear from the upper part, and when these have penetrated the damp ball, the new plant is completely removed and potted separately. An axillary bud below the cut becomes the new growing tip of the original plant.

Water. Vandas require abundant water during their growing season, with somewhat less during the winter, though not to the point of dryness. Syringing is necessary during bright weather, both to keep the atmosphere damp and to furnish water to the aerial roots. The atmosphere must be kept fairly saturated.

Temperature. Vandas like to be warm. Conditions suited to Phalaenopsis will also suit this genus. They may be adapted to a warm spot in the Cattleya house. An exception is *V. caerulea* which should be grown cool, as described for Cymbidium.

Light. Natively the Vandas grow in full sun, and they are so grown in warm regions where they may stay out-of-doors all summer, even all year round. In a greenhouse, they require 20–30% of outdoor light during the summer, and as nearly clear glass in the winter as they can stand. The amount of light they receive may make the difference between few or many flowers, and between weak or strong plants.

Ventilation. Good ventilation is necessary for Vanda to help prevent ailments likely to occur under humid conditions.

Feeding. In addition to the more abundant potting medium, Vanda thrives with extra nutrients. Feeding with a dilute fertilizer or with manure water once a week is beneficial during the months of rapid growth.

Vandas may be readily propagated from seed, using the method recommended for Phalaenopsis. The wide variety represented in the genus gives promise of lovely things to come. Many successful hybrids have already been made, but as yet these are not as numerous in culture as the species. The terete leaved species when crossed with strap leaved species yield an intermediate type called semi-terete. Vanda has been successfully crossed with Renanthera, the resulting hybrids being called Renantanda.

The Species

There are about twenty-five species, many of which are found in collections. The list given here comprises those most frequently grown, both by amateurs and to some extent by commercial growers.

Vanda caerulea. This is the lovely blue orchid, whose color varies from clear cobalt to both paler and deeper shades of blue. Its rather dense sprays carry ten to twenty flowers, each 3 to 4 inches across. The sepals and petals are nearly equal and overlap each other. The effect is a round, flat, compact flower. The little lip is three lobed, the front lobe a rich deep blue. The flowers last about a month when kept cool. Occurs under cool, sunny conditions at high elevations in northern India and Burma. Flowers anytime from fall through winter and spring.

Vanda Hookeriana. A terete species, with a long, climbing stem and short leaves. The attractive flowers are 3 to 5 inches across and are notable for the huge lip, which is as large as the rest of the flower. The dorsal sepal and petals are white dotted with purple, the lateral sepals pure white. The middle lobe of the lip is fan-shaped, with three deep scallops, and is white spotted with purple. Only a few flowers are produced to a stem. The famous hybrid Vanda, Miss Joaquim, is *Vanda Hookeriana alba* × *Vanda teres alba,* large quantities of which are grown commercially in Hawaii. Occurs in Borneo. Flowers in the fall.

Vanda Kimballiana. A terete species requiring cool conditions. The plants are slender, and rarely grow taller than 15 inches. The lovely flowers are pure white except for the lip, the middle lobe of which is deep rose, marked with darker veins, and the side lobes yellow. The base of the lip forms a distinct spur about an inch long. Grows on the face of cliffs, exposed to the sun, in high altitudes of Burma. Flowers in late summer or early fall.

Vanda Roxburghii. This is the Vanda of Bengal, whose name has been given to the genus. It is a medium-sized plant that produces spikes of six to eight greenish yellow flowers. The wavy sepals and petals are white on the back, reticulated with olive brown on the front. The long middle lobe of the lip is violet. Occurs in Bengal. Flowers from May to August.

Vanda Sanderiana. One of the most highly esteemed of the species, and next only to *Vanda caerulea* in popularity. The beautiful, 5-inch flowers occur a dozen or more to the spike. The pinkish lilac petals and dorsal sepals are dotted with red-brown at the base. The large lateral sepals are yellow-

Vanda teres, one of the terete leaved species. (Courtesy of H. A. Dunn)

green, suffused and reticulated with reddish brown. The little lip is dull crimson, with a squarish middle lobe and the side lobes formed into a cup under the tip of the column. The color variations in this species are quite remarkable, some tending to purple, others to red. Occurs in the Philippines. Flowers in the fall.

Vanda suavis. This is a variety of *Vanda tricolor,* but usually listed by its varietal name. The plant reaches a height of 6 feet, with leaves 12 to 16 inches long. The fragrant flowers are 2 to 5 inches across, borne on drooping spikes and last 5–6 weeks. The wavy sepals and petals are white, barred and spotted with reddish purple. The front lobe of the lip is pale rosy-purple, the side lobes deep purple. This species requires slightly cooler conditions. Occurs in Java. Flowers in spring and summer.

Vanda teres. A tall, terete species, with distinct flowers. The oval, wavy sepals and petals are about equal in size. The sepals are white, tinged with rose, while the petals are a rich deep rose. The large lip is an outstanding feature of the flower. The rounded side lobes which curl over the column are yellow, spotted with crimson. The long middle lobe is rose, veined and spotted with yellow, spreading at its outer end, and split in the center. The flowers last about a month. Occurs in Burma. Flowers from May to September.

Vanda tricolor. A tall, stout species, with fragrant, long lasting flowers. A dozen or more blooms, 2 to 3 inches in diameter, occur on a drooping stem. The sepals and petals are oval, slender at the base, white on the back, and creamy-yellow spotted with reddish brown on the front. The middle lobe of the lip is lyre shaped, rich purple, and decorated with elevated lines. Occurs in Java. Flowers in the spring and summer.

OTHER MEMBERS OF THE AERIDES TRIBE

Aerides, the type genus of the tribe, is very much like Vanda, and is grown under the same warm conditions. *Aerides odoratum* has dainty sprays of small fragrant flowers that are white marked with carmine and purple. *Aerides Fieldingii* has been nicknamed the "fox-brush orchid" because of its extraordinarily dense flower sprays that reach a length of 18 inches. The blooms are white marked with rose-pink. These are but two of the thirty odd species that range natively from the Malay Archipelago to India, East Asia, and Japan.

Angraecum is a genus of about twenty species native to tropical Africa, Madagascar, and the Mascarene Islands. The oddly shaped flowers are sometimes beautiful, often a bit grotesque. In habit and cultural requirements the genus is similar to Vanda, except that they are somewhat more tender. *Angraecum sesquipedale* caused Darwin to wonder whether an insect existed in nature that could reach the nectar in the bottom of its 11-inch spur. After he published his fascinating book *On The Fertilization of Orchids by Insects,* the specific moth that performed the function was indeed located. The flowers of *Angraecum sesquipedale* are 5 to 7 inches in diameter, shaped like a six-pointed star, and are of such heavy texture that they appear to be made of white wax.

Renanthera is another genus similar to Vanda, grown for its brightly colored flowers. Subtle variations of yellow marked with red, and red with orange, are the general color schemes of the species. The purpose of crossing this genus with Vanda is to introduce deep red tones into the hybrids.

Saccolabium has long dense sprays of small flowers, which are rose, orange, or white tipped with blue (*Saccolabium coeleste*). The genus succeeds in the Cattleya house, with plenty of water during the growing season and considerably less during the winter.

Vandopsis is a genus that differs from Vanda in having no spur at the base of the lip. The plants are large, the flowers yellow, marked with red. A single plant may flower throughout the year.

The remaining genera of this tribe have similarities to those already described, but are less often grown. They are Acampe, Camarotis, Cleisostoma, Listrostachys, Luisia, Mystacidium, Polyrrhiza, Rhynchostylis, and Sarcanthus.

Chapter X

THE CATTLEYA TRIBE

The Cattleyas and Laelias, the showy members of this tribe, have already been described, as have Brassavola and Sophronitis and the part they play in making the marvelous bi- and tri-generic hybrids. However, these handsome orchids should not be allowed to overshadow completely their lovely, but less striking, cousins.

EPIDENDRUM

The Epidendrums, a wide-spread genus of one thousand species, are loved by amateurs everywhere. They are easy to grow, and flower profusely, some producing their beautiful clusters of brightly colored flowers almost all year round. The flowers vary from 1½ inches, each a dainty miniature, to 6 inches in diameter. Many are worth growing for their fragrance alone.

They grow wild in tropical and subtropical America, from Florida south to Brazil. They are so abundant in parts of Central America that they could almost be classed with weeds. Yet when they are transplanted to our greenhouses, they match their true quality with that of their more exalted relatives. Epidendrums were among the first epiphytes to be imported into Europe. In fact, the first epiphytic orchid to flower in England was *Epidendrum cochleatum,* in 1787.

There is some variation among the widely distributed species as to cultural needs, but in general a Cattleya house suits them well, with a night temperature of 55°–60° F. They may be potted in osmundine, in suspended baskets or in pots, according to your choice. The latter might be used for those resembling Cattleyas in shape and size, and the former given to those that have drooping flower sprays. Repotting and propagation should be done just at the start of new growth.

THE SPECIES

Out of such a large genus it is possible to give here only a handful of species, which have been selected for their variety and popularity.

Epidendrum atropurpureum. One of the loveliest of the genus. The mahogany and green sepals and petals spread wide, the tip of each curving forward gracefully. The spreading lip is white with crimson stripes. Six to ten of these attractive, long-lasting flowers are borne at the end of a long spray rising from the top of the short, oval pseudobulb. Ranges from Mexico to Venezuela. Flowers in late spring and early summer.

Epidendrum atropurpureum, a lovely addition to a small collection in case or greenhouse. (Courtesy of H. A. Dunn and H. Griffin)

Epidendrum aurantiacum. Often classed as *Cattleya aurantiacum* because of its similarity to that genus, and rather resembles *Cattleya Skinneri.* Striking red-orange flowers are borne in drooping clusters. Occurs in Guatemala. Flowers in late winter.

Epidendrum ciliare. One of the best-known, and loved for its easy-going habit. The plant looks like a Cattleya and grows about a foot tall. The slender, graceful flowers are about 5 inches across and are borne in clusters of three to seven. The sepals and petals are yellow-green, set off by a dainty, three-lobed white lip, whose lateral lobes are prettily fringed. Grows abundantly in Mexico. Flowers in the winter.

Epidendrum cochleatum. Attractive, upside-down flowers whose shape suggests an octopus. The slender, yellow-green sepals and petals stream down from the shell-like, green and purple striped, lip. The flowers grow in clusters of four to seven, each 3 to 4 inches across. Ranges from Florida to Colombia. The variety, *triandrum* is one of Florida's favorite native orchids. Flowers nearly all year round.

Epidendrum fragrans. Spicily scented, pretty but not very showy. The small creamy upside-down flowers are set off by a red peppermint-striped lip.

Epidendrum fragrans will flower in home, greenhouse, or out-of-doors in the summer. (Courtesy of H. A. Dunn and H. Griffin)

Several lovely clusters occur on each flower stem. Occurs from Guatemala through the West Indies to north Brazil. Flowers in late summer and early fall.

Epidendrum prismatocarpum. One of the most showy of the genus, with large clusters of small, strikingly colored flowers. The pale yellow-green sepals and petals are spotted with purple-black. The spear-shaped lip is pale purple with a yellow tip and a white border. Occurs in Central America. Flowers in the summer.

Epidendrum radicans. A semi-climbing plant, with stems that reach 5 feet. This species is often used as an example of a true epiphyte, for aerial roots are produced opposite each leaf all along the stem. The flowers are brilliant red, about 2 inches in diameter, and open one at a time in attractive clusters. It must have plenty of light and a cool spot in a Cattleya house. The tall stems need support and are quite decorative in a corner or against a wall. New plantlets that grow along the stem may be removed and potted separately. Grows among weeds and grass in Guatemala. Flowers in late spring and summer.

Diacrium bicornutum, little known but lovely. (Courtesy of H. F. Loomis)

Epidendrum Stamfordianum. Large panicles of fragrant flowers, yellow, spotted with crimson, make this a most attractive species. It occurs from Mexico to Colombia, and flowers in the spring.

Epidendrum vitellinum. Sprays of bright orange-red flowers, ten to fifteen to a stem. This species requires cooler conditions than most of the genus, with a night temperature of 50° F. *Epidendrum vitellinum,* var. *majus,* is superior to the type and is the one usually imported. Occurs in Mexico at high altitudes. Flowers in early fall.

Epidendrums are usually grown as species. Although they have been crossed with Cattleyas and Laelias, the resulting Epicattleyas and Epilaelias are more or less of a curiosity. Hybridization may have future possibilities. Neither the species nor the hybrids have commercial value as yet. Some day a more orchid conscious public may appreciate these dainty flowers in arrangements to be worn in the hair or in table decorations combined with other flowers.

Schomburgkia Luedemanii, the ultimate in ruffles.
(Courtesy of H. A. Dunn and H. Griffin)

OTHER MEMBERS OF THE CATTLEYA TRIBE

Broughtonia is a genus native to the West Indies, containing two or three species sometimes included with Epidendrum. *Broughtonia sanguinea* is an attractive little plant, with pseudobulbs 2 inches long, leaves 2 to 4 inches long, and clusters of small crimson-purple flowers.

Diacrium is another genus whose four species are sometimes given with Epidendrum. The superbly beautiful *Diacrium bicornutum,* called the "Virgin Orchid," is one of the loveliest of the Cattleya tribe. The fragrant, sparkling white flowers have a dainty sprinkling of red on the lip. The delicate spray holds twelve to twenty buds which open in succession over a period of two months or so. They do well in the Cattleya house. The species is found in northern South America, Trinidad, and Tobago.

Schomburgkia, a genus of about fifteen species, is similar to Laelia. *Schomburgkia Luedemanii* has tall flower sprays that bear large clusters of ten to twenty beautiful flowers each. The extremely wavy sepals and petals are brown. The three-lobed lip is purple, trimmed with yellow. Occurs from Panama to Venezuela. Flowers in the summer.

The last member of the Cattleya tribe is Leptotes, of which there are about six species. The leaves arise from stems, not pseudobulbs, that grow from a creeping rhizome. *Leptotes bicolor* is a pretty little plant, bearing small white flowers with a bright rose lip. Not very floriferous.

INTER-GENERIC CROSSES IN THE CATTLEYA TRIBE

The bi- and tri-generic crosses between Cattleya, Laelia, Brassavola, and Sophronitis have already been described. In addition to these, many others have been made, most of which are, however, purely of botanical or historical interest. Diacattleya and Dialaelia are crosses between Diacrium and Cattleya and Laelia, respectively. Epicattleya, Epidiacrium, Epilaelia, and Epiphronitis reveal their origin as crosses between Epidendrum and Cattleya, Diacrium, Laelia, and Sophronitis. Leptolaelia is the hybrid between Leptotes and Laelia. The ease with which the various genera may be crossed shows how closely related they are. An amateur might have a good bit of fun trying various combinations.

Chapter XI

THE CYMBIDIUM TRIBE

Of the four members of this tribe, the genus Cymbidium far surpasses the others. Two of the latter are seldom cultivated, and the fourth is so huge that one plant alone would take up most of the space in an amateur greenhouse.

Cymbidium

Cymbidiums are among the loveliest of orchids and the most useful. Their tall, arching sprays of waxy, delicately colored flowers make a wonderful display in shades of yellow, green, rose, and white, plainly or subtly blended. The plants themselves are attractive for their grassy foliage. The keeping quality of Cymbidiums is unusual even among orchids, and the blooms last in perfection a minimum of six weeks and sometimes as long as three months.

The serene beauty of the flowers gives them a charm quite different from that of the showy, ruffled Cattleya or the curiously flagrant Cypripedium. Their oval, pointed sepals and petals are of nearly equal size and shape and are colored similarly. The dorsal sepal often bends slightly forward over the lip. The lip is fleshy, with side lobes that stand erect beside the column, and a front lobe that bends down in tongue-like fashion. It is from the somewhat boat-shaped lip that the genus gets its name (*Cymbid,* Greek for boat). The lip is usually marked with a pattern of spots and lines, bears one or more ridges, and is sometimes downy. The column is nearly erect, often flushed with color, and frequently speckled or lined with the same shade that marks the lip. Each spray bears from five to thirty blooms.

The Cymbidiums range natively throughout the high elevation of the Khasia Hills and the Himalayas, and are found in greatest abundance in Assam, Annam, and Burma. A few species spread to Australia and the coast of Africa. They are epiphytic, though they are occasionally found growing on the ground, and in cultivation are quite indifferent as to whether they are grown in pots or beds. This geniality of habit makes it possible for flower lovers who live in some frost-free areas to have them in their gardens. They are often grown thus in parts of California. Most of us must grow them in

Cymbidium Peri, variety *Beefeater.* A very floriferous hybrid.
(Courtesy of Armacost and Royston, Inc.)

greenhouses, however, and no orchid gives greater satisfaction to the amateur.

Cymbidiums are evergreen plants, with abundant large, fleshy, vigorous roots. The pseudobulbs vary according to the species from globe-shaped to quite slender and barely apparent. They are sheathed with the base of the leaves, which remain green for several years. As the leaves fall, their dried bases remain attached to the pseudobulb. New growths arise laterally from the base of mature pseudobulbs. The plants are compact and cover a circular area. The slender leaves taper to a point, and are from 1½ to 3 feet long, of leathery texture, but not fleshy. A 5-foot spread is not unusual for a vigorous plant. The species differ in the number of leaves produced per pseudobulb. In some, the pseudobulb matures when it has produced a dozen or so leaves, whereas in others twenty or thirty leaves may appear before growth is complete.

The flower spikes appear from the base of the pseudobulb, from June through October, according to the habit of the plant. Spikes that appear in early summer will probably flower in the fall. Those that come along later may flower through the winter and spring. The spike is at first similar in appearance to a vegetative growth, but as it progresses to a length of 3 or 4 inches its character becomes apparent. It remains closely pointed, instead of showing opening leaf tips, and is thickened a bit where it encloses the developing flower buds. As the spike lengthens, the tip of each new sheathing scale may split the end of the one just formed. When the spike has attained about half of its total length the flower buds come out of the last protective sheath. The stem now rapidly lengthens, becoming 18 inches long on a small plant, to a yard long on larger ones. The flower buds open beginning usually with those near the basal end, but often one opens here and there along the stem with the others not far behind, and those at the tip last of all. A stem may be cut after most of the flowers are open, and the end buds will open later. For perfect quality in each flower, however, it is best to let the whole spray open on the plant.

GREENHOUSE CULTURE

Potting. Selection of compost for Cymbidiums is a matter of personal choice. Straight osmunda fibre is preferred by some, to which may be added a generous sprinkling of well-dried cow manure. This method assures them the porous medium they require. Other growers like a mixture of half osmundine and half fibrous loam, while still others make a compost of one-third shredded osmundine, one-third loam, with equal parts of sand and cow manure making up the last third. The latter two composts must be mixed thoroughly before use.

Cymbidiums do not like to be disturbed too often. Therefore, mature plants should be given a pot large enough to accommodate a good many new bulbs. Often two growths come from each pseudobulb so that the plant rapidly increases in size. For instance, from two pseudobulbs, four may come, and from these four eight, so that in two years' growth the plant may greatly

Remove old fibre from center, and re-place with fresh fibre. Loosen up roots a little if possible.

Add a three inch pot full of screened, dried cow manure to the amount of fibre necessary to fill the six inch pot in which the plant is to go.

Center the plant in the new pot and stuff fibre around it.

Tie the fibre in with a potting stick, and work in enough more to make it firm.

multiply its size. The plants do better when carried on into 10- or 12-inch pots instead of being divided and kept in smaller pots. Repotting should be done just as flowering is finished, at intervals of two years.

Prepare the new pot by enlarging the drainage hole and putting in plenty of crock. If you desire to use straight osmundine and manure, put a thin layer of fibre over the crock, and then add a layer of manure mixed with fibre. About a 3-inch pot of manure is about right for a 6-inch pot, and for larger pots more in proportion. If you use one of the mixed composts, pour some in the pot over the crock before setting the plant in it.

Knock the plant out of its pot. Try not to disturb the good roots as you trim off any dead ones and remove what you can of the old fibre or compost. Loosen up the ball here and there, spread the roots a bit, and stuff fresh fibre around them. Now hold the plant in place in the new pot. Work in fresh fibre using your hands. Next firm the fibre with a potting stick but do not pot as hard as for Cattleyas. If you use a compost, pour it in around the plant, firming it with a tamper. The base of the pseudobulbs should be just at the level of the potting medium, or only slightly within the surface. Cymbidiums do not do well when the pseudobulbs stand on a pedestal of roots.

Put newly potted plants in a warmer spot (58° F. by night) and give extra shade and frequent syringings. Water only lightly until new growth starts, and then increase the amount of water and move the plants to a cooler spot (50° F. by night).

When division is necessary, separate the pseudobulbs that have lost their leaves and put them in a flat of moist sphagnum moss. Each one will send out a new green shoot, at which time it may be put in a 4-inch pot with the regular compost. These will reach flowering size in two or three years. Cut the section containing green pseudobulbs in two or three pieces, keeping a fair number of bulbs together, and pot each part in regular compost.

Temperature. Here again, growers do not concur on the best temperature for Cymbidiums, except that they must be kept as cool as possible in the summertime. The majority of growers find that their success with the plants depends on keeping them at a night temperature of 50° F. and a day temperature of 60° F. This is a simple matter in the wintertime, and remains the ideal to strive for in the summer. However, few regions allow the maintenance of a day temperature of 60° F. in the summer, and fortunately Cymbidiums will tolerate an increase up to 80° F. for the better part of the day, and even higher temperatures during the noon hours. Growers who cannot prevent greater increase in temperature in their greenhouses may avoid injury to the plants by putting them out-of-doors. The pots may be set on wire stands under large trees, or in a lath house.

An occasional grower succeeds with Cymbidiums at a night temperature of 58° F., which may depend on special conditions. While the lower temperatures recommended above assure good growth and flowering, an amateur who cannot furnish these conditions might experiment with the warmer method. Young seedlings make vigorous growth with a night temperature of 58–60° F., but most growers find that flowering is delayed or even inhibited entirely unless the plants are grown cooler as they reach maturity. The growth of mature plants frequently remains vegetative. Fine, big plants result, but flowering is poor when raised at high temperatures.

Water. Water should be given abundantly. The type of compost and environmental conditions will have to be the guide in formulating a schedule. Cymbidiums use a great deal more water than Cattleyas, and should never be allowed to dry out. Yet the compost must not become soggy lest root aeration be hindered. In warm, bright weather 5- and 6-inch pots might be flooded nearly every day and larger pots twice a week.

Frequent syringing of the foliage is beneficial in warm weather, to check red spider, the chief enemy of Cymbidiums, and to help lower the greenhouse temperature, as well as to supply atmospheric moisture. Damping down the walks and benches is also necessary.

If your plants do not flower as profusely as you desire, you might try a technique practiced by some growers. Toward the end of the summer, sort out those plants that have made up their growth and reduce the amount of water given them for a period of a month. This may help to initiate flowering. Do not let them get entirely dry, but handle them something like Cattleyas, allowing the compost to approach dryness before watering. It might be interesting to treat some of your plants this way, and compare the results with those that are carried on the regular watering schedule.

Light. Cymbidiums grow and flower more satisfactorily when they receive as much light as they can stand, about 30% of outdoor light in the summer, and if possible clear glass in the winter. Local conditions will dictate the necessary modifications. Somewhat heavier shade may be necessary to keep down the greenhouse temperature during hot weather, but this should not be carried to excess. Rather, do everything possible to cool the greenhouse by ventilation and damping down, so that the plants may benefit from good light. Otherwise, move the plants out-of-doors. Winter shading in the form of a thin skim on the glass or roller blinds, should be used only in regions of extremely bright winter sun, and then only if yellow foliage dictates it.

Ventilation. Cymbidiums need the good air circulation furnished by proper ventilation both winter and summer. The ventilators may be left open at night when the outside temperature permits.

Flowering season. Research is being done to learn what factor or group of factors controls the flowering of Cymbidiums. Whether it is day length, or day and night temperature relationship, or a combination of these, remains to be seen.

GARDEN CULTURE

In regions where the temperature does not fall below 26° F., Cymbidiums may be grown out-of-doors. Large trees will furnish good shade with a little sunlight filtering through, or a lath house may be used in lieu of trees. The laths should run north and south so that the sun will cast moving shadows, and should be spaced about an inch apart. When the thermometer shows signs of falling below 26° F., the plants should be covered for frost protection.

The plants may be grown in beds, with soil prepared in a ditch 1 foot deep and 1 foot wide. In the ditch put a layer of leaf mold 6 inches deep, and then a layer of horticultural peat to an equal depth. This is tramped down, and a layer of sandy soil added on top. Then, the compost is thoroughly mixed by turning it over two or three times with a shovel. Moisten the compost and wait a day or two before planting.

Remove the plants from their containers, and carefully loosen up the ball of fibre or compost. If it is possible to do so without injuring the roots, spread them out about 3 inches below the surface, cover them with pure peat, and put some peat directly around the pseudobulbs. Then fill in with the compost. If the roots are too tightly tangled, set the loosened ball in the trench and fill the compost in around it. Water lightly until new growth starts, giving frequent syringings of the foliage. When the plants are established, they may be watered rather abundantly.

Cymbidiums are attractive grown among rocks along with other plants, where their location is carefully prepared with sufficient compost.

FEEDING

Cymbidiums benefit from the addition of a fertilizer (manure water or a prepared fertilizer) during their growing period. Applications may be made at biweekly intervals. Withhold fertilizer for the two months preceding formation of the flower spikes. Then, when the spikes have formed, feeding may be resumed to aid in flower production.

SEEDLINGS

Cymbidium seed is obtained by hand pollination and sown in flasks after the method described for Cattleyas. It sticks to the sides of the tube of disinfecting solution, but may be handled either by keeping it agitated when a dropper is used, or by picking it up with a platinum loop. The seed is somewhat slow to germinate, but the seedlings grow well.

Cymbidium seedlings, a flask soon after germination, and two- and three-year-old plants.

When the seedlings are removed from the flasks, they may be put either into 5-inch community pots, or, better, in flats. Pure osmunda fibre is satisfactory for their growth, or one of the composts described earlier. The community pots should be kept in a covered box, or the flat covered with a pane of glass, to furnish them the close, damp atmosphere conducive to rapid growth. At this stage they benefit from a night temperature of 58–60° F. When the plants are 3 or 4 inches tall they may be moved from the community pot into 3-inch pots. If those in flats still have room to grow, they may be left there for a while longer.

Seedlings may be shifted to larger pots as the need requires without disturbing the ball around the roots. They grow rapidly, and often flower at five years of age, though the naturally slower ones may take seven or eight years.

Cymbidium seedlings are reasonably priced and are a good buy for the amateur. Since it takes propagations two or three years to become re-established, two- or three-year-old seedlings will actually flower about as soon. Unless you have a particular interest in obtaining propagations from certain plants, the young seedlings will give the greatest satisfaction.

THE SPECIES

Of the sixty or more species, only ten or so have gained importance from a cultural point of view, and only a few of these have played a really important role in the making of our present-day hybrids. Even these appear less and less in cultivation, for the hybrids surpass their parents in beauty and quality. Those species that are still widely grown are *Cym. insigne, Lowianum,* and *Tracyanum.*

Cymbidium seedlings flowering for the first time. In spite of the difference in size, these plants are the same age, six years from seed.

Some of the species that have contributed to the hybrids were for a long time quite rare, and the few that were collected brought very high prices. Their discovery was often accidental. A single plant might have been collected along with other things, and its identity not known until it flowered. By that time it was impossible to trace its origin, and years of search were necessary to yield another specimen. Sometimes these were hard to find because they actually did not occur abundantly. At the same time, some other species were found in large numbers.

The selected list of species given below will prove interesting to those who, though they may not grow them, will find in them the characteristics manifested in their hybrids.

Cym. eburneum. This species seems to be rather hard to grow, and is now rarely cultivated. But it has had a great influence on hybrids, in fact it was one of the parents (with *Cym. Lowianum*) of the first Cymbidium hybrid, made in 1889, the famous *Cym. eburneo-Lowianum*. The broad flower parts of *Cym. eburneum,* its round shape, and delightful fragrance have come down through a long line of hybrids, largely through mating other species with the primary hybrid *Cym. eburneo-Lowianum*. Its flowers are rosy-white, or pure white, with a creamy lip, dotted with rose-purple and having a yellow ridge down the center. The flowers are 3 to 4 inches across, usually only one to a stem. The flower spike rises in the axil of the second to fourth leaf. The plant is rather weak growing, with slender pseudobulbs and leaves 1 to 2 feet long. Occurs in the Khasia Hills at elevations of 5000–6000 feet. Flowers in late winter and early spring.

Cym. erythrostylum. So called because of its red column. The flowers are white with a few rose colored dots at the base of the petals and sepals, and the creamy lip is heavily lined with red-violet. The petals are held forward, meeting at the top edges, and give the appearance of a hood over the lip. This hooded aspect is often inherited by hybrids that include this species. The early flowering habit of this species is one of the characteristics sought in its hybrids. The plant is small, with pseudobulbs 1½ to 2 inches tall, and leaves 10 to 15 inches long. The arching flower spike rises from the axil of the second or third leaf, and bears four to eight flowers. Occurs in Annam. Flowers in the fall and winter.

Cym. giganteum. In spite of its large, fragrant flowers and early flowering habit, this species is not used as much now as it was at one time. It has not the good keeping qualities that we now expect, and its hybrids are often dull in color. It is found in the ancestry of many hybrids, however, to some of which it has contributed its yellow-green color. Occurs in Nepal. Flowers in fall and winter.

Cym. grandiflorum. Handsome plants, which are distinguished by having the base of each leaf expanded into a ribbed sheath, striped yellow and green. Their growth is tufted, the pseudobulbs scarcely thickened. The fragrant flowers reach 5 inches in diameter, and occur five to fifteen on a curving spray that originates from the base of the newly formed pseudobulbs. The petals and sepals are clear green, and the large lip is pale yellow spotted with red-purple. In using this species in breeding, growers have had to eliminate its only poor feature, that of frequently dropping its flower buds before they open. Sometimes the buds sit on the stem for weeks apparently ready to open, only to turn pink and fall off. The hybrids we now have flower satisfactorily, and many of them trace their green color to *Cym. grandiflorum.* Occurs in Nepal, Sikkim, and Bhotan.

Cym. l'Ansoni. This species was once thought to be a variety either of *Cym. Lowianum* or *Cym. Tracyanum,* but its distinct differences make it a valid species. Its striking flowers have yellow sepals and petals, heavily lined with purple-brown, and the large spotted lip is pale in contrast. Its most outstanding hybrid is *Cym. Ceres (Cym. l'Ansoni* $\times$ *Cym. insigne)* which ranges from pink to red and which, in turn, has been a most successful parent. Occurs in upper Burma, but only a few plants have ever been found.

Cym. insigne. One of the most valuable of the species because of its vigor, its compact growth, and its tall, upright spikes of twelve to twenty flowers. The spikes grow 3 to 4 feet tall and arise from the base of mature pseudobulbs. The flowers range in color from white (var. *album*) and near white, to rose-lilac, with rosy dots at the base of the sepals and petals. They are 3 to 4 inches in diameter. The lip is rounded, dotted with rose, and has a yellow keel. Both the white and colored forms have been used in making many fine hybrids, which have since been combined in various ways to give a wide variety. Two of the important hybrids are *Cym. Alexanderi Westonbirt* variety (*Cym. eburneo-Lowianum* $\times$ *Cym. insigne*), and *Cym. Pauwelsii,* var. *Compte de Hemptinne (Cym. Lowianum* $\times$ *Cym. insigne). Cym. insigne* was discovered comparatively recently, in 1901. Occurs in Annam. Flowers in early spring.

Cym. Lowianum. This is another handsome and much used species. The plants are large, with pseudobulbs up to 9 inches tall and leaves 2 to 3 feet long. The flower spike arches gracefully, and bears 15–35 large flowers. It arises from the base of a newly matured bulb. It has many varieties that are almost as desirable as its hybrids. The flowers keep for two months or more, and this desirable quality, along with its floriferousness, has been handed down to its progeny. The flowers are greenish-yellow with faint red or brownish veins. The rather pale yellow lip is downy and has a V-shaped red-brown blotch on the front lobe. One of its often-used varieties, var. *concolor,* has clear yellow-green petals and sepals, and its lip is marked with a light orange-buff patch. Occurs in Burma. Flowers from late winter to early summer.

Cym. Parishii. This rather rare species resembles *Cym. eburneum,* except that the pseudobulbs and leaves are larger, and the spike bears three to six flowers instead of one or two. The fragrant, white flowers are 4 inches in diameter, with the lip decorated with large purple spots. The parent of the many hybrids made from this species was the var. *Sanderae,* distinguished by much more color in the lip, and broader and more pointed petals and sepals. It has been combined with many of the other fine species. Occurs in Annam. Flowers in the summer.

Cym. Schroederi. This species is found in the ancestry of many hybrids, but does not add much to them in quality. Therefore it has not continued in use. It has greenish yellow flowers and a lip marked with dull red blotches. Occurs in Annam.

Cym. Tracyanum. This species has contributed its early flowering season to its descendants. The yellow-green flowers are fragrant and occur five to twenty-five on a spray. The spike arises from the axil of the first or second leaf on a rather immature pseudobulb. The plants are vigorous and are grown with ease. It is said that, while the species is often used out-of-doors, its flowers keep better in the damper conditions of a greenhouse. The flowers are yellow-green, marked with bright red, and have a yellow lip also marked with red. Occurs in Burma and Siam. Flowers in the fall.

An interesting observation has been made on the number of flowers produced to a spike in the primary hybrids. You might expect that if you crossed a species that usually produced one bloom with one that produced twenty-five, the resulting hybrid would give something close to the mean (average) between these two, or thirteen. But that is not the way it happens. Actually, a hybrid between a species that gives one and a species that gives twenty-five will itself produce about five or six flowers to a spike. Mathematically, five is the geometrical mean between 1 and 25, arrived at by multiplying 1×25 and taking the square root of the sum. Studies of various crosses have shown that Cymbidiums follow this general rule, and the rule may be used to predict the number of flowers you will get in any primary hybrid. As inheritance becomes more complicated in advanced hybrids, it is not possible to trace this feature through the maze of habits represented in any one plant.

OTHER MEMBERS OF THE CYMBIDIUM TRIBE

Cyperorchis is a genus closely related to Cymbidium, and native also to the Khasia Hills and the Himalayas. It has very few species. The flowers differ from Cymbidium in having narrower sepals and petals, which remain closed for nearly their entire length, spreading apart only at the tips. The flowers are small and are borne close together on the stem.

Grammangis differs from Cymbidium in that the leaves arise from the apex of the tall pseudobulb. About four species are known, and these are native to Madagascar and Java. The genus is seldom cultivated.

Grammatophyllum is a genus noted chiefly for one member which is a giant among orchids. This is *Grammatophyllum speciosum,* which has pseudobulbs 6 to 10 feet tall, to which the leaves add even greater height. One specimen in cultivation grew to a height of 18 feet, and produced as many as fifty flower spikes simultaneously, each of which carried 70 to 100 flowers. The 6-inch flowers are clear yellow, spotted with purple. Obviously this is not a species to be grown in a small greenhouse. *Grammatophyllum Fenzlianum* is not as large a plant but produces flower spikes 5 feet long bearing sixty flowers each. They are green or yellow-green, spotted with brown. Unfortunately neither of these is a frequent bloomer, but one plant in flower must indeed be a glorious show.

Chapter XII

THE CYPRIPEDIUM TRIBE

The Cypripedium tribe consists of four terrestrial genera, one genus native to the north temperate zone, one to southern Asia, and two to South America. The first two genera are well known, and both are called Cypripedium in common usage. However, the name Cypripedium belongs accurately only to the ladyslippers of the north temperate zone, found in the woods of North America. The Asiatic genus is Paphiopedilum, and this name will be used here. The South American genera are Phragmopedilum and Selenipedium.

The Paphiopedilums (Asiatic) are the ones cultivated by amateur and commercial growers, and nicknamed the "Cyps." Included in this genus are some of the most striking of all orchids. In florist shops they compete for admiration with Cattleyas and Cymbidiums and are becoming increasingly popular. Their marvelous range of colors, from yellow, green, brown, red, and purple, to white, is often subtly combined in single flowers. Phragmopedilum and Selenipedium are genera interesting to collectors, although not widely grown. The true Cypripediums are known by all who love and study wild flowers and may be grown with special care in our gardens.

The flowers of the Cypripedium tribe are distinct, differing markedly from those of other tribes. The most appealing floral part is the lip, which is shaped like a pouch or slipper and which suggested their name (Cyprus, sacred to Venus, and *pes, pedis,* Latin for foot). Conspicuous, too, is the dorsal sepal standing guard above the lip, often broad and brilliantly marked. The petals extend laterally and are slender in proportion to the dorsal sepal. The other two sepals are fused together and lie behind the pouch. Usually they are hidden in a front view of the flower, but when they are enlarged, they add one more touch of beauty.

It would seem that these structures would be enough to distinguish the tribe. But botanically speaking, more important than these is the number of fertile anthers. All members of the Cypripedium tribe have two fertile anthers, whereas other tribes have only one. A third anther, which is sterile, is modified to form the conspicuous shield-like body called the staminode,

COLOR PLATE 7   Cymbidium Jocosity.

which projects forward from the column and covers the reproductive parts. (See Fig. 1.)

The members of the Cypripedium tribe lack pseudobulbs and so are not equipped for storing water. There is a short stem from which grow the leaves. After the leaves have formed on a new growth, the flowering stem arises from the tip of the stem, between the leaves.

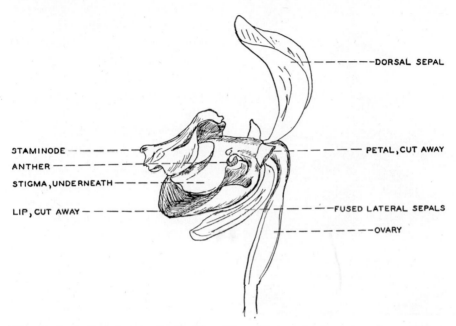

Fig. 1. Reproductive parts of a Paphiopedilum. The staminode projects forward from the tip of the column. The folds of the lip (not shown) lie between the staminode and the stigma, so that an insect caught in the lip must crawl up under the stigma. If it bears pollen from another flower, this is wiped off on the stigma. As the insect leaves through the openings at the upper end of the lip, it brushes against the sticky pollen held by the anther in just the right position.

PAPHIOPEDILUM

This genus of handsome Asiatics has an almost lurid beauty. The heavy-textured flowers are unexcelled in keeping quality and may be enjoyed on the plant or cut for a month or more. Some few remain fresh for as long as three months. The species vary in their flowering season so that blooms may be had at any time during the year. One of their chief attractions is their ease of culture. They are a good choice for amateurs who do not have a greenhouse, for a pot or two of Paphs will grow beautifully on a window sill or in a Wardian case. The species are inexpensive, and a few dollars will buy many years of pleasure. The hybrids are more costly, particularly the more recent ones.

The fifty or so species are native to tropical Asia, Malaya, and the near-by islands. Some are found at relatively high altitudes in the mountain chains, where rainfall is abundant and temperatures cool. Here they grow on accumulations of decaying vegetation on ledges or in crevices of limestone rocks, partially shaded by overhanging cliffs or trees. Other species occur at lower elevations where the temperatures are higher.

A Paphiopedilum makes a good house plant. Set the pot over water in a saucer by raising it on stones, or devise some other means to keep the pot above the water.

Temperature. Culturally, the cool- or warm-growing ones may be distinguished by their foliage. Those with plain green leaves require a night temperature of 50°–55° F., and the day temperature should be kept below 75° F. if possible. An occasional midday rise of temperature above this reading will not be detrimental, but shading and ventilation should be carefully adjusted to prevent excess heat. In order to protect the cool Paphiopedilums where the heat of summer is prolonged, some growers put the plants out-of-doors in the shade of large trees. The pots may be set on cinder beds, to assure drainage, or, better yet, they may be set on wire supports to keep them away from slugs and cutworms. The species with mottled leaves may be grown comfortably with Cattleyas, with a night temperature of 60° F. and the daytime conditions that suit the Cattleyas.

The good keeping qualities of the Paphiopedilums make it possible to have them for most holidays. Occasionally, however, it is desirable to slow down the opening and prolong the life of the flowers in order to hold them for a certain purpose. When the stem has reached its full length and the buds are almost fully developed, the temperature may be lowered a few degrees and kept down until flowering is finished. Flowering is thereby slightly delayed. The temperature must not be lowered too soon or the stems will remain short and the plant will not be as handsome in bloom. Exercise care in watering and syringing while the temperatures are lowered.

Potting. Paphiopedilums thrive when potted in soft, brown osmunda fibre. Some growers prefer to use a mixture of three parts of osmundine to one of live sphagnum moss, but it is difficult to keep the sphagnum alive. Another compost used successfully by some is two parts of shredded osmundine, one part of fibrous loam, and one part of clean, sharp sand, with an added sprinkling of dried cow manure. The choice of compost becomes a personal thing, and those who succeed with one type may not like another.

The plants are best repotted soon after flowering, at which time they may be divided into groups of not less than three growths. Remove all dead leaves and roots and all decayed osmundine or old compost. After adding crock for drainage and the appropriate amount of fibre to the new pot, hold the plant at such a depth for potting that the base of the plant will be about one-half inch deep in the fibre. If the plant is set too high the new roots will not thrive, and, if too deep, the base of the plant may rot. If fibre is used, pot firmly, but not as hard as for Cattleyas. Mixed compost should be firmly tamped. After potting, keep the plants on the dry side until root action starts; that is, water only lightly and do not flood the pots until growth begins. In the meantime, syringe the plants lightly several times a day. The plants will be thoroughly re-established in about three months.

Water. Since growth is continuous in this genus, and because the plants have no pseudobulbs, the potting medium should not be allowed to dry out. The frequency of watering depends so much on environmental conditions that it is difficult to give any set schedule. During bright weather two waterings a week may be sufficient, with longer intervals between times in dull weather. Syringing is beneficial on bright days, with the finest mist possible so as to avoid collection of water in the leaf axils. When the flowering scapes start to push from the center of the growth, the greatest care must be used in syringing lest the flower buds should rot.

Light. Paphiopedilums do best when shaded throughout the year, but this is a matter for judicious handling. During seasons characterized by long spells of cloudy weather, or where the sky is habitually hazy, less shading will be needed or the shading may be entirely removed. In the summer, the shading will perhaps have to be heavier than desirable in order to keep the greenhouse temperature down. When temperature is not a problem, the shading should be adjusted to the needs of the plants. From February to November the plants should receive from 20% to 30% of full sunlight, between 2000 and 3000 foot-candles. With such light intensities the plants will make more prosperous growth and produce more flowers. However, in all cases, let the plants themselves be the guide. The foliage should be a deep green color, and the light should be adjusted to keep this color.

The genus is divided, purely for convenience, into three sections according to certain features of the flowers.

Section I has flowers nearly round, made so by the large, round petals. All have mottled leaves and require somewhat warmer temperatures than the plain leaved species.

Section II has elongated, slender petals, and a plain pouch with the top not eared. All have plain green leaves and require cool treatment.

Section III has the pouch eared or notched on the posterior edges. Plants with both mottled and plain leaves are represented.

SECTION I

Paphiopedilum bellatulum. A species attractive for its foliage as well as for its charming flowers. The leaves are up to 10 inches long and are 3½ inches wide. They are deep green, mottled with lighter green on the upper surface, purplish underneath. The flower is round, shaped like a deep saucer, with the almost egg-shaped lip backed by the broad petals. They are white to pale yellow marked with purple spots, which run nearly into lines on the dorsal sepal, and which are smaller on the lip. Occurs in China. Flowers in the summer.

Paphiopedilum Godefroyae. A smaller species, with leaves 6 inches long by 1½ inches wide that are mottled green on the upper surface, and green spotted with brown-purple underneath. The short flower stem bears one or two white or pale yellow flowers that are lightly spotted with magenta. The petals are oval and point downward. Occurs in Cochin-China. Flowers in the summer.

Paphiopedilum concolor. The plants are about the same size as *P. Godefroyae,* with leaves mottled green on their upper surface and spotted with deep crimson below. The flowers are yellow, spotted with purple. The dorsal sepal is concave and almost round, and the broad petals point downward. The paler lip is nearly cylindric, somewhat flattened on the sides. Occurs in Moulmein. Flowers in the fall.

Paphiopedilum niveum. The plants are about the same size as the two preceding species, with the foliage strikingly colored, green mottled with gray-green above and brilliant purple underneath. The flowers are white with a scattering of purple dots, and the dorsal sepal is red on the back. The edges of the flower are prettily waved. Occurs in the Loncavi and Tambilan Islands. Flowers in the spring.

SECTION II

Paphiopedilum praestans. The striking flowers are large and brightly colored. The 2-inch tall dorsal sepal is whitish, decorated with sharp lines of purple. The spirally twisted petals are yellowish, veined with brown, and are about 5 inches long. They have hair-bearing warts on their margins. The lip is rather long, somewhat flattened on the sides, and is shiny yellow, suffused with red. Occurs in New Guinea. Flowers in August.

Paphiopedilum Rothschildianum. A handsome species with 2-foot long, green leaves, and a flower spike that may bear several flowers. The flowers are stunningly colored. The dorsal and lateral sepals are yellow striped with black-purple. The fused lateral sepals in this species are larger than in many others and give the effect of a mirror image of the dorsal. The long, slender petals extend 5 inches and are pale green, spotted with purple, distinctly lined or nerved with dark green. The long lip is purple, veined with a darker shade and yellow toward the top. It stands sharply forward. Occurs in Borneo and Sumatra. Flowers in the winter.

Paphiopedilum Sanderianum. A remarkable species. The petals are 1½ feet long, twisted, pale yellow, barred and spotted with purple. The dorsal sepal is narrow and pointed, yellow-green with brown stripes. The long, projecting lip is brown-purple and yellow. Occurs in the Malay Archipelago. Flowers in early spring.

Paphiopedilum Stonei. Three to five stunning flowers are borne on a stem. The dorsal sepal is white, trimmed with two or three crimson streaks and the lateral sepals almost equal it in size. The twisted petals are 5 to 6 inches long, tawny with crimson spots for two-thirds of the length, and solid crimson at the end. The lip is rose, reticulated with crimson; the upper sides fold in and are white. Occurs in Borneo. Flowers in the fall.

SECTION III

Paphiopedilum Argus. Distinctive, medium-sized flowers. The dorsal sepal is oval and pointed, white striped with green, or sometimes with both green and purple. Occasionally it is spotted with blackish purple at its base. The wavy petals have a white ground with green veins for two-thirds of their length, and clear purple tips. Blackish warts decorate the inner surface of the petals. The lip is brownish purple, green underneath, and the narrow, infolded lobes are light purple spotted with a deeper shade. The foliage is mottled. Occurs in Luzon. Flowers in April.

Paphiopedilum barbatum. An attractive species whose deep purple tones often approach red. The nearly round dorsal sepal is folded at the midvein. It is white, green at the base, stained and striped with purple. The petals, which bear blackish warts on their upper edges, are brownish green at the base changing to purple at the tip. The lip is deep brownish purple. The foliage is mottled. Occurs in the Malay Peninsula. Flowers usually in the summer.

Paphiopedilum callosum. Beautiful, large flowers, noted for their huge dorsal sepal, which may be 3 inches across. It is folded at the midvein and somewhat wavy at the top, white, with alternately long and short veins changing from purple at the base to green above. The petals are pale green with purple tips and have a sprinkling of blackish warts on the upper margin. The brownish purple lip is green beneath. The foliage is mottled. Occurs in Siam. Flowers in the spring.

Paphiopedilum Charlesworthii. A charming species with mottled foliage and medium-sized flowers. The large and spreading dorsal sepal is white, suffused and spotted with rose-purple. The petals are yellow-green, reticulated with brown, and the lip is rosy-purple. Occurs in Bengal. Flowers in the fall.

Paphiopedilum Dayanum. An attractive species with mottled foliage and slender flowers produced on a long stem. The dorsal sepal is prettily shaped, with the lower sides folded back and the upper edges folded forward to form a point at the top. It is white with green veins. The long, slender petals are greenish brown changing to rose purple. The slender lip is somewhat pointed at the tip, brownish purple, veined with green. Occurs in Borneo. Flowers in May and June.

Paphiopedilum exul. The lightly marbled foliage is bordered with white. The yellow-green dorsal sepal has a white margin and brown spots. The petals and lip are yellow with faint brown markings. Occurs in Siam.

Paphiopedilum Fairieanum. Small plants with light green leaves and attractive, medium-sized flowers. The nearly round dorsal sepal is large in proportion to the size of the flower, with an undulating margin. It is greenish white, reticulated with violet. The upward-curving petals are yellow to white, streaked with purple, bearing tufts of hairs on their wavy margins. The smallish lip is green and white. Occurs in Assam. Flowers in the fall.

Paphiopedilum hirsutissimum. Large, dark colored, hairy flowers make this a striking species. The roundish dorsal sepal is heavily marked with black-purple and bordered with green. The petals are slender near their base, wider toward the end, and somewhat twisted. They are mottled with deep purple on a green ground near the base, becoming bright purple at the tip. The deep green lip is tinged with purple. The foliage is plain green. Occurs in Assam. Flowers in the spring.

Paphiopedilum insigne. The easiest to grow and one of the most popular of the genus. It appears everywhere, in collections and in the florist's show window. Perhaps its most attractive feature is the shiny appearance of the flowers, almost as if they had been varnished. The broad, oval dorsal sepal has the top turned slightly forward. The central part is apple green, spotted with purple along the darker green veins, and the upper part is white. The wavy petals are pale yellow-green, veined with brown. The lip is also yellow-green, suffused with brown. Occurs in Nepal and Assam. Flowers in the winter. *Paphiopedilum insigne* has many named varieties, of which var. *Harefield Hall* has proved to be outstanding both in itself and as a parent of hybrids. This form is larger than the type, and recent studies have shown it to be a natural triploid (having three times the usual haploid number of chromosomes). The standard chromosome number of Paphiopedilum is 26 in the vegetative cell, 13 in the reproductive cells. The variety *Harefield Hall* has 39, or three times thirteen. It transmits its large size to a large number of offspring when used as a parent. The hybrid, *Paphiopedilum insigne,* var. *Harefield Hall* × *Paphiopedilum Spicerianum* has also proved an excellent parent. Its large size (from var. *Harefield Hall*) plus the large dorsal sepal (from *Spicerianum*) have been carried down to many of our present-day hybrids.

Paphiopedilum Lawrenceanum. A handsome species with mottled yellow-green foliage and large flowers. The beautiful dorsal sepal is nearly round, white with deep purple, flame shaped veins reaching nearly to the tip. The straight, veined petals are green with purple tips, and both margins carry black warts. The lip is dull purple, tinged with brown and green. Occurs in Borneo. Flowers from April to July.

Paphiopedilum Lowii. Quite an unusual species in that three to six dainty flowers are borne on a long nodding stem. The leaves are light green. The flower parts are slender. The oar-shaped petals are yellow with black spots toward the base, violet at the outer ends. The dorsal sepal is slender at its base, spreading at the top, yellow-green, veined with brownish purple. The lip is brown. Occurs in Borneo. Flowers in the summer.

Paphiopedilum Spicerianum. Medium-sized flowers, distinguished for the large dorsal sepal which is markedly wider than it is tall, yet is folded in a turret-like manner. The foliage is dark green. The dorsal sepal is white, with a simple crimson-purple band down the center. Its basal region is green, spotted with red. The petals have wavy margins and are pale green spotted and striped with purple. The lip is rather long, dull purple marked with green. Occurs in Assam. Flowers from October to December.

Paphiopedilum villosum. Large, glossy, hairy flowers are produced on rather large plants whose leaves are green above, purple spotted beneath. The dorsal sepal is brownish purple with a green tip. The longish petals are wavy, yellowish brown with a prominent central band of purple. The lip is brownish yellow. The variety, *Paphiopedilum villosum,* var. *Boxallii* is sometimes given as a separate species. In this the dorsal sepal is marked in the center with numerous black spots. Var. *Boxallii* has been a frequent parent of hybrids. Occurs in Moulmein. Flowers in January and February.

GROWING PAPHIOPEDILUM FROM SEED

When a group of species as distinct and as beautiful as the Paphiopedilums displays itself before you, you cannot down the urge to make hybrids with them. Growers have long worked to combine the best features of several into one superb flower, and there are today some stunning hybrids. But the casual observer cannot know the patient work and the many disappointments that lie behind the flower he sees.

The first Paphiopedilum hybrid was made in 1869, a cross between *Paph. barbatum* and *Paph. villosum.* Since then, many successful hybrids have appeared, of which one of the most famous is *Paph. Maudiae,* the so-called green orchid. Its parentage was *Paph. callosum,* var. *Sanderae* × *Paph. Lawrenceanum,* var. *Hyeanum.*

A number of difficulties exist in the breeding of Paphiopedilum hybrids. A great deal of effort has gone into the making of crosses in this genus, with less relative success than with other genera. Many of the beautiful hybrids shown today are almost sole survivors of the matings that made them. In the first place, the hybrids are frequently partially or entirely sterile, according to their genetic make-up (see p. 166). This means that often only a small amount of viable seed is produced. In the second place, Paphiopedilum seed is hard to germinate, so that much good seed never results in seedlings.

This does not mean that an amateur cannot breed Paphiopedilums, for he may hit on a combination that gives a fair amount of good seed. But even if he achieves only a few plants for his effort, he will be rewarded by a justifiable thrill at success under such challenging circumstances.

The pollen of Paphiopedilums does not keep as well as most pollen. Hence it should be used shortly after it has been removed from the two anthers.

A toothpick can be used to transfer the granular pollen directly to the stigma.

A seed pod matures in approximately nine to eleven months, occasionally in a shorter or longer time. The technique used for sowing the flasks is essentially the same as that described for Cattleya. Calcium hypochlorite solution is usually used as the disinfecting agent. The coat of Paphiopedilum seed is unusually hard and moreover is protected by hairs which make it more difficult to wet with a disinfecting agent. Some workers add a drop or two of a wetting agent, such as Santomerse, to the 140 c.c. of hypochlorite solution to aid its penetration. The exposure to the disinfecting solution is 10 to 20 minutes.

The best growing medium produced so far is Knudson's "C" solution, with the addition of .05 gram of peptone to 1 liter of the agar-nutrient mixture. The *p*H should be adjusted to 6 to give the more nearly neutral conditions suited to Paphiopedilum.

Paphiopedilum Leeanum.

Often out of a large number of seed sown, only a scant few ever germinate. Sometimes seeds germinate after months or even years, but it is almost impossible to maintain the proper growing conditions over such long periods. It is, therefore, suggested that a generous amount of seed be sown in each flask.

The reluctant germination suggests the possibility of the presence of an inhibitor in the seed. Burgeff used a soaking technique which improved the percentage of germination. He allowed the seed to stand in sterile water for two weeks to two months before sowing it in the flasks. His growing medium differed slightly from Knudson's "C," and he kept the flasks in the dark until the embryos began to lengthen.

Using unripe seed is another method suggested to improve germination. The pod is removed from the plant just before it is ready to split open. Have the flasks ready to receive the seed. Pass the pod quickly through the flame, being careful not to let it stay long enough to raise the temperature within it to the death point. Or dip the pod in a solution of one part of Clorox to nine of water. Then slit it open with a sterile knife, and transfer the seed directly to the flasks by means of a sterile platinum loop. If desired, the seed may be first removed to a tube of sterile water, and then sown either with a loop or a pipette (dropper).

Obviously, one method of getting better germination would be to obtain a higher percentage of good seed from the cross. And here is your chance to experiment. As will be seen below, chromosomal aberrations are the cause of a good bit of partial or complete sterility in Paphiopedilum. Abnormalities in the reproductive cells may cause any one of the following kinds of incompatibility. The pollen may fail to produce pollen tubes, or the tubes may not grow long enough to reach the ovary. If they reach the ovary, they may fail to penetrate the ovules. Perhaps the growth of the pollen tubes is so slow that the ovules degenerate before the tubes reach them. Even after penetration of the ovules, the reproductive cells may not be able to unite. Sometimes, after the reproductive cells have united, an embryo fails to develop.

There is little you can do in a mechanical way about such incompatibilities as the last two mentioned. But research on other types of plants that have difficulty in setting seed suggest a few tricks to try on Paphiopedilums. As far as I know, they have not been tried on orchids. Supposing that the cross you particularly want to make has failed because of the undue length of time it takes the pollen tubes to reach the ovules, or suppose that seed is formed only in the apex by the first tubes to reach the ovary, the others being too slow in growing down. You might try bud pollination, which has been successful in some other cases. The flower to be pollinated is opened while still in the bud stage and the pollen placed on the stigma. The extra time gained may be just the critical difference between success and failure of the cross.

Another method to try is the application of a growth promoting substance to the ovary. Mix thoroughly 1 gram of naphthalene acetamide with 99 grams of lanolin. Smear a small amount of this on the base of the ovary at the time of pollination. Its stimulating effect may enable seed to be formed where it might not otherwise develop.

GENETICS OF PAPHIOPEDILUM

Some matings yield rather a high percentage of good seed, whereas others give little viable seed or prove to be completely sterile. Crosses between *Paph. insigne, Paph. villosum, Paph. Boxallii,* and *Paph. Spicerianum,* or between hybrids which have only these as parents are usually quite successful. The matings of other hybrids, particularly those more advanced or of more complex lineage, are often less compatible or prove sterile.

It often happens that a handsome, show quality hybrid cannot be used as a parent, which is discouraging both to commercial and amateur growers. Seed production drops proportionally when horticulturally more desirable flowers are used in breeding. A number of cytogeneticists (who study genetics with a microscope) are working to find out what lies behind this sterility. They have turned up some clues, and with their aid growers may in the future be able to plan their crosses so as to produce more viable seed.

The clues lie in the genetic make-up of the species and their hybrids. Usually, plants have two sets of chromosomes in each of their body cells, one from the female and one from the male parent. These two sets comprise the diploid number. While the number of chromosomes is not the same for all the species in the genus, yet each species has its own standard number. *Paph. insigne* and its close relatives have the standard diploid number of 26, yet the variety *Hare-field Hall* of *Paph. insigne* contains 39. Instead of having only two sets of 13 chromosomes, it has three, and is a triploid.

Paphiopedilum Gratixianum. (Courtesy of Clarelen Orchids)

While twenty-six chromosomes is the standard number for *Paph. insigne, villosum, Boxallii, bellatulum, Dele-natii,* and *Fairieanum,* other species have different basic numbers. *Paph. barbatum* has 38, *Paph. callosum* has 32, and *Paph. Curtisii* and *Paph. Laurenceanum* have 36.

Associated with polyploidy (triploids, tetraploids, etc.) are larger, thicker leaves, and larger flowers. These characteristics are found in most of the choice present-day hybrids, which suggests that they are either triploid or tetraploid, and this has been found true in many hybrids examined.

Sometimes in reduction division (see Chapter V) at which time the reproductive cells are formed, the chromosomes are not equally distributed. A cell that has a diploid number of 30 chromosomes usually gives single sets of 15 to each daughter cell. Occasionally the division may result in cells with 14 and 16, or rarely a reproductive cell may be given the double set and carry the full 30. It is easy to see that the chromosome content of a complicated hybrid may be quite different from what would be expected.

The accumulation of additional chromosomes may take place either by having a triploid or tetraploid parent, or by the chance fertilization of a normal cell by one that has a double complement, or more than the usual number of chromosomes. When *Paph. insigne,* var. *Harefield Hall* is used as a parent, its 39 chromosomes may conceivably separate into sets of 26 and 13, so that some of its offspring would receive a double set. Triploids also occur when a tetraploid is mated with a diploid, so that each offspring receives two sets from one parent and one from the other. The triploids are larger than the diploids and produce more flowers than the tetraploids. (In practical application, use the tetraploid as the female parent.)

A case has been reported showing how nonreduction may function. *Paph. Maudiae* is a hybrid between *Paph. callosum* (32 chromosomes) and *Paph. Lawrenceanum* (36). Examination of plants of *Maudiae* showed them to have 34 chromosomes, which would be the expected number (a set of 16 from one parent and 18 from the other). When *Maudiae* is used as a parent it should contribute 17 chromosomes, but a case has been found where *Maudiae* × *insigne* (*Sanderianum*) produced a plant with 46 or 47. Since the insigne used was evidently not a polyploid (as shown by its size) it must have given the normal 13 chromosomes to the cross, showing that the other 33 or 34 must have come from *Maudiae* in a reproductive cell carrying the double set. *Maudiae,* incidentally, is partially sterile.

While sterility usually results when the chromosome numbers are erratic, sterility may also be caused by irregularities in the chromosomes themselves. The work on genetics has far to go before the whole story is known, but an excellent beginning has been made.

PHRAGMOPEDILUM AND SELENIPEDIUM

Phragmopedilum, one of the South American genera of the Cypripedium tribe, has about 11 species. It differs from Paphiopedilum in that the dorsal sepal is more or less like the petals, and the edges of the lip are infolded giving it a more slipper-like appearance. An important botanical difference is that the flowers are deciduous. They may be grown with plenty of heat and moisture from March to November, shaded from the direct rays of the sun. Osmunda fibre with a little leaf mold mixed in is a good compost, and it should be allowed to rise above the rim of the pot. The pot should have good drainage. After potting, keep on the dry side until growth starts.

Phragmopedilum caudatum. Rather stiff, upright leaves, and flower stems 1 to 2 feet tall. Remarkable for its long, ribbon-like petals which grow to a length of 3 feet. The petals are yellow shaded with brown and tinted with crimson toward the tips. The dorsal sepal is slender and wavy, about six inches long, pale yellow veined with green. Occurs in Peru.

Phragmopedilum Sargentianum. The leaves are tufted, 6–8 inches long, with golden margins. The flower stem bears two or three blooms. The oval dorsal sepal is pale yellow with red veins. The petals are slightly longer, twisted at the ends, yellow with red margins and veins. The lip is rather long, also yellow marked with red. Occurs in Brazil.

Selenipedium, the other South American genus of the Cypripedium tribe, is so similar to Phragmopedilum that it is included by many botanists in the latter genus. Some of the species given under Phragmopedilum may therefore sometimes be found classified as Selenipedium. Selenipediums are often too large to be adaptable to small greenhouses, for example, *Selen. Chica* of Panama reaches 12–15 feet in height.

CYPRIPEDIUM

These are the moccasin-flowers or ladyslippers of our own woods and moist meadows. They may be transplanted to our gardens if their new locality is made to imitate their native spot. There are about 30 species. Like the other members of the tribe, these are becoming less numerous with the passing years. Man probably has something to do with this, by using for himself the sunny areas where the plants would do best, so that they are forced to exist in the woods. They are sun-loving plants and do not grow as well in heavy shade. Lovers of these plants ask that instead of removing the wild clumps to your garden, plants be purchased from nurseries. The latter may even do better for you, for they will have been adapted to garden conditions.

These native Cypripediums require plenty of moisture. A dam built around their bed will help to retain water. They do best with some shade at noon.

Cypripedium acaule. Pink moccasin-flower. The single flower grows on rather a tall stem. The color is usually pale pink with deeper veining, but deep pink with light veins and pure white are also found. The lip is closed except for a slit in front. This species requires an acid soil and is the most difficult to grow. Often it will last for a year or two and then die out. It should be aided by the addition of such acid material as pine needles to the soil. Occurs from Newfoundland to North Carolina, and west to the Great Lakes region. Flowers in May and June.

Cypripedium californicum. Tall plants with leaves produced alternately on the stem. From six to twelve flowers occur about an inch apart on the stem. They are small, with green sepals and petals and a white lip. Occurs in California.

Cypripedium candidum. Green flowers with a pretty lip that is white, striped inside with purple. Found in New York, Pennsylvania, Minnesota, Missouri, and Kentucky.

Cypripedium montanum. A handsome, fragrant species that grows rather tall. One to three flowers are produced on a stem. The petals are wavy-twisted, dull brown, and the lip is whitish veined with purple. Found from California to Washington.

Cypripedium parviflorum. The beautiful yellow ladyslipper, one of the most handsome of the species and the easiest to grow. The whole flower is bright yellow, with narrow, somewhat wavy petals and a wider dorsal sepal. In culture it requires a porous neutral soil, with plenty of moisture and some shade. Found almost everywhere from Kansas eastward.

Cypripedium pubescens. This species is also given as a variety of *Cyp. parviflorum.* Its flowers are similar but a little larger. The roots and rhizomes have some medicinal properties.

Cypripedium reginae, or *Cypripedium spectabile,* is truly named the "Queen" ladyslipper. It is tall and robust and produces a wealth of large flowers. The white sepals and petals are set off by the rosy shades of the lip. It requires a sunny spot in the garden and moist, neutral soil. Occurs from Maine to the Middle West. Flowers in June.

Chapter XIII

THE DENDROBIUM TRIBE

The Dendrobium tribe includes the marvelous genus, Dendrobium, and two genera of definitely lesser importance. The name is derived from *dendro,* tree, and *bios,* life.

DENDROBIUM

Dendrobiums have been popular with amateurs for over a hundred years, and for good reason. Their flowers, though sometimes small, are charmingly colored and vividly marked. Even one small plant in bloom catches the eye of the casual observer, and a plant that has long, drooping racemes of flowers is a sight not soon forgotten. Not the least of the charms of the Dendrobiums is the rapidity of their growth and the ease with which they can be propagated. From a few plants they may soon be increased to a large number.

The very size of this genus of epiphytes promises a wide variety of types, for it numbers more than 1000 species. The plants vary in size from small, with thin wiry pseudobulbs, to those whose pseudobulbs are as large as young trees. The pseudobulbs are usually stem-like and jointed, producing leaves at the joints. The flower stems usually arise from the juncture between leaf and pseudobulb. In some the pseudobulb is short and erect, so that the flowers appear in an upright cluster. In others the pseudobulb is long and pendulous, producing a long, drooping spray of blooms. Characteristics of the flower are that the lateral sepals are united at the base to form more or less of a spur, and the lip narrows at its base to a mere stalk.

The genus ranges wild over western Asia and the Pacific Islands, from the Himalayas through Burma to the Malayan regions, Australia, New Zealand, China, Japan, and the Philippines. Obviously, the variety of climatic conditions gives a variety of plant habits. However, the Dendrobiums can be conveniently divided into two sections, the evergreen and the deciduous, according to their habit either of keeping their leaves throughout the whole year or losing their leaves before flowering.

The evergreen Dendrobiums come from warm, humid regions where the climate is similar all year round, for instance from the Malayan regions and the Philippines. During part of the year the rainfall may abate somewhat, but there is no dry season. The deciduous Dendrobiums come from warm regions such as Burma where there is a definite wet season (as much as 250 inches of rain a month) followed by a season of little rain and slightly lower temperatures.

A young plant growing on the pseudobulb that produced the season's flowers. The plantlet may be removed and potted by itself.

For these two types general cultural rules can be evolved, which must be varied a bit here and there for individual species. The evergreen type must not be allowed to dry out. It requires abundant water all year round, and for the most part a night temperature of about 60° F. The deciduous type requires abundant water during the growing season, and considerably less water while at rest. During the growing season these plants like a night temperature of 60°, but must be given a winter night temperature (50°) to encourage flower formation. Their growing period follows the seasons of spring and summer in our country, when night temperatures are naturally warm.

Dendrobiums are grown in osmunda fibre, requiring good root aeration. They like warm sunny positions in the greenhouse, with the shading adjusted to their needs.

Repotting should be looked after every two years, when flowering is just finished, or as new growth begins. The pot is chosen according to the size of the plant. More growths can be accommodated in a small pot when the pseudobulbs are close together than when the sections of rhizome are longer between bulbs.

Propagation is done in two ways—by division, as in Cattleyas, in which case new growths arise from the base of older bulbs, and by offsets. The latter are young plants that arise along the pseudobulb, at the nodes. These plantlets often come after flowering is finished, when new growth starts. They may grow on the pseudobulb as it stays on the plant, or the pseudobulb may be cut into sections and laid on moist sphagnum moss to encourage sprouting. When the little plants are 3 or 4 inches long they may be potted up in

COLOR PLATE 7A.   Cymbidium Nell Gwynne.

osmundine. They attain flowering size rapidly and may bloom the following season. To make a large display, a number of young plants may be put in the same pot.

Hybrids are easily made and are becoming more and more numerous. With such a large number of species to choose from, the amateur has a bright future in this field. His joy should be increased by the fact that Dendrobium seedlings mature and flower in about three years from seed. The seed germinates readily in flasks prepared as for Cattleyas.

More than two hundred of the thousand species are grown and enjoyed by amateurs. Representative ones from each of the two types are given here, but can be only an introduction to this large genus.

DECIDUOUS DENDROBIUMS

The leaves of these species fall sometime during the period of lessened activity before the flower buds appear, or during the blooming period. When growth is finished, the plants are rested at a cooler night temperature (50° F.), and given only an occasional watering to keep them from shriveling. If it is not possible to change the greenhouse temperature, find as cool a spot for them as you can. During this period they should be given plenty of light and especially good air circulation. When the flower buds begin to show, water more frequently again, and gradually increase the night temperature to 60° F.

Dendrobium Findlayanum. Daintily colored flowers are produced in a large, open cluster. The sepals and petals are white, tinted with lilac, and the heart-shaped lip is white, tipped with pink and yellow in the center. The slender, curved pseudobulbs have swollen nodes and grow 2 to 3 feet long. The rather long flower stems bear two or three blooms each, and arise from the several nodes near the end of the pseudobulb. Occurs in Burma. Flowers in late summer.

Dendrobium nobile. A species with over eighty named varieties. It is the most widely grown of all the Dendrobiums and has some commercial cut-flower value. The charming, brightly colored blossoms are produced in rounded clusters from the nodes toward the tip of the 18-inch pseudobulbs. The little stems curve at the top, giving the flowers a slightly nodding posture. Individual flowers are 3 inches in diameter. The rounded, velvety lip is deep purple in the throat and bordered with white. The pointed sepals and petals are white tipped with rosy purple. The flowers last a long time and lend themselves to dainty corsages. Occurs in India. Flowers in the spring.

Dendrobium Pierardii. Long, drooping pseudobulbs that grow to a length of 3 feet produce a wealth of flowers, each 2 inches across. Pale pink sepals and petals, set off by a yellow lip striped with purple, make the sprays most attractive. Old pseudobulbs often flower for two or three successive years. Occurs in India. Flowers in early summer.

Dendrobium superbum. Handsome, drooping sprays of fifty or more flowers grow along the 3- to 4-foot pseudobulbs. The magenta-rose flowers are 3 to 5 inches across, and have a delightful spicy fragrance. The lip is pointed and grooved, downy on its upper surface, and has two red-purple spots in the throat. Sometimes the tube is also red-purple. Occurs in the Philippines. Flowers in March and April.

Dendrobium Wardianum. Flowers slightly larger than in *Dendrobium nobile,* and with good keeping qualities, make this another species of commercial value. The curving, 3-foot-long pseudobulbs produce a lovely array of blooms that grow in groups of two or three nearly the length of the stem. Waxy sepals and petals are white, tipped with magenta. The large lip is white, tipped with purple, the throat orange marked with purple eyes. Occurs in Assam and Burma. Flowers in late spring.

THE EVERGREEN DENDROBIUMS

These species retain their leaves while flowering. They need warmth and water all year around, with an occasional exception in the matter of temperature. The evergreen Dendrobiums have not entered much into the commercial market, though some compare favorably with *D. nobile* and *D. Wardianum* as to keeping qualities, and certainly deserve a place among florists' orchids from the point of view of beauty.

Dendrobium aggregatum. A dwarf-growing species, with short, wrinkled pseudobulbs crowned with a single, short leaf. The flower stems arise from the side of the pseudobulb, and each bears a dozen or so clear yellow flowers in a graceful, drooping cluster. The shell-shaped lip is downy, deeper than the petals and sepals in color. Occurs in India and China, and flowers in late spring and early summer.

Dendrobium aureum. (Also called *Dendrobium heterocarpum.*) Fragrant, creamy yellow flowers, whose brighter yellow lip is streaked with purple, are borne in two's and three's from the nodes of the previous year's bulbs. Each flower is about 2 inches across. Pseudobulbs are erect, yellow, and grow to 18 inches in height. Occurs from the Himalayas to the Philippines. Flowers in late winter.

Dendrobium bigibbum. Clusters of bright magenta-purple flowers are borne at the end of the slender 18-inch pseudobulbs. The flowers have a waxy appearance, except for a downy white crest on the darker lip. Occurs in Australia.

Dendrobium Dearii. White flowers, whose lip is marked with a yellow-green band, grow in clusters from the tops of both new and old pseudobulbs. The latter reach a height of 3 feet, tapering upward from a thickened base. The spur (the base of lateral sepals) is long and funnel-shaped. Occurs in the Philippines. Flowers in summer.

Dendrobium fimbriatum. The softly fringed lip of these golden yellow flowers adds a delicate touch to the thick clusters of blooms that spring from the ends of the long, drooping pseudobulbs. The lip has an orange spot in the center, which in the variety *oculatum* is replaced by a maroon spot that gives a most striking appearance. This is a very vigorous species. Occurs in Nepal. Flowers in winter.

Dendrobium formosum. A species having large flowers, 3½ to 4 inches in the type, and up to 5 inches in the variety *giganteum.* The handsome

Dendrobium fimbriatum, var. *oculatum.*
(Courtesy of Jack Sweet)

flowers are white, with a bright yellow groove down the center of the broad lip. They are produced in clusters of three to five from the tops of rather short, stout, hairy pseudobulbs. Occurs in Burma. Flowers in the fall.

Dendrobium Phalaenopsis. A beautifully colored species, whose flowers are borne in delicate sprays of ten to fifteen blooms, from the top of both old and new pseudobulbs. The sepals are white, tinted with rose, the petals mauve, veined with a deeper shade. The lateral lobes of the lip are deep maroon-purple while the slender, pointed middle lobe is pale purple with deep veins. Occurs in Australia. Flowers in fall and winter.

Dendrobium Thyrsiflorum. Beautiful long, dense sprays of twenty to forty flowers arise from the axils of the leaves near the top of both old and new pseudobulbs. The flowers are white with a lovely round, rich yellow lip. The variety *Walkerianum* carries long sprays of fifty or more flowers. Occurs in Burma. Flowers in late spring.

OTHER MEMBERS OF THE DENDROBIUM TRIBE

Other genera of the Dendrobium tribe are Inobulbon and Sarcopodium, but neither is as floriferous or as striking as the Dendrobiums. *Inobulbon munificum* produces scanty racemes of greenish flowers spotted with brown. *Sarcopodium amplum* has greenish-white flowers. Both genera has unusually short pseudobulbs.

Chapter XIV

ODONTOGLOSSUM TRIBE

An artist with words might contrive a new adjective to describe the wonders of this tribe of epiphytes. The adjective would have something in it of feathers and pixies, butterflies and pansies, filigree work and the classical ballet. Woven through it would be a feeling of golden sunlight and cool, frosty nights. And when its syllables were cleverly fitted together, it would mean Odontoglossum, Oncidium, and Miltonia, the three important members of the six belonging to this tribe.

Odontoglossums and Miltonias were widely grown in nineteenth century England, in the house, the garden, and the greenhouse. A writer of the times described a plant that grew wonderfully in the sitting-room of his home, where it was covered with frost on winter nights and had no heat until the fire was lighted for tea. Sprays of Odontoglossums were made into bouquets for "lady musicians" and were used in arrangements for decorations. Single blossoms were considered quite the best boutonnieres for gentlemen. While other kinds of orchids were admired and even grown in quantity, the Odontoglossums and Miltonias were really the popular orchids of the day.

Oncidium, the third important member of this tribe, offers variety scarcely to be matched elsewhere in the orchid family. An amateur could easily become an Oncidium fancier, for possession of a few of the species provokes a curiosity to know the other elfin forms of the genus. Legend has it that it was an Oncidium that started the craze of amateur orchid growing.

The genera belonging to the Odontoglossum tribe are so closely related that some botanists consider it merely one large and varied genus. The genera may be freely crossed with one another. So many natural hybrids have been found that the job of marking these from distinct species is far from finished. Whether the tribe is considered one genus or several, certain characters separate the types from each other, and the generic division is helpful in classifying the hundreds of species.

The tribe inhabits tropical America, from Mexico to Bolivia, and climbs from the hot, coastal regions to the cool, misty heights of the Andes. The warm-growing species may be easily grown in the ordinary greenhouse, but those that come from the highest altitudes require conditions not found everywhere in this country. It has been said that the latter, particularly certain Odontoglossums, may be grown only in New England and the Pacific Northwest, and that elsewhere air-conditioned greenhouses are necessary. However, amateurs here and there across the northern part of the country seem to grow them successfully. Certainly parts of the Rocky Mountain region are beautifully adapted to their culture. The critical factor is, of course, cool summers. Amateurs who are attracted by Odontoglossums and Miltonias, and who live in regions blessed with the proper climate, should certainly give them a try.

MILTONIA

The Miltonias are affectionately called the "pansy orchid," and their charms are indeed similar to those of the much beloved pansy. Their flowers open flat, with the same frank expression, and their rounded parts are as softly colored. The blossoms are held gracefully on stems about as long as the leaves, that rise from the base of the pseudobulb. They vary in number from one to ten according to the species, and last nearly a month on the plant. The leaves are slender, two or more at the apex of the pseudobulb and a few small ones sheathing its base. A flowering plant has the graceful symmetry of a hand-arranged bouquet.

Miltonias thrive under the same cool conditions described for Cymbidium. They require some shade during the summer, partly to keep down the greenhouse temperature, but need more light during the winter. The new growths must be well matured in order to give rise to flower spikes.

The best potting medium is black osmunda fibre, packed hard. Avoid overpotting, choosing pots large enough barely to provide for two years' growth. Some growers repot every year and give the plants scant growing space. The plants may be divided at repotting time, after flowering is finished.

Abundant water during the growing period is a necessity, with plenty of atmospheric moisture and syringing on bright days. Water is withheld somewhat after flowering and until new growth commences.

The plants are especially susceptible to red spider and thrips, against which they must be protected.

Miltonia hybrids are numerous, and crosses have been made with other genera in the tribe. Both hybrids and species are widely grown, and the most popular of the latter are described below.

THE SPECIES

Miltonia candida. A striking species that produces generous numbers of flower spikes, each with six to ten blooms. The flowers are about 2½ inches across, yellow marked with large red-brown blotches. The large oval lip is white tinged with yellow and has a wavy margin. The pseudobulbs arise at intervals of about an inch along the rhizome, and the foliage is characteristically yellowish. Occurs in Brazil. Flowers in the fall.

Miltonia Charlesworthii, a lovely hybrid. (Courtesy of Frederick T. Bonham)

Miltonia Clowesii. This species resembles the preceding one and has the same yellow-green foliage. The flowers are a bit larger and are of a shade approaching orange. The lip is fiddle-shaped, white, with a violet base. Occurs in Brazil. Flowers in September and October.

Miltonia Phalaenopsis. This species is less robust than some, with pale green, grass-like foliage. The short flower spikes produce one to three beautiful flowers, which have daintily pointed white sepals and petals, and a spreading lip that is white streaked with crimson. Occurs in Colombia. Flowers in the spring.

Miltonia Roezlii. A lovely species, often found in the lineage of hybrids. The foliage is green and the pseudobulbs are tightly clustered. Two to four large flat flowers are borne on each spike. The sepals and petals are white, the latter having a purple band at the base. The large lip is two lobed, white with a tinge of purple. It becomes yellow at the base, where two little horns project backward on each side of the column. This species requires especially free ventilation, and plenty of moderated light. Occurs in Colombia. Often flowers twice a year, winter and spring. The popular hybrid *Miltonia Bleuana* is a cross between *Miltonia Roezlii* and *Miltonia vexillaria*.

Miltonia spectabilis. This was the first Miltonia introduced into culture. It is indeed a spectacle when in flower, for large, sturdy plants may bear as many as fifty flowers, each on a separate stem, and all opening at once. The flowers are large, white or cream color, with a large, wavy lip that is rose-purple veined with a darker shade. The pseudobulbs are an inch apart, and the foliage is yellow-green. Occurs in Brazil. Flowers in the fall.

Miltonia vexillaria. This species has the largest flowers of the genus and is the most popular. It is also the most frequently used in hybridization. The plants are sturdy, easily grown, and generous in the numbers of blooms produced. The richly colored flowers are 4 inches or more in diameter, and occur two to seven on a spike. A single pseudobulb may give rise to several spikes. The small sepals and petals are bright rose in color, sometimes with a white margin. The huge, bilobed lip is the striking feature of the flower and the character desired in its hybrids. It, too, is a rich shade of rose, shading to white at the base, and streaked with yellow and red. Two small horns project from the base of the lip on either side of the column. The plant has pale green foliage. Occurs in Colombia. Flowers in spring and summer.

ODONTOGLOSSUM

Some of the loveliest orchids known to man belong to the genus Odontoglossum. Their culture is easy, provided you can give them the conditions they require, cool summer days and nights for those that grow natively in the high altitudes of the Andes and warmer conditions for those that occur on the lower slopes or near the coast.

The low altitude ones are perhaps the best for the amateur to try, as they may be grown with a general collection at a night temperature of about 60° F. and considerably more warmth in the daytime. These are rather the exceptions among the hundred species belonging to the genus. *Odontoglossum citrosmum* with its sprays of beautifully rounded, white and purple flowers, and *Odontoglossum grande* with its huge yellow and brown flowers are striking additions to any collection.

A second group, that requires cool conditions similar to those described for Cymbidium and Miltonia, may be grown where the night temperatures in the summer can be kept around 50° F. and the day temperatures ideally between 60° and 70° F. This group is worth the exploration of amateurs who live in the northern parts of the United States, or at high altitudes, where the summers are naturally cool. Experimentation should perhaps be on a small scale, just a plant or two of various species, until the grower has established which ones will do well in his locality. Some of the loveliest species in this group are *Odontoglossum bictoniense, Harryanum, Insleayi, nobile, Pulchellum, Rossii, Schlieperianum,* and *Uro-Skinnerii. Odontoglossum nobile,* which is found at an altitude of 8000 feet, has been used in many hybrids. It is a vigorous species, and its hybrids are readily adapted to the conditions suggested for this group.

The cold Odontoglossums require an ideal night temperature of 40°– 45° F. winter and summer, and a day temperature of 60° F. Many of these are grown successfully in the cooler regions of this country, where it has been found that the plants will tolerate somewhat warmer summer temperatures if they are not prolonged. However, everything should be done to keep the temperature as close to the ideal as possible, without shading the greenhouse too heavily. It is suggested that amateurs who are successful with the second group try a few of the cold-growing species on the happy chance that they might thrive for them. Fortunate indeed is the amateur who can have the lovely *Odontoglossum crispum, luteo-purpureum,* and *odoratum* in his collection. Where conditions are too warm for these species artificial methods of producing cool temperatures may be employed. Air-conditioned greenhouses, or the installation of pipes above the ridge which keep a steady stream of water flowing over the glass, are means employed by some growers. However, it is questionable whether having these particular species, beautiful as they are, is worth the expense of special construction for the amateur.

All Odontoglossums require plenty of modified light, good fresh air, and atmospheric moisture. Shade is necessary all year round, but can be lessened during the winter. Local conditions in some areas may allow almost complete removal of shading during December and January.

The warm-growing group requires only a moderate amount of water, and the pots should be allowed to approach dryness between waterings. The cool and cold groups grow natively with their roots embedded in mosses that cling to the trees. Cool mists keep the mosses continually damp. These two groups therefore require more frequent watering, and their compost should never be allowed to dry out.

Abundant atmospheric moisture is necessary and must be coupled with good ventilation. To protect the plants, particularly the cool groups, from disease, it is wise to syringe the foliage only on bright days, and to provide most of the humidity by under-bench sprayers and by damping down the walks, etc. Collection of water in the foliage or around the roots invites infection.

The best potting medium is black osmunda fibre, well firmed, and somewhat higher in the center. The plants should be put in as small pots as possible, and these should be provided with ample drainage. Repotting is done in the fall, if the plants need more space. Otherwise the plant need not be disturbed, but instead the surface fibre may be replaced with fresh material.

Odontoglossums are not easily propagated by division. They are, however, readily grown from seed. The flasks of young seedlings must be carefully protected against heat. They mature more quickly than many other genera, in about half the time required for Cattleyas.

The smooth, bright green pseudobulbs of the Odontoglossums are oval to round, usually compressed to a sharp edge at the sides. They bear one to two fleshy leaves at the apex, and often have small sheathing leaves at the base. The remarkably varied flowers have sepals and petals that are free and spreading, but an occasional exception has the sepals somewhat united. The base of the lip is parallel to the column, with its outer lobe spreading. This habit of the lip is one of the ways by which Odontoglossum is distinguished from Oncidium, where the lip is never parallel to the column.

The flower stems arise from the base of the mature pseudobulbs (except that in *Odontoglossum citrosmum* they come from the new ones) and may be either erect or drooping. They are usually many flowered, often branching, always graceful, and the flowers are long lasting.

THE SPECIES

Odontoglossum bictoniense. This was the first Odontoglossum to survive the voyage to England and has been popular through the years. It bears 3-foot sprays of small yellow-green flowers with a white or rose colored lip. Occurs in Guatemala. Flowers in the fall.

Odontoglossum citrosmum. The drooping stems carry thick clusters of rounded flowers of pastel hues. The sepals and petals are white to rose, and the extended lip is violet and spreads into two lobes at its apex. Occurs in Guatemala. Flowers in late spring.

Odontoglossum crispum. Connoisseurs often name this species the most beautiful of all orchids. Its lacey 2½-foot sprays are crowded with flowers, each 2½ to 3 inches across. The sepals and petals are pointed, daintily ruffled, with their borders toothed or notched. In color they are white, sometimes tinged with rose, and may be spotted with crimson or brown. The flower is centered by a speckled lip that is fringed with teeth, and whose borders are even more finely notched than the petals. This species is extremely variable, and more than a hundred varieties have been named. Occurs in Colombia, at an elevation of 12,000 feet. Flowers at any time of the year.

Odontoglossum grande. Large, brilliantly marked flowers make this one of the most widely grown species. The flowers are from 5 to 9 inches across, and occur from four to seven on a spike. The sepals are long and rather slender, yellow, barred with chestnut brown. The wider, wavy petals are brown at the base and yellow at the outer end. The generously rounded lip is white or cream colored, spotted with brown. The flowers last for two weeks or so, and are very decorative. Occurs in Guatemala. Flowers from October to December.

Odontoglossum Harryanum. The variegated coloring of this species together with its striking shape make it

Odontoglossum citrosmum. (Courtesy of H. D. Sawyer)

the valued parent of many hybrids. Four or five 3-inch flowers occur to a stem. The wavy sepals and petals are brown with irregular bands of yellow-green. The large shield-shaped lip is flat and wavy, its lower half white, changing to yellow, and its basal part brown, veined with purple. Seven serrated crests decorate its base. Occurs in Colombia. Flowers in the fall.

Odontoglossum Insleayi. A species with flowers that resemble *Odontoglossum grande,* but which are smaller, reaching 4 inches in diameter. The sepals and petals are yellow, spotted with brown, and the lip orange-yellow spotted with red-brown. Occurs in Mexico. Flowers from October to December.

Odontoglossum luteo-purpureum. A striking and varied species whose flowers are produced in horizontal sprays. The wavy, oblong sepals are brownish-purple with a yellow margin. The petals are toothed, spotted with purple-brown. The deeply scalloped yellow lip is fringed and is spotted with purple or rose. Occurs in Colombia. Flowers in winter and spring.

Odontoglossum nobile. This species is a good substitute for those who cannot grow *Odontoglossum crispum,* but who can furnish quite cool conditions. The long flower spikes carry up to a hundred blooms, each 3 inches in diameter. The sepals and petals are usually white, sometimes faintly tinged with rose. The kidney-shaped lip is white with a few crimson spots. Occurs in Colombia. Flowers usually in the spring.

Odontoglossum odoratum. The flowers of this species are small, but produced in great numbers on branching sprays. They are golden yellow, marked with red-brown, and the wavy narrow lip is covered with down. Occurs in Mexico. Flowers in winter and spring.

Odontoglossum pulchellum. This species is easy to grow and flowers readily. Slender sprays carry six or seven small, rounded white flowers, each 1½ to 2 inches in diameter. Their fragrance suggests lily-of-the-valley. Occurs in Guatemala. Flowers in the spring.

Odontoglossum Rossii. One of the loveliest of the genus. The short flower stems bear only two to five blooms, each 3 inches in diameter, but lack of numbers is compensated for by the beauty of the individual flowers and by their good keeping quality. The sepals are pointed, cream colored to greenish yellow, and barred with dark brown. The blunt, somewhat curled petals are white with a few brown spots at their base. The large, round, wavy lip is pure white. Occurs in Mexico. Flowers in the winter.

Odontoglossum Schlieperianum. Another species that resembles a small *Odontoglossum grande,* except that the yellow-green ground color is carried into the lip and the markings are orange rather than brown. Its flowering season makes it a worthwhile addition to a collection. Occurs in Costa Rica. Flowers in the summer.

Odontoglossum Uro-Skinnerii. Ten to thirty flowers of striking coloring are produced on long spikes. The sepals and petals are green, marked with chestnut-brown, and the large, heart-shaped lip is rose, mottled with white. Occurs in Guatemala. Flowers in the spring.

ONCIDIUM

Whatever Nature's mood may have been when she created the other orchids, surely it was fanciful when she designed the Oncidiums. She seems to have caught dancing rays of light, flickering patterns of sun and shadow, little fairy forms not seen by man, and made them into friendly, whimsical, thoroughly delightful little flowers. They are meant to be enjoyed with smiles and chuckles. Still generous after endowing so much beauty elsewhere, she seems to have poured out her warmth in the showers of gold given us by this genus.

At least three hundred species of Oncidiums have been discovered. The description of a mere handful is only a tantalizing glimpse of the whole genus. Favorites among the species are easy to find, and no two fanciers will list the same ones as deserving of attention.

The genus ranges throughout tropical America, from Florida and the West Indies, through Central America to the southern part of Brazil. As in the Odontoglossums some are found in low, hot regions, others in the cool upper altitudes. They are more amenable to changes in temperature, however, and most of them will adjust themselves to a moderate greenhouse condition. This makes it easy for the average amateur to include a few Oncidiums with almost anything else he grows. As cut flowers, the possibilities they offer are limited only by the imagination of the person working with them. Their filigree-like sprays are charmingly decorative when used alone or as a foil for other flowers. Dainty arrangements for the hair or stunning corsages can be made with groups or single blossoms.

This genus of epiphytes includes great variety. The pseudobulbs are rounded and flattened at the edges, similar to Odontoglossum, but some species are without pseudobulbs. The foliage is usually clear green, but is sometimes mottled. The leaves are usually fleshy, oval and pointed, with a single prominent mid-vein, but species occur with thinner, many-veined leaves, and some with terete (cylindrical) foliage. The flower sprays are long, sometimes drooping, often erect. Flowers may be large and showy, or small and dainty. The unvarying feature that distinguishes the Oncidiums from the Odontoglossums is that in Oncidium the lip is never parallel to the column, in fact forms a right angle to the column. The column is short and winged.

Oncidiums do well in straight osmundine, with firm potting and good drainage. Large, robust plants need more fibre in proportion to their size than do smaller ones. Those that produce drooping, many-flowered sprays may be suspended in pots or baskets, while those that have tall, erect flower stems need plenty of head room.

A winter night temperature of 50°–55° F. will suit most kinds, with the day temperature running between 65° and 70° F. They will stand higher daytime temperatures in the summer, but it is best to keep the greenhouse as cool as the weather permits.

Abundant water is necessary during the growing period, moderated somewhat during the period of lessened activity, but the pots should never be allowed to become bone-dry. The atmosphere must be kept humid, and the

Oncidium ampliatum. (Courtesy of H. A. Dunn and H. Griffin)

plants may be syringed lightly in bright weather. Good ventilation is important, as Oncidiums need free circulation of air.

Oncidiums seem to need rather more light than other orchids, and shading should be applied only sufficiently to prevent leaf burn or to keep down the temperature in the summer.

In the list of species given below, an attempt has been made to select representative types, as well as to include those which are most easily grown.

THE SPECIES

Oncidium altissimum. This species is often called the giant of the genus. The robust plants produce flower sprays that sometimes reach 12 feet in length, but usually grow close to 6 feet. They are gracefully arched or drooping and bear many small blooms. The small sepals and petals are pale yellow spotted with olive-brown, and the larger lip is a brighter yellow with a brown band. Occurs in the West Indies. Flowers in August.

Oncidium ampliatum. Magnificent panicles, attractively branched and arched, reach a length of 3 feet. The attractive little flowers are clear yellow, spotted with red toward the base of the small sepals and petals and the round flat lip. The pseudobulbs are green spotted with purple. Occurs along the coast of Nicaragua. Flowers from March to May.

Oncidium excavatum. A hundred or more gold and brown blossoms are produced on each 3- to 5-foot panicle. Each flower is 1½ inches across. Occurs in Peru. Flowers in the fall.

Oncidium flexuosum. A small member of the popular "dancing doll" orchids. Because of the reduced, arm-like sepals and petals and the voluminous lip, this group resembles a miniature ballet. The tiny, 1-inch flowers of this species occur in dainty showers on a loose, airy panicle atop a tall stem. The sepals and petals are yellow, barred with brown, and the broad, full lip is yellow with a few red spots.

Oncidium Kramerianum. (Courtesy of H. A. Dunn and H. Griffin)

It grows and flowers with great freedom and, because of its small size, is welcome in little greenhouses. Occurs in Brazil. Flowers at various seasons.

Oncidium incurvum. This species, which does best when grown a little cooler than the average, produces many dainty, gracefully branched panicles of rosy-purple and white flowers. Occurs in Mexico. Flowers in late summer and fall.

Oncidium Kramerianum. The "butterfly orchid," which description it shares with its more famous relative, *Oncidium Papilio*. Although this species does not grow with the abandon usual to the genus, it rewards careful attention with a few spectacular butterfly flowers. The petals and the dorsal sepal are drawn out to look like antennae. The lateral sepals are broad, golden yellow spotted with brown, and the large, round, ruffled lip is yellow with the finely toothed border decorated by a band of brown spots. The foliage of the plant is green, mottled with brown. Occurs in Central America. Flowering season variable.

Oncidium Lanceanum. An odd combination of colors makes this a very striking species. The showy flowers are 2 to 3 inches across. The sepals and petals are blunt and fleshy, yellow, spotted with chocolate brown or crimson. The spreading lip stands in contrast to the rest of the flower with its rose margin and violet base. The robust plants have no pseudobulbs, and the wide, fleshy leaves are mottled with brown. The rather short, stout, erect flower stems bear a generous number of blooms. Occurs in British Guiana. Flowers in the summer.

Oncidium ornithorrhyncum. The long specific name means "bird beak," and the drooping, tightly clustered sprays resemble a flock of birds. The rather small plants are easily grown and flower freely. The tiny, fragrant flowers are colored in shades of soft rosy purple. The species likes to be grown a little on the cool side. Occurs in Mexico. Flowers in fall and winter.

Oncidium Papilio. This butterfly orchid is said to be responsible for the orchid craze that has swept the world. It is much like *Oncidium Kramerianum,* described above, but flowers more freely. It was shown at an exhibition of the Royal Horticultural Society soon after its introduction to England in 1823. Here its striking appearance so intrigued the Duke of Devonshire that he was inspired to start an orchid collection of his own. Thus was the fashion for private collections started among wealthy Englishmen. *Oncidium Papilio* has longer antennae than *O. Kramerianum,* and the lateral sepals and lip are banded, rather than spotted, with brown. The flowers are produced singly at the tip of a tall stem. Occurs in the West Indies. Flowers at any season.

Oncidium pumilum. A miniature species, scarcely 6 inches tall, without pseudobulbs, and whose tiny flower spray is less than the height of the leaves. The minute blossoms grow in tight little clusters along the stem, each ⅛ inch across. The sepals and petals are rounded, and the lip has three deep scallops. This species is a beautiful "botanical" that would be a valuable addition to a small-scale collection. Occurs in Brazil. Flowers in the spring.

Oncidium sphacelatum. A "dancing doll" on a larger scale than *O. flexuosum.* The airy ballet is dressed in butter-yellow, the upper part of the costume sprinkled with brown, and the skirt with a few large brown spots. The flower stem holds a loose panicle of blooms, generous in number, and produced freely. Occurs in the West Indies and Honduras. Flowers in the spring.

Oncidium splendidum. Stunning flowers of blended green and brown and yellow gold. The greenish upper part is heavily barred with brown, against which stands the large pure yellow lip, decorated with a long white crest.

The 3-inch flowers are of heavy texture, and a single bloom makes a striking lapel pin. A flowering plant is a handsome sight, with its 30-inch, branched flower stem crowded with blooms. This species is often given as a variety of *O. tigrinum,* below, and is cultivated commercially to some extent. Occurs in Guatemala and Mexico. Flowers in the spring.

Oncidium tigrinum. The startling flowers are among the most showy of the genus. They have the appearance of being made of two flowers wired together. The rather large sepals and petals are rich brown, barred with slender lines of yellow. The large bright yellow lip is in complete contrast to this dark backing. The flowers are about 2½ inches across, produced rather few to a stem. Occurs in Mexico. Flowers in the winter.

Oncidium varicosum. One of the most beloved of the genus, a "dancing doll" in a beautifully swirling skirt. Literally clouds of these sunny little flowers are borne in lacy, branching sprays. One to two hundred may occur on a single panicle. The upper part of the flower is yellow-bronze barred with brown. The lip is pure yellow, sometimes with a brown spot or band at its base, and a curiously toothed crest. The variety *Rogersii* is considered by some to be the best of all the Oncidiums. It is one that should be included in all Oncidium collections. Occurs in Brazil. Flowers in winter and spring.

BI-GENERIC HYBRIDS

Bi-generic hybrids are common in this tribe. A cross between Miltonia and Odontoglossum is called Odontonia. Odontoglossum combined with Oncidium receives the compound name Odontocidium.

A small tribe of orchids, Aspasia (which will not be described elsewhere), is important in relation to the Odontoglossum tribe. One of its two members, the genus Cochlioda, is used in making hybrids with the genera that have just been described. Cochlioda is similar to Odontoglossum in appearance, habitat, and cultural requirements. Its long sprays of small flowers come in shades of rose, red, and red-orange, and it is for the sake of the colors that its species are bred with those of other genera. Cochlioda combined with Miltonia gives the bi-generic hybrid Miltonioda. Odontioda is Odontoglossum crossed with Cochlioda.

Some of the bi-generic crosses are beautiful things. More and more of this work is being done, and it is a field in which the imagination of the amateur may have free play. The warm reddish tones of Cochlioda may be added to almost any of the species to brighten and deepen their own coloring. The soft hues and ample proportions of Miltonia give a touch of lushness to their hybrids, for instance to the star-like Odontoglossums.

Other Genera of the Odontoglossum Tribe

A fourth member of this tribe is Brassia, whose spidery flowers are most unusual, and make an attractive showing in spite of their lack of richness of coloring. The sepals and petals are attenuated, giving the appearance of spider legs, and the lip is indeed shaped like the body of a spider. There are about thirty species, all easy to grow with a mixed collection of orchids. They require abundant water during the growing season, and must never be allowed to dry out.

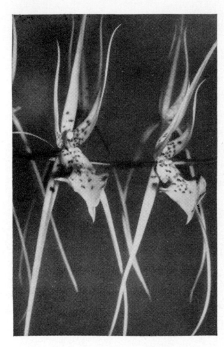

Brassia verrucosa has its own special appeal in spite of its pale colors. (Courtesy of Mrs. James J. Waring)

Brassia verrucosa. The whole flower is 7 or 8 inches long with the dorsal sepal and the shorter petals accounting for 3 inches of the length, and the longer lateral sepals for the other four. They are pale yellow-green, spotted at the base. The lip is pinched in in the middle and is white with dark green warts. The phalanx of eight to ten flowers is borne in a neat row on a horizontal stem. Occurs in Guatemala.

Brassia longissima. Deep orange-yellow with a pale yellow lip that bears purple spots at its base. The extreme length of this species makes it a curiosity. The dorsal sepal and petals are 2 to 3 inches long, whereas the lateral sepals reach 7 or 8 inches. Occurs in Costa Rica.

Gomesa and Palumbina are the remaining genera of the tribe. Both are pale by comparison to those already described and are therefore seldom grown.

Chapter XV

COLLECTORS' ITEMS

Ada Tribe

The tribe contains few orchids that are generally grown, but since they are cool growing orchids, they will add variety to an Odontoglossum house. There are three genera, consisting of very few species.

Ada has only two species, of which one seems to have been lost. The known species, *Ada aurantiaca,* bears sprays of orange flowers, which add a bright spot of color to the greenhouse. The petals and sepals are pointed and are held almost closed, barely showing the small, pointed lip. Occurs in Colombia at elevations of 8500 feet.

The genus Mesospinidium has five species, of which the species *Meso-spinidium sanguineum* is cultivated for its sprays of bright rose-colored flowers. Occurs in the Peruvian Andes.

The third genus of this tribe, Quekettia, is similar to Ada but little known horticulturally.

Bulbophyllum Tribe

Two genera make up this tribe, Bulbophyllum and Cirrhopetalum. They include some of the smallest orchids known, and some whose very odd shapes add variety to a collection. They are epiphytes, found in tropical Asia and Africa, and may be grown on osmundine attached to pieces of wood. They require a warm, moist atmosphere, with ample water and frequent syringing during their growing period. During the winter they may be kept a little cooler at night, but should not be allowed to dry out, and should be frequently syringed.

BULBOPHYLLUM

Single leaves are produced from pseudobulbs along a creeping rhizome. The flower stems grow from the base of the pseudobulbs and produce either several small flowers or a single large flower. The flowers are characterized by having the lateral sepals joined to the column at their broadened base, and by the small lip which is attached to the foot of the column. There are about 125 species.

Bulbophyllum grandiflorum bears a single 8-inch flower to the stem. The long, slender sepals are pale brown and yellow, the dorsal sepal bending forward, and lateral ones bending backward. The petals and lip are very tiny.

Bulbophyllum Careyanum. One of the smallest of orchids. The flowers are only ½ inch in diameter, borne in a dense cluster. They are orange-yellow or greenish, spotted with red-brown or purple.

CIRRHOPETALUM

These rambling plants receive their name from their tendril-like lateral sepals, which grow like long, twisted tails away from the minute petals and lip. The little lip is often oscillating. Among the ninety species are found some weird and fascinating forms.

Cirrhopetalum Medusae. Also called *Bulbophyllum Medusae.* The plants are about 6 inches tall, and have odd little flowers, cream-colored, spotted with yellow or purple. The lateral sepals are hair-like, 4 or 5 inches long, and give the tight clusters of flowers the appearance of tiny Medusa heads. The lip and petals are almost microscopic. Occurs in Singapore.

Cirrhopetalum picturatum. A small plant with pseudobulbs 2 inches long and leaves 3 to 5 inches. The coloring is striking. The sepals and petals are green, the dorsal sepal spotted with purple and topped with a purple-knobbed thread. The little lip is blood red. Occurs in India.

CATASETUM TRIBE

The Catasetum tribe is made up of three genera, each with striking peculiarities. Catasetum and Cycnoches produce flowers of separate sexes, and Mormodes has flowers with the lip and the column twisted in opposite directions. All are native to the American tropics and are mostly epiphytic. They may be grown with Cattleyas. Catasetum and Cycnoches need a little warmer temperature and more water during the growing period than does Mormodes.

CATASETUM

Catasetum is a genus that has puzzled orchidists for generations, and the species are not completely designated even yet. A few species produce perfect (bi-sexual) flowers, but most species have separate male and female flowers. Confusion among the latter arises from the fact that female flowers are rarely seen. Supposedly a plant may produce both male and female flowers at the same time or in successive years. But unless plants are found bearing both kinds of flowers, it is difficult to know which male form goes with which female form. Plants in cultivation have been known to give rise only to male flowers for periods of from twenty to forty years. At present, species are classified according to the male form, and a description of the female is given if it is known.

Male flowers are produced on a somewhat arching raceme bearing several blooms. They may be identified as such by the slender beak-shaped column, bearing at its base two curving antennae. These antennae serve as triggers which, when touched, cause the pollinia to fly out with some force. In nature the pollinia strike the back of a visiting bee and adhere to it by means of a sticky disc at the end of the caudicle. If you substitute a pencil to touch the antennae, the pollinia will strike and stick to it, or may shoot past it to a distance of two or three feet. Should you be holding the flower when you make it perform, the recoil will give you quite a start.

The males of some species (such as *Catasetum Oerstedii* and *C. viridi-flavum*) have a helmet-shaped lip, with the antennae curling around within it. The petals and sepals curve down in a semicircle. In other species (such as *C. bicolor*) the male form is slender and delicate, with a fimbriated lip closely flanked by the lateral sepals. The petals and dorsal sepal overlap behind the upstanding column, whose antennae are completely exposed.

Female flowers occur only two or three to an erect raceme. They are similar for all species, all having a helmet-shaped lip and a fat, blunt column.

In some species the female flowers have the lip uppermost (nonresupinate), while the male flower holds itself with the lip hanging down (resupinate). In other species the condition is exactly reversed, and in still others both male and female flowers are nonresupinate.

Colors tend to green, white, and yellow, often spotted with brown or purple, and the flowers last only a short time. The rather broad, pleated leaves are deciduous, and when they fall the bases that are left attached to the pseudobulb are armed with sharp spines.

Catasetum viridiflavum. The upside-down flowers are green and very fleshy, with a short, thick column. The large helmet-shaped lip is yellow inside. The oval sepals and petals overlap each other in a semicircle under the lip. Occurs in Central America.

CYCNOCHES

These are very lovely orchids, worth cultivating for their beauty as well as for their interesting habit. The name means swan's neck, referring to the arching column, and they are familiarly called the "swan orchid." Flowers of each sex are produced on the same plant, and occasionally a perfect flower (carrying both sexes) shows up. The plants have stout pseudobulbs that bear ribbed (pleated) leaves at the nodes.

Cycnoches chlorochilon. The graceful, fragrant flowers are borne upside

Cycnoches chlorochilon. (Courtesy of H. A. Dunn and H. Griffin)

down in a spray. The sepals and petals are yellow-green and spread wide open, with the dorsal sepal curved slightly forward. The lip is white and its sides turn down, leaving a dimple in the top surface from which arises a dark-green cone-shaped callus. The column is slender with the tip enlarged. In this species the male and female flowers are alike in appearance. Several sprays of from two to ten flowers are produced from October to January. Occurs in Central America.

Cycnoches pentadactylon. The male and female flowers differ in coloring and structure. The male flowers are produced in many-flowered racemes, usually drooping. The sepals and petals are greenish-yellow barred with brown. The lip is white, spotted with red, and has five finger-like projections. The female flowers are produced on an erect spike, only a few to the stem, with sepals and petals broader than in the male, and spotted. The lip lacks the projections. Occurs in Brazil.

MORMODES

The name means grotesque creature, descriptive of the distortion of the lip and column. The flowers, contrary to those of the other two genera, are not separately male and female. The leaves are deciduous.

Mormodes luxata. The fragrant, rather fleshy, globular flowers are lemon-yellow with a streak of brown down the center of the lip. The twisting of the lip and column is quite marked. Flowers in July. Occurs in Mexico.

Coelogyne Tribe

The Coelogyne tribe contains several genera, of which the most popular is Coelogyne. The members of the tribe grow natively from Australia north to China. All are characterized by short, rounded or oval pseudobulbs, topped by two bright green, attractively ribbed leaves. Their small flowers are produced in dainty sprays.

COELOGYNE

The genus Coelogyne is native to North India and Ceylon. There are over a hundred species, and though the species *Coelogyne cristata* is the best known, many are attractive and popular. They are easy to grow, and reward the amateur with a profusion of blooms for very little effort. Osmundine is a good potting medium, and pots, shallow pans, or baskets may be used. They have rather a rambling habit, and should be given plenty of room in the pot. Divisions are made after flowering, when necessary, by cutting the plant into groups of three pseudobulbs behind each new growth. They like firm potting and good drainage.

The species vary in exact temperature requirements. Many of them can be grown in the Cattleya house, however. They need copious water during their growing period, but are kept on the dry side, with only occasional waterings, during their period of lessened activity. They require some shade, adjusted to their needs. In some regions they may be placed out-of-doors in protected, shady places during the hottest months.

Coelogyne cristata. Considered by some to be the most beautiful of East Indian orchids. The combination of sprays of snow-white flowers, apple-green pseudobulbs, and dark green leaves is most attractive. The blooms measure 3 to 5 inches, and occur many to the spray which arises from the base of the pseudobulb. The petals and sepals are wavy, and project forward. The lip is three-lobed, the middle lobe decorated inside by five yellow, fringed keels. They keep beautifully and are highly decorative as sprays or for corsages. *Coelogyne cristata* likes fairly cool treatment and does not thrive in great heat. Occurs in the Himalayas. Flowers in the winter.

Coelogyne pandurata. Sometimes called the "black orchid," although there are others that fit the name as well. The sepals and petals are emerald-green, and the fiddle-shaped lip is heavily veined and stained with black on a greenish ground. The middle lobe of the lip is ruffled and fringed and carries black warts and ridges. This species does well in the semitropical states. Occurs in Borneo. Flowers in the summer.

Coelogyne tomentosa. Pendulous sprays of fifteen to twenty pale orange-red flowers are quite striking in appearance. Occurs in Borneo and Sumatra. Flowers in the summer.

Coelogyne Dayana. A large plant, with pseudobulbs 5 to 10 inches long and leaves 2½ feet. The long sprays bear many flowers which are pale yellow except that the lip is decorated with brown fringed ridges and has brown lateral lobes. Occurs in Borneo. Flowers in the spring and summer.

OTHER MEMBERS OF THE COELOGYNE TRIBE

The four other members of the Coelogyne tribe are of lesser importance.

Neogyne is a genus of one species, *Neogyne Gardneriana,* which produces small white flowers that quickly wither.

Pholidota has acquired the name "rattlesnake orchid," because the scales of the unopened flower raceme are reminiscent of the rattles of that snake. The genus is native to India and China. The small (¾ inch) flowers are borne in short little sprays and are rather insignificant. The species *Pholidota chinensis* is seen in old Chinese drawings.

Platyclinis produces very delicate fragrant sprays of tiny white or yellow flowers, set close together on a thread-like stem. The pseudobulbs are crowded, each producing a single tall broad leaf. Occurs in India, China, and the Malay Islands.

Pleione, "mother of the Pleiades," has rather large, attractive flowers and unusual plant characters, but seems to be seldom grown in this country. The pseudobulbs, which last only a year, are persimmon-shaped, sometimes warty, topped by a single leaf that is large in proportion. The leaf falls as the bulb matures. The flowers arise singly or in pairs on short stems that grow from the base of the bulbs.

Pleione praecox. The slender sepals and petals are pink, and the trumpet-shaped lip is fringed at the edges and striped yellow and white. Requires cool treatment as the species comes from high altitudes of India. Flowers from October to November.

GONGORA TRIBE

The eight genera of the Gongora tribe spread from Mexico to South America. They are distinguished for the curious formation of the lip, which is different in each genus, and which in some cases gives a reason for the cultivation of the flower. The plants have oval to globular pseudobulbs from which arise broad, pleated leaves. All are epiphytic. Those with pendulous flower stems should be grown in baskets, or at least in suspended pots. They like abundant moisture while growing, with somewhat less during their periods of inactivity. Cattleya conditions suit them, that is, a night temperature of 55°–60° F.

PERISTERIA

A genus of stately plants, which produce their flowers on tall stems from the base of the pseudobulb. Of the five species, one is very popular.

Peristeria elata. The waxy creamy-white flowers are often nicknamed the "dove orchid" or the "Holy Ghost flower." The purple-spotted lip is cup-shaped, with two wing-like append-ages that stand up beside the column. The effect is that of a pulpit, in which stands the dove-shaped column. The sepals are round and, together with the smaller petals, form a solid background. The flowers are fragrant, about 2 inches in diameter, and are produced on a tall, straight spike. They open slowly, and each lasts a long time, so that the whole spike may be en-joyed for two or three months. After growth is made, water is cut down until the flower spike appears and is then resumed. Water is again reduced

Peristeria elata. (Courtesy of H. A. Dunn and H. Griffin)

while at rest. Repot in the spring, in large pots, using osmundine. Flowers in the summer.

STANHOPEA

The flowers of this genus possess a fleshy, horned lip which curves down under the long, arching column. The column is sometimes so long that it sweeps in a good half-circle and reaches out almost to touch the tip of the lip. The sepals and petals are thin textured, and the flower lasts only a few days. However, for its fragrance and curious shape it is worth having even for that short time. The flower stems bore their way down through the potting medium and emerge at the bottom of the basket, for which reason the plants must be grown in some such open container.

Stanhopea oculata. Three to six flowers are borne on a sheathed stem. They are 5 inches across and very fragrant. The petals and sepals are yellow, lightly

spotted with purple. The column is tall and arching, with two little pointed projections at its tip. The lip has a boat-shaped basal part, in front of which are two curved horns. The tip of the lip is triangular. Occurs in Mexico and was highly revered by the Aztecs. Flowering time variable.

Stanhopea tigrina. Startling, 6-inch flowers, whose delightful fragrance seems in odd contrast to their weird coloring. The sepals and petals are deep purple at the base, the purple breaking up into blotches on a yellow ground at the tips. Occurs in Mexico.

Stanhopea Wardii. Fragrant, yellow to golden-orange flowers are borne three to nine on a stem. Scattered

Stanhopea Wardii. (Courtesy of H. A. Dunn and H. Griffin)

crimson spots accentuate their brilliance. Occurs from Mexico to Panama. Flowers in August.

CORYANTHES

A genus in which the flowers last too short a time to be much enjoyed, but interesting because of their remarkable modifications to insure pollination. Part of the lip is transformed into a bucket, which is filled with fluid secreted by two glands near the base of the column. Insects that visit the flower slip off of the smooth sides of the bucket and fall into the fluid. Then, their wings wet, and also apparently intoxicated by the fluid, they are forced to crawl out through a narrow spout just under the tip of the column. Here they remove the pollinia. Often they return to the bucket and when they emerge the second time they effect pollination. Closely related to Stanhopea. Occurs in tropical America.

OTHER GENERA OF THE GONGORA TRIBE

Acineta, a genus whose flower stems grow down through the potting medium. The species produce flowers that are yellow or brown, variously spotted with brown, red, or purple. Rarely grown.

Aganisia, a genus of but two species, rarely grown. The small flowers are white or mauve, marked with red or purple.

Gongora is an interesting genus that carries its attractive flowers in a drooping spray. Each bloom is held gracefully on a stem that curves down and then turns up, so that the open flower has the position of a little old-fashioned candle holder. The petals and the back sepal are joined to the column, and the small lip is horned, and has other curious structures. The flowers are various shades of yellow and brown, usually spotted. The genus ranges from Mexico to Brazil.

Houlletia, a seldom grown genus, produces small, richly colored flowers.

Lacaena, a little-known genus, whose flower stems grow down in the manner of Stanhopea. The flowers are brightly colored, often with a downy lip.

IONOPSIS TRIBE

The four genera that make up this tribe range natively from Mexico to Brazil. All are small, even dwarf, epiphytes and produce sprays of dainty flowers. Some are quite striking, whereas others are interesting purely as botanicals.

RODRIGUEZIA

The most popular genus, and the most showy, is Rodriguezia. The plants are small, with delicate sprays of dainty flowers. The lateral sepals are united, and the lip more or less spurred. Their culture is similar to that of Laelia and Cattleya.

Rodriguezia secunda. The whole plant is dwarf in habit, and the 6-inch-long spray carries twenty to thirty rose-colored flowers, all carried on one side of the stem. Occurs in Trinidad and Guiana. Flowers in August.

Rodriguezia venusta. The flowers are a little larger than in *secunda,* and the sprays more open. They are white, tinged with pink, and the lip is marked with yellow. Occurs in Brazil. Flowering time variable.

COMPARETTIA

These are graceful little plants, whose small flowers are brightly colored and curiously constructed. The lateral sepals are united and form a horn at their base. The petals and upper sepal form a sort of hood over the column. The lip has a double spur at its base which fits into the horn made by the sepals. The front lobe of the lip is broad and somewhat heart-shaped. They will grow well in a Cattleya house and must never be allowed to become dry. The flowers last well.

Comparettia coccinea has pretty little flowers, 1 inch in diameter, light yellow margined with orange, with a crimson lip.

Comparettia falcata is similar to *coccinea,* but with flowers entirely deep crimson or purple.

IONOPSIS

The third genus of the tribe is Ionopsis. It is interesting because of its many-branched flower stem, which rises to two or three times the height of the small plant, and carries almost innumerable delicate flowers.

Ionopsis paniculata. The tiny petals and sepals are pointed, and overlap one another. The lip is large and spreading and curves downward. It is downy, usually white, sometimes with a patch of purple or yellow.

TRICHOCENTRUM

This genus is characterized by its odd trowel-shaped lip which is prolonged at its base into a prominent spur. The sepals and petals are free, sometimes longer than the lip and spreading, sometimes smaller and overlapping. The flowers are brightly colored.

Trichocentrum albo-purpureum has stunning little flowers greenish on the outside, maroon-brown within, and a white lip decorated with two purple spots.

Trichocentrum panduratum. A recently described species whose sepals and petals are extremely short and overlapping, and whose lip is long and narrow with a long tail-like spur. The general appearance of the flower is that of an old-fashioned salt shovel.

LYCASTE TRIBE

Most orchid collections contain a few members of the Lycaste tribe, particularly of the genus Lycaste itself. They are grown not only for their ease of culture, but for their distinct individuality and charm. All members of the tribe are natives of Central or South America or the West Indies. They are mostly high altitude plants, and therefore grow best under fairly cool conditions. The coolest spot in the Cattleya house may suit them, with night temperatures in the winter of 50°–55° F. They like to be cool in the summer, too, and shaded from direct sunlight both winter and summer.

Finely chopped osmunda fibre is a good potting medium. Watering must be handled judiciously so as not to let the fibre become soggy. Propagation is by division, cutting through the rhizomes to separate the bulbs in groups of two. Repotting and division should be done just as new growth starts.

LYCASTE

The oval, somewhat corrugated pseudobulbs bear broad, pleated leaves similar to those of Calanthe. When the bulbs are newly growing they are sheathed with smaller leaves which soon fall. The quaint flowers are borne singly on stems that arise from the base of the pseudobulbs preceding the new leaves. The broad sepals stand out gracefully, while the petals and lip give the impression of a sunbonnet in the center. The petals stand forward, each with its tip gracefully turned out, and surround the small lip which just protrudes from within. The lateral sepals are united at the base to form a short spur or chin. The blooms last a long time.

Lycaste Dowiana. (Courtesy of H. A. Dunn)

Lycaste aromatica. An attractive species with flowers about 3 inches across, yellow, tinged with green. The lip is spotted with orange. It has a strong, pleasant fragrance. During its resting period it should have considerably less water but should not be allowed to remain dry for long periods. Occurs in Mexico. Flowers in winter and spring.

Lycaste Deppei. An interesting species with curiously colored flowers. The sepals are dull green, spotted with chocolate-purple. In striking contrast, the petals are white, and the little lip, with its middle lobe waved, is yellow. Occurs in Guatemala. Flowers nearly all year round.

Lycaste Dowiana. Prim, quietly colored flowers are produced in profusion. The sepals are olive green on the back, brown in front, and the petals and little fringed lip are pale yellow. Occurs in Panama.

Lycaste Skinneri is the species most often grown. Its flowers are larger than those just mentioned, reaching 6 inches in diameter. They are waxy, white, tinged with rose. The middle lobe of the lip is tongue shaped, marked with a purple callus, or variously dotted with purple. *Lycaste Skinneri* is one of the easiest of all orchids to grow. Its flowers last well and can be enjoyed for a long time. There are many named varieties, which range from pure white to dark purple. This species requires a much less intense rest period than the more deciduous ones. Occurs in Guatemala. Flowers in the spring.

ANGULOA

The genus Auguloa is native to the Andes. It has only three species, but each is attractive and easy to grow. They are noted for their fragrance, and for their peculiar globular shape which has given them a number of nick-names, such as "tulip orchid" or "boat orchid." Their hinged lip oscillates gently with the least movement. The plants themselves are rather striking, with their long, broad, pleated leaves, and the tall, sheathed flower stem rising from the base of the conical pseudobulbs, bearing a single flower. Although they are more or less terrestrial in habit, they will grow in osmunda fibre, to which may be added a third part soil, or possibly some well-dried cow manure. A night temperature of 50° F. in the winter is desirable, and a cool, shaded environment in the summer. They require ample moisture and water all year round.

Anguloa Clowesii has lemon yellow flowers that are green inside with a white downy lip.

Anguloa uniflora is creamy white, flushed or dotted inside with pink.

Anguloa Ruckeri is greenish-yellow, flushed with brown on the outside, spotted inside with red.

BATEMANNIA

A genus with but a single known species, rarely seen in cultivation, *Batemannia Colleyi.* Its flowers are strikingly colored and make it worthy of attention. The sepals and petals are red, backed and tipped with green. The dorsal sepal and the petals are about equal in size and form a solid background for the cup-shaped lip which is white sprinkled with red dots. The lateral sepals are longer and trail down under the lip. Occurs in Guiana.

BIFRENARIA

Another genus that is rarely grown, though of interest to a botanical collection. The pseudobulbs are shorter and thicker than in Lycaste, and the leaves broader. The flowers have a definite spur where the lateral sepals enclose a foot-like projection at the base of the column.

Bifrenaria aurantica has clusters of little yellow flowers spotted with bronze-purple.

Bifrenaria indora has small apple green flowers with a white, yellow, or rose lip and a long spur.

PAPHINIA

A genus native to South America that resembles small Lycastes and similar to them in requirements. The flowers have the lip uppermost, which gives them a curious appearance.

Paphinia cristata has sepals and petals of white streaked and striped with chocolate purple, and a small, three-lobed crested lip of chocolate purple.

Paphinia rugosa is creamy white, spotted with red.

Paphinia grandiflora has flowers of chocolate brown. The sepals and petals are bordered with greenish yellow, and banded on their lower halves with this same color. The lip is purple with a white middle lobe.

MAXILLARIA TRIBE

The two members of this tribe, Maxillaria and Scuticaria, are appealing to those who enjoy a wide variety in their collections. They grow natively from Central America to Brazil. They can be grown in osmunda fibre, prefer shallow pots with good drainage or baskets, and are kept moist all year round. They may be grown with Cattleyas and should be well shaded.

MAXILLARIA

There are two sections of this genus of over a hundred species—those which have more or less climbing stems and those which grow with clustered pseudobulbs. The flowers of both types are somewhat similar to Lycaste.

Maxillaria Houtteana is an example of the climbing type. The pseudobulbs rise out of a sheathed stem. The flowers are oddly colored. The spreading sepals are dull yellow on the outside, marked with a purple patch on the upper inside half, and purple spots toward the base. The smaller petals are similarly marked and curve toward each other. The tongue-like lip is yellow with red-brown spots. Occurs in Guatemala. Flowers in April, and the flowers last a month if kept cool.

Maxillaria Sanderiana. This is the finest of the nonclimbing type. The pseudobulbs are small, and the leaves are about 6 inches tall. The large flower is borne on a short stem, so that it appears to be nestled at the base of the plant. The large, wide sepals and the smaller petals are white, spotted with purple near the base. The lip curves upward forming almost a cup, and exposing the chin formed by the base of the sepals joined to the column foot. Occurs in Ecuador.

SCUTICARIA

The two species of this genus are characterized by their whip-like leaves, which are about as thick as a goose quill, and by their lack of pseudobulbs. *Scuticaria Steelii* has leaves 1½ feet long, whereas in *Scuticaria Hadwenii* they are 4 feet long. The flowers of both are similar to those of Maxillaria, and their culture is the same.

Phaius Tribe

This tribe of mostly terrestrial orchids covers a large part of the world with its various genera. Many are deciduous, and flower after the leaves have fallen. Two of the genera are rather widely grown, Phaius and Calanthe.

PHAIUS

A genus of large, handsome plants comprising some twenty species that produce tall spikes of showy flowers. There are among the species some that are epiphytic as well as the better known terrestrial ones. The former are seldom grown.

The terrestrial species are native to tropical Asia, Africa, Australia, Madagascar, China, and Japan. They have been cultivated since 1778, when *Phaius Tankervilliae* (*grandifolius*) was imported from China. This is commonly known as the "nun's orchid" or the "veiled nun."

This genus likes an intermediate greenhouse with adequate shade, and night temperatures that do not fall below 55° F. The potting compost is a mixture of sandy loam, well-rotted cow manure, and shredded peat moss or osmundine, in equal parts. The pots must have plenty of drainage crock in the bottom. To insure adequate nutrition, the top surface of the soil is covered with a mulch of cow manure. A nutrient solution or manure water may be added after the flower spikes have started. The plants grow vigorously, and require plenty of water all year round.

Plants of Phaius may be divided every two or three years, when the blooming season is over. Young plants may be grown from dormant buds on the flower scapes, much in the manner described for Dendrobiums. After the flowers have withered, cut the stem, lay it on moist sand in a flat. Cover with glass or muslin to keep in the moisture and provide shade. The little plants that grow from the dormant buds will be large enough in a few months to be potted up.

Dwellers in the southern states may grow members of this genus out-of-doors under the trees. In some regions they may be kept (in their pots) in the

CYP. TONBRIDGE
R.H.S. A.M. FEB. 11. '36

CYP. TONBRIDGE
Massive, well-set
flower.

PRINTED IN GREAT BRITAIN

garden at least for the summer, being brought into the greenhouse before the nights turn cool.

Phaius maculatus. Attractive yellow flowers, 2 to 3 inches in diameter, are borne in clusters of ten to fifteen on spikes 2 feet tall. The lip is erect with the front lobe recurved and streaked with orange. The base of the lip forms a prominent spur. The foliage of this plant is attractively variegated with yellow. Occurs in North India and Japan. Flowers in the spring.

Phaius Tankervilliae (*grandifolius*). Majestic plants, familiarly known as the "nun's orchid." The tall flower spike carries ten to fifteen flowers whose petals and sepals are white on the back, reddish brown inside. The lip is tubular, with a short spur, with a yellow throat and crimson sides. Occurs in China and Australia. Flowers in winter and spring.

A number of bigeneric hybrids have been made between Phaius and Calanthe, which are named after both genera, Phaio-Calanthe.

CALANTHE

The name Calanthe means "beautiful flower," and each of the species known in cultivation lives up to this name. The genus contains some forty or fifty species, some of which are deciduous and some evergreen, but all are terrestrial. The deciduous species have tall, conical pseudobulbs that reach 8 or 9 inches in height, from which rise the handsome, heavily ribbed leaves. The leaves fall before or at the time of flowering. In the evergreen species the pseudobulbs are lacking and the leaves grow directly from the creeping rhizome.

Mr. Dominy, the original orchid hybridist, made his first cross with Calanthes. In 1856 *Calanthe Dominii* (*Calanthe Masuca* × *Calanthe furcata*), the first hybrid orchid, flowered.

Calanthe is potted in the same manner as Phaius. The bulbs may be separated once a year, when growth is just starting in the spring, or the plant may be repotted without being divided. New growths come from the base of the old bulbs. A method often used is to separate the bulbs and put several in one large pot, to be assured of a good display of flowers. Water sparingly until growth starts, and give the new leaves extra shade for a while. After the leaves are well along, the plants need more light, but, as for Cattleyas, the light must be properly moderated. Calanthe thrives in warm places in the greenhouse, with a temperature of 55° to 60° F. at night and with generous daytime humidity.

During their growing season, water the deciduous species generously. The frequency of watering is reduced when the foliage begins to turn yellow in the fall. When the flower spikes show, increase the watering and continue until the blooms are finished. After their winter flowering, the plants must have a decided rest. The pots are laid on their sides in a cool place and given no water until the following spring. As soon as root growth begins, the plants must be repotted. The evergreen species are watered all year round.

Calanthe vestita. Once one of the most widely grown of all orchids and still very popular. The lovely sprays of white flowers keep well and lend themselves to decorations for holiday social affairs or to dainty corsages. The sepals and petals are more or less overlapping, and hold themselves up and back from the long, beautiful lip. The front lobe of the lip is scalloped, and flaring, with a touch of yellow or crimson in the throat. The pseudobulbs are silvery green and the deciduous leaves nearly 2 feet long. The flower spike rises to a height of 2 or 3 feet. Occurs in Malaya. Flowers in the winter.

The hybrid *Calanthe Veitchii, Calanthe rosea* × *Calanthe vestita,* is one of the most popular, and is as widely grown as *Calanthe vestita* itself. The flowers are rose colored, and the lip is decorated with a white spot near the base.

The parents of the first hybrid orchid were evergreen Calanthes. *Calanthe furcata* bears creamy white flowers generously distributed on a long spike. The plant has large fan-like leaves. *Calanthe Masuca* has deep violet flowers on spikes somewhat shorter than those of *C. furcata.* Both require warm, humid growing conditions.

OTHER MEMBERS OF THE PHAIUS TRIBE

Bletia is a genus of twenty species native to tropical America. The plants have spherical pseudobulbs, from the apex of which the tall flower spikes are produced.

Bletia verecunda produces rose-colored flowers, the blooms of *Bletia Shepherdii* are deep purple, and those of *Bletia Sherrattiana* are bright rose. These plants all have leaves from 3 to 4 feet long.

Chysis is a genus of attractive epiphytes native to tropical America. They are deciduous, and require warm growing conditions (60° F. at night) and plenty of water. After flowering, they should be given little or no water and kept cool. The flowers are brightly colored, of heavy, waxy texture, and are produced in clusters from the axils of the leaves.

The species, *Chysis aurea, laevis,* and *Chelsonii* have yellow flowers marked with red.

The species, *Chysis bractescens, Limminghei,* and *Sedenii* have white flowers marked with red or purple.

Aplectrum is a genus that grows wild in our own northern woods. The single species, *A. hyemale,* produces a single evergreen leaf and in the spring a spike of brownish flowers. Commonly called "Adam and Eve."

Acanthophippium, in contrast to Aplectrum, comes from the hottest moist jungles of Java, where they grow in heavy shade. The odd flowers are borne on a stem that grows from the base of the pseudobulb. The broad, fleshy sepals enclose the petals and lip, giving the flower the shape of an urn. The species *A. javanicum* has yellow flowers flushed and striped with red.

Spathoglottis is a genus of terrestrial orchids native to India and China. They have small corm-like pseudobulbs and grassy foliage. The small, bright flowers are produced usually in small numbers on rather tall spikes. Where they may be grown out-of-doors, for instance in our warm states where the climate is humid, they might be worth a try, for their foliage is quite attractive.

PLEUROTHALLIS TRIBE

This tribe is interesting because of one member in particular, the genus Masdevallia. They are native to high altitudes in tropical Central and South America and are all cool-growing.

MASDEVALLIA

The over one hundred and fifty species of this genus are distinguished by their weird and grotesque shapes, to which some of them add brilliant coloring and fragrance to make them spectacular and amusing additions to collections. The plants have no pseudobulbs. The stems grow from the rhizome in a bushy or tufted manner and bear ribbed leaves. A first glance at a flower reveals little of the familiar orchid shape, for the petals, and often the lip, are so tiny that they are hardly visible. The conspicuous parts of the flower are the sepals, which are transformed in a most unusual manner. They are united at the base to form a calyx tube, and the spreading parts are often prolonged into horns or tails. The petals and lip are usually hidden within the calyx tube, and the lip is sometimes sensitive.

The plants may be grown in pots or baskets in osmunda fibre to which is added one-third chopped sod. Winter temperatures should be 50° F. at night and 60°–65° F. in the daytime. In the summer the temperatures should be kept as cool as possible in the manner of Odontoglossum culture. They need a generous supply of water all year round, with good air circulation and atmospheric moisture.

Masdevallia coccinea. The small flowers are crimson-magenta. The dorsal sepal is slender and tail-like, bent backward from a triangular base. The lateral sepals are broad and ribbed, tapering to a point, the tips curving somewhat toward each other.

Masdevallia Chimaera. This grotesque species has the sepals prolonged into tails sometimes nearly a foot long. The yellow tails taper away from a continuous, out-turned base that is heavily spotted with purple. These must be grown in baskets as the flower stems sometimes grow down through the potting medium.

Masdevallia elephanticeps. The formation of the flower suggests an elephant head with the trunk raised. The dorsal sepal is yellow, the other two crimson.

Masdevallia muscosa. The sensitive lip has a raised yellow disc. When the disc is touched the lip moves upward with a jerk. The sepals are alike, triangular, with the tips prolonged into tails and curving backward. The leaves are covered with round papillae, and the flower stem is hairy.

Masdevallia Roezlii. The flowers are similar in character to *M. Chimaera*, but are the darkest in coloring of the genus. The yellow ground color is almost obscured by the brown cross-bars. The long tails are solid brown, and the small lip is pink.

OTHER GENERA OF THE PLEUROTHALLIS TRIBE

The genus Pleurothallis has 400 species, but most of them have inconspicuous flowers and for this reason are seldom cultivated. One species, *Pleurothallis ornata,* is interesting for its dwarf habit. The tufted leaves are barely an inch tall, and the tiny flowers are produced in a little feathery spray. They are yellow, spotted with brown, and the sepals are fringed with silvery hairs.

Restrepia is a genus whose members look like little Masdevallias. They are dwarf plants, with interesting flowers that are less spectacular than the latter.

Scaphosepalum is distinguished from Masdevallia by having the dorsal sepal nearly free, and the lateral sepals united into a boat-shaped body. The plants are less compact, and the flowers are borne on a long spray on which they open in succession over a period of several months.

SOBRALIA TRIBE

The Sobralia tribe is a group of terrestrial orchids which includes two genera, Sobralia, native to Mexico and tropical America, and Calopogon, native to North America.

SOBRALIA

Sobralia is a genus of reed-like plants, whose stems grow close together in thick, bushy clumps. They take up quite a bit of room in a greenhouse, but if space can be afforded they are worth growing for their handsome foliage and large, Cattleya-like flowers. They vary in height from 1 foot to 10 feet, and the flowers are from 1½ to 9 inches in diameter. The individual flowers do not last long, but the plants produce a succession of blooms that give a continuous show.

The Sobralias lack pseudobulbs. They require a rich, porous compost, a mixture of loam, leaf mold, osmunda shreds, and cow manure. The pots should be large, with ample drainage to allow for the copious water supply they need during their growing period. During the winter they require somewhat less water, but should never be allowed to become dry at the roots. They may be grown out-of-doors in our subtropical states, but require cool greenhouse treatment farther north.

Sobralia fragrans. One of the smallest of the genus, with flowers of sulfur yellow, 1½ to 2 inches in diameter, borne two to a stem. One of their charms is the fringed lip, which is decorated with many fringed crests. Occurs in Costa Rica, Panama, and neighboring countries.

Sobralia leucoxantha. Plants 3 feet tall, with a profusion of flowers. The sepals and petals are pure white. The gracefully waved lip is white, with its golden throat striped with brown. Occurs in Costa Rica and Panama. Flowers in August.

Sobralia macrantha. Tall, handsome plants that reach a height of from 4 to 7 feet, with rose-purple flowers often 9 inches in diameter. The sepals are slender and twisted, the petals broader and wavy. The front lobe of the lip is almost round, deep purple, and beautifully ruffled. The throat is whitish with several yellow ridges. Occurs in Mexico and Guatemala. Flowers from May to July.

CALOPOGON

Of the several species in this genus, the well known *Calopogon pulchellus* grows from Newfoundland to Florida in bogs and moist meadows. It will do well in a shaded place in your garden in a porous soil, with ample water. The plants should not be disturbed very often, but offsets may be separated from the large clumps occasionally. The small offsets take several years to reach blooming size, whereas large clumps bought from collectors will flower immediately. *Calopogon pulchellus* grows in clusters of solid bulbs or corms, each producing a single, grassy leaf. The flower stem carries two to twelve attractive flowers that vary in coloring from magenta-crimson to white. The lip is uppermost in the flower, and is bearded with white, yellow, or purple hairs.

TRICHOPILIA TRIBE

This tribe has but a single genus, Trichopilia. The fragrant flowers are charming, daintily colored, with a large wavy lip curled around the column.

Trichopilia suavis. (Courtesy of H. A. Dunn and H. Griffin)

The plant has smooth, oval, flattened pseudobulbs, dipped in at the top where the single broad, keeled leaf arises. Their culture is easy. They may be potted in osmunda fibre and grown in the cooler part of a Cattleya house, being kept cool in the summer. Water should be given moderately.

Trichopilia suavis. This lovely orchid was named by John Lindley in 1850. The flowers occur three or four to a stem that droops gracefully over the edge of the pot. The sepals and petals are white or cream colored, and the spreading, ruffled lip is white, prettily spotted with pale purple. Occurs in Central America. Flowers in early summer. The flower stems lie on the substratum or hang down close to the pot until just before the buds open.

At this time each bud lifts itself and turns slightly, to present the open flowers with the lip held invitingly forward.

Trichopilia tortillis. The brown sepals and petals are attractively bordered with yellow and are spirally twisted. The large lip is four lobed, white, spotted with crimson, and entirely crimson in the throat. Occurs in Mexico. Flowers profusely in the summer, and sometimes again in the winter.

Vanilla Tribe

The most interesting genus of this tribe is Vanilla, the only orchid at present to yield an important commercial product other than its flowers. The long seed pods are the source of the flavoring vanilla. The tall, climbing, plants, with their heavy velvety leaves are quite ornamental. The leaves are produced all along the stem and in their axils occur the sprays of small, yellow Cattleya-like flowers. The vine is grown from cuttings which are tied a little above the soil to some sort of support. In greenhouses the plants will grow in a compost of leaf mold and chopped osmundine. The aerial roots sent out from the cutting grow down into the compost. As the vine grows, it is trained around a post. The plant begins to produce about three years after becoming established, and continues to flower for thirty or forty years.

Vanilla planifolia is the only species cultivated commercially from the twenty or so species that represent the genus. It is native to Mexico and is cultivated in many of the tropical islands. It may be grown in greenhouses and does best with warm humid conditions. Pollination baffled growers who cultivated Vanilla away from its native habitat, for the insects required for the function were not transported with the plants. Hand pollination was a mystery. Placing the pollen on what appeared to be the stigma produced no results. Finally, a creole worker discovered that the stigma was covered by a shield, which had to be lifted in order to place the pollen on the stigma. After pollination, the shield snaps back into place. Now native workers go down the rows of plants, pollinating thousands of flowers in a day.

Zygopetalum Tribe

The only member of interest in this tribe of epiphytes is the genus which bears the name of the tribe, Zygopetalum. They have heavy textured flowers whose curious markings make them most interesting and whose ease of culture make them a welcome addition to an amateur collection. The flowers last a long time and are adaptable to corsages or to decorative arrangements.

Zygopetalum is distinguished for its large, vividly marked lip which spreads out broad and flat, and which is always a contrast in color to the sepals and petals. It bears a ridge-like crest or callus at its base. The sepals and petals are small, equal in size, and are more or less united at the base. The rather tall flower stem grows from the base of the rounded pseudobulb and carries

Zygopetalum Mackayi. (Courtesy of Jack Sweet)

several of the jaunty blooms near its top. The leaves of the plant are like those of Lycaste.

This genus does well with Cattleyas. They like a night temperature of 60° F. and prefer to be kept cool in the summer. They need especially good drainage and may be grown in osmunda fibre, or you may mix fibrous loam half and half with the osmundine. The plant is potted so that its base is even with the rim of the pot. The usual care in watering is important so that the fibre does not become soggy, and water is supplied all year round.

Zygopetalum crinitum. The sepals and petals are green, barred with brown. The wide, downy, lip is white, with purple veins radiating from the thick crest at its base. Occurs in Brazil. Flowering time variable.

Zygopetalum Mackayi. The sepals and petals are dull yellowish green, marked with blotches of purple. The large, round lip is smooth, white, veined or spotted with deep blue. Occurs in Brazil. Flowers in the winter, often in December. The flowers last eight or nine weeks.

The genus Colax has only two known species, of which *Colax jugosus* has striking red, white, and blue flowers. The sepals are pure white, the petals white spotted with red or red-violet, and the fiddle-shaped lip striped and spotted with blue-violet. Occurs in Brazil.

Eriopsis is the third genus in this tribe, and is characterized by bright orange colored flowers borne in arching or drooping sprays.

Chapter XVI
MINERAL NUTRITION

Man cannot live by love alone. Nor can a plant live by air and water. Every living thing, both animal and plant, depends on certain minerals for the development of its body structure and the maintenance of the living substance within it, protoplasm. Even plants that hang on such a sterile perch as a telephone wire (Tillandsia) have a source of minerals to nourish them, dust settling on the wire and minerals dissolved in rain water—small amounts, to be sure, but enough for these particular plants.

It used to be thought that orchids lived entirely on materials taken from the air. Observers overlooked the accumulation of humus material present in breaks in the bark of trees or crevices in weathered rock, the fertilizing minerals dissolved out of bird droppings and washed down to the plants by rain, and the yearly collection of dead leaves among the bulbs of the plants themselves. Even rain water is not pure, since rain droplets form on dust particles and take up more dust on their way earthward.

A 10-ounce orchid plant consists of 9 ounces of water and 1 ounce of sugars, starches, proteins, fats, waxes, and numerous other substances. This single ounce represents the other chemical substances accumulated by the plant during its lifetime plus the amount of food it has on hand at the moment of weighing. To find out what part of the dry weight of the plant is mineral, the dried plant is ignited and burned to remove carbon, hydrogen, nitrogen, and oxygen. The ash remaining is the total mineral content of the plant, and amounts to approximately 0.076 of an ounce for a 10-ounce plant. A fraction of a cent would buy the chemicals that make up the plant. The value of the living plant is based on the marvelous things its protoplasm, governed by its genes, can do with that minute quantity of nonliving substances.

The minerals, in the form of mineral salts, are absorbed by the roots from the medium in which they grow. The salts are released from the organic matter by slow decay and are put in solution by moisture in the soil. The salts in solution are then taken up by the roots, and transported to every part of the plant, where they enter into various vital activities.

In addition to the minerals, the plant needs two things absorbed from the air, oxygen and carbon dioxide. Oxygen, necessary for respiration, is absorbed by the leaves and stems from the atmosphere and by the roots from air in the soil. Carbon dioxide is absorbed by the leaves (and other green parts of the plant) and combined with water taken up by the roots to form sugar, the food of the plant. This process is called photosynthesis because it is carried on only in the presence of light. The simple sugars are turned into complex sugars, starches, and cellulose, and various products formed from carbohydrates are combined with nitrogen, sulfur, and phosphorus to form proteins.

The major mineral elements, necessary in relatively large amounts, and their activities, follow:

Calcium, for cell wall formation and for regulation of cell activities. If calcium is deficient the new growths are stunted and distorted.

Nitrogen, an essential ingredient of proteins and of chlorophyll, and necessary for good vegetative growth. When nitrogen is deficient the plants are stunted and mature too early. Older leaves turn yellow and drop off. Too much nitrogen produces excessive vegetative growth and delayed flowering.

Sulfur, also an ingredient of proteins. Sulfur deficiency may stunt root growth.

Phosphorus, the third important mineral in protein formation, and a catalyst and regulator of vital activity. Sometimes called the "dynamite of living cells." Phosphorus deficiency leads to stunting, but the leaves, instead of turning yellow, become dark green.

Potassium, another important catalyst, regulating many activities. Deficiency results in dwarfness with the edges of the leaves frequently scorched and dead.

Magnesium, part of the chlorophyll molecule, and therefore necessary to the manufacture of food. With lack of magnesium the older leaves become yellow between the veins and the plant does not thrive.

Iron, a catalyst in many reactions, including the formation of chlorophyll. Iron is seldom deficient but is insoluble unless the soil is sufficiently acid. Deficiency of iron causes the younger leaves to become yellow.

Certain other minerals are also necessary, but in extremely minute amounts. Very little is known about their specific activities, and it is thought that they act as catalysts in vital chemical reactions. These minor elements are *boron, manganese, copper,* and *zinc.* They are seldom deficient, for the faint traces found in most soils, and even as impurities in most chemicals, are enough to supply the needs of the plants. It is therefore not necessary to add them to nutrient solutions, with the possible exception of manganese. Research workers who are studying the activities of these four elements find it necessary first to purify their own chemicals to free them from any faint traces,

and even to redistill water many times for their experiments. Complete absence of these minor elements causes poor growth and amounts over the smallest trace are toxic.

In order for a plant to thrive, all of the minerals mentioned must be present and available to the roots. Not only must they be present, but they must be present in definite amounts and in the proper ratio to each other, so much nitrogen to so much phosphorus, for example. In other words, the diet must be balanced. Too much of a given element is often just as injurious to a plant as too little, some-

Mineral deficiency can be caused by too loose potting, as shown by the stunted growth of the loosely potted plant at the left. In contrast, the vigorous plant at the right, has made excellent growth in fibre packed hard.

times more so. Hence the grower must beware of the idea that if a little is good, more is better. Orchid plants have been severely weakened by over-fertilization.

Fortunately, the usual potting medium, osmundine, gives a well-balanced diet for orchids. By analysis it proves to be the equal chemically of good black garden soil. It has a pH of about 5.6. Under proper growing conditions, that is, with light, heat, water and aeration given in the right amounts, the plants will not suffer from mineral deficiencies.

Oddly enough, orchids can sometimes suffer from deficiencies in the face of plenty, not because the minerals are lacking, but because under some conditions the plants are unable to take them up. The most serious factor in this is overwatering. Roots are living, "breathing" organs. They need oxygen to carry on the process of respiration (they absorb oxygen and give off carbon dioxide), and without oxygen they cannot function. Continued overwatering causes the air spaces in the fibre to be filled with water to the exclusion of air. The roots are unable to perform their duties and the plants begin to show starvation symptoms, yellow leaves, for instance, because the necessary minerals are not being absorbed. If lack of aeration at the roots continues for too long, the roots will die. The sodden, poorly drained fibre becomes overacid and toxins are formed. The best thing to do is to repot the plant, and give it fresh fibre in which to start a new, healthy root system.

The opposite of overwatering, underwatering, is not nearly so dangerous to the health of Cattleya plants. Yet it, too, deprives the plant of enough minerals, which together with the lack of water, results in a stunted plant. The leaves and bulbs will shrivel, and if drying is continued for too long, the plant will become dormant. Mature plants can stand drying better than seedlings. The latter can be severely checked by lack of water, to the extent that it may be difficult to return them to an actively growing condition.

Some growers have been experimenting with the addition of a nutrient solution to the osmundine. A few feel that it is beneficial for seedlings. In some cases the small gains made could be more than duplicated with greater attention to light and water, not to mention care in repotting. However, in the work done at Ohio State University, some beneficial results occurred with some plants, so that further work on the subject seems merited.

Here is a chance for amateurs to experiment on their own. It should be said that results are difficult to evaluate, due to the variability among plants. And if an experiment is to be carried on, the grower should be absolutely honest with himself and the orchids. He should select a group of plants, if possible all of the same age, that are as nearly identical in size and condition as can be judged. Then he should separate them into two groups, one to be given nutrient solution and the other to be watered as usual. He should decide on a definite time interval for applying the nutrient solution (at every watering, once a week, or once a month), and whether it is to be used only during the growing season of the plant, or all year round. Then he should carry out this plan religiously, in the meantime watching and noting the progress of each plant. Obviously, both groups should be kept under the same external conditions of light, heat, and humidity. The control group is as important as the experimental one, for it is the only basis of comparison.

A good solution to use is the Ohio W. P. solution given later (p. 218) under gravel culture, and applied half strength. Hyponex, or any other complete garden fertilizer, may also be used, applied one-half the strength recommended for other plants. For Hyponex, one teaspoonful to a gallon of water is the concentration to use.

At the completion of the experiment if the majority of the experimental plants show better development than the majority of the control group, it can be assumed that the nutrient solution was beneficial. If the two groups are essentially the same, then in this particular experiment the addition of nutrient solution was not effective. Beware of jumping to conclusions on the basis of just one or two plants that may have outstripped the others. Unless most of the plants show a gain, the unusual growth of the exceptional ones will have to be put down to individual variation.

GRAVEL CULTURE

Gravel culture is a more or less new way of raising plants, a form of hydroponics, that has caused considerable excitement among horticultural- ists. At first hydroponics was greeted as a magic method that would do away with soil culture in short order. Crops were expected to be larger and better, with science taking control to eliminate the elements of chance. However, wherever there is a human element there is an element of chance. Where solutions must be mixed and tested, and where their application depends on human judgment, there are chances for errors. And errors in making and applying nutrient solutions can be fatal to crops just as drouth and flood can be.

Those who have worked experimentally with the gravel culture of orchids are divided in opinion as to its benefits, but all remind novices to go slowly. Some have had remarkable results that lead you to think that gravel culture is the only true way to grow orchids. Others report that gravel culture seemed beneficial for some plants but not for others. The grower trying gravel cul- ture for the first time should do so with an open mind to find out for himself how it works on his own plants. Obviously, he should try it on only a few plants to start with.

The essential differences between gravel culture and the use of osmunda fibre are: Osmunda fibre is itself the source of minerals for the plants. Once potted in this medium you have only to water the plants with care, until they need to be repotted. In gravel culture the plants are potted in an inert medium and nutrients are furnished in a solution with which the plants are watered. It means measuring and mixing chemicals, or, in its easiest form, using a ready-mixed fertilizer, to be added regularly to the water.

A skilled "peat" (osmundine) man and a skilled gravel culture man will both give you good reasons for his choice of medium. And the best plants grown by one will not outrank those grown by the other. Gravel does over- come one of the most common faults of those who use osmundine, that of overwatering. There is nothing in gravel to become soggy, drainage is more rapid and complete, and aeration of the roots is better assured. Potting with gravel is less of a chore than potting with fibre. However, when plants are in gravel, not only do they need to be watered more often, but mixing and applying the nutrient solution regularly is a necessity.

The amateur might first pot a few plants in gravel and feed them nutrient solution with a watering can. Then if he wants to try it on a larger number, he might put in a tank to hold the nutrient solution, and apply it with a hose, making up the solution fresh each time, and allowing the pots to drain on the ground. Later, if he feels that he wants to go into gravel culture on a large scale, he might build special benches for subirrigation and install a pump to take the nutrient solution to the plants. In this type of system, the same solution is used over and over, draining back into the tank from the benches after each flooding. The solution must be tested at regular intervals for quantities of the various minerals, so that those that become depleted may be renewed. Or the solution must be made up fresh every few weeks. Some growers feel that the ease of handling the plants offsets both the initial expense and the constant attention to the nutrient solution.

NUTRIENT SOLUTIONS

Any complete fertilizer, such as Hyponex, may be used in weak dilutions for orchids. The fertilizer should contain nitrogen, phosphorus, and potassium in the proportions of 4-12-4, along with other necessary minerals. There are other complete fertilizers besides Hyponex on the market, and many more being newly added to the lists. Solutions of these fertilizers should be one-half the strength recommended for other types of plants. For Hyponex, one teaspoonful to one gallon of water is entirely sufficient, in fact a stronger solution may not only give poor results but may even be injurious.

We have been talking of elements necessary to plant nutrition, nitrogen, phosphorus, iron, sulfur, and so on, but actually these are not adaptable to plant use unless they are in the form of mineral salts. Oxygen is the only substance used by the plant as a pure element. The soil elements exist in various combinations, and different formulae for hand-mixed nutrient solutions also vary in the specific salts used. Potassium may be furnished to the plant in the form of potassium sulfate, potassium nitrate or potassium chloride. Nitrogen is available in nitrate salts or as ammonium sulfate, calcium as monocalcium phosphate or calcium sulfate, and manganese, magnesium and iron as manganese sulfate, magnesium sulfate and ferrous sulfate. Phosphorus and sulfur occur in the phosphate or sulfate part of these salts.

A standard nutrient solution, used with success on orchids, is the Ohio W. P. solution. The formula for this is as follows:

The Ohio W. P. Solution (to be used half strength)

Name	Symbol	Amount
Potassium nitrate	KNO$_3$	2.63 grams
Ammonium sulfate	(NH$_4$)$_2$SO$_4$	0.44 grams
Magnesium sulfate	MgSO$_4$·7H$_2$O	2.04 grams
Monocalcium phosphate	CaH$_4$(PO$_4$)$_2$·H$_2$O	1.09 grams
Calcium sulfate	CaSO$_4$·2H$_2$O	4.86 grams
Iron sulfate (Ferrous sulfate)	FeSO$_4$·7H$_2$O	0.5 grams
Manganese sulfate	MnSO$_4$	Make a 1% solution and add 2.5 c.c. of this
Water	H$_2$O	1.0 gallons

In preparing this solution dissolve each salt completely in the gallon of water before adding the next salt. Manganese is added by first dissolving one gram of manganese sulfate in 99 c.c. of water then 2.5 c.c. of this solution is used per gallon of nutrient solution. It is not necessary to use C. P. grade chemicals in mixing these nutrient solutions. Nor is it necessary to add the minor elements, boron, zinc, and copper, since they occur as impurities in the chemicals, in tap and rain water, and in Haydite and most gravels.

INDIVIDUAL POTS ON OPEN BENCHES

This is perhaps the most usable method for amateurs who have a variety of species and hybrids. It is adaptable to few or many plants. Application of the nutrient solution is done with a watering can or a hose connected to a gravity tank. The solution is made up fresh each time and allowed to drain through the pots onto the ground.

The most satisfactory material for use in gravel culture is Haydite, a porous, relatively inert commercial product used in making lightweight concretes. It comes in various sizes, and the following are recommended: for community pots, $\frac{1}{16}$ to $\frac{1}{8}$ inch in diameter; for seedlings three to four years old, $\frac{1}{8}$ to $\frac{1}{4}$ inch; and for larger seedlings and mature plants, $\frac{1}{4}$ to $\frac{1}{2}$ inch. Gray granite gravel may also be used, but dries out more slowly than Haydite. Limestone and silica gravels should not be used. Beginners are advised not to try other gravels because some require modification of the nutrient solution according to the mineral content of the gravel.

Haydite may be used alone, or as some growers prefer, mixed with chopped osmunda fibre and granite gravel in equal parts. The mixture is especially good for community pots as the surface does not dry out as fast as that of plain gravel or Haydite and gives the little roots the benefit of more constant moisture.

Flask seedlings are transplanted directly to shallow, 5-inch pots containing the mixture prepared as follows. Make three piles, one each of: Haydite $\frac{1}{16}$ to $\frac{1}{8}$ inch in diameter, granite gravel of the same diameter, and finely chopped osmunda fibre that has been screened through a $\frac{1}{8}$-inch mesh screen. Mix equal parts of these together in each pot, first putting four or five large pieces of crock in the bottom. Settle each seedling firmly into the surface, about one-half inch apart. The pots should be kept in a box or covered bench as recommended earlier for care of community pots using osmunda fibre. They should be given the nutrient solution of your choice not oftener than once a week. The plants may be lightly syringed on bright days. If they need watering between applications of nutrient solution, add a little plain water to each pot, not enough to run through. Drying will be a little more rapid than with plain osmundine, but the mixture of fibre and gravel will in turn not dry as fast as plain gravel. The fine gravel used here will hold water longer than the coarse size used for larger plants, so watch the watering carefully.

Gravel culture, individual pot method. The plant in Haydite is tied to a rigid wire support such as that shown at the right. The support is clamped to the pot by means of a sliding ring that pulls the wires together as it is forced down.

From the gravel community pot (in which the plants can stay longer than in osmundine) the plants are moved to 3-inch pots. Plain Haydite may be used, or the mixture described above. The Haydite is now $\frac{1}{8}$ to $\frac{1}{4}$ inch in diameter, and it is not necessary to screen the chopped fibre. Separation of the roots is an easy matter, and little bits of gravel or fibre clinging here and there need not be removed. Only one piece of crock over the hole in the pot is now necessary. The plant is held at the desired level and the gravel poured into the pot and around the roots. The plant may be a little deeper in the gravel than in fibre, but the rhizome should not be buried. The plant will have to be supported by a rigid wire frame. Plants may stay in these

3-inch pots for two years or until they outgrow the pot. Again, the nutrient solution is applied once a week, with light syringing in bright weather, and plain water added to the pots when needed.

Another method of handling seedlings from the flask or community pot is to put them in gravel filled flats. The same type of Haydite or Haydite-fibre mixture is put into the flat, and the plants put directly in this. The flat is given nutrient solution once a week, and the same additional care as single pots. A large number of seedlings may thus be handled with ease. When it comes time to move the plants, either for wider spacing in another flat or to single pots, the roots are easily separated.

Transplanting to 5- and 6-inch pots involves the same procedure as given for 3-inch pots, but the Haydite should now be $\frac{1}{4}$ to $\frac{1}{2}$ inch in diameter. Again, plain Haydite may be used, or mixed with chopped fibre. The latter is not really necessary now, and time may be saved by omitting it. The larger pots may need only one watering between the weekly applications of nutrient solution, but here your judgment and the conditions in the greenhouse must be your guide. Whenever the gravel begins to dry out, add water to the pot.

Mature plants in gravel should be divided and moved whenever their growth merits it. Plants receive little shock when moved from one gravel pot to another. Although there is not as much danger from overwatering in gravel, there is still no advantage in using too large a pot. Nutrient solution is still given once a week, with water added between times when needed, just enough to wet the gravel without draining out. During periods of inactivity (rest periods) give no nutrient solution. Instead water when needed with plain tap or rain water.

Plants in osmundine may be moved into gravel whenever the plants themselves are ready for transplanting. The shock is greater in moving a plant from osmundine than in moving one out of gravel. Most of the fibre must be removed. A small ball, just enough to decrease the shock, may be left, but a large ball is a distinct disadvantage. Plants thus moved should be kept on the dry side until root activity is regained, and then given nutrient solution according to schedule.

In all cases, once a week has been given as the interval for applying the nutrient solution. But the interval may have to be stretched occasionally. For instance, you would not give nutrient solution except in bright weather. In dark, wet or cold weather, when the plant should not be watered anyhow, nutrient solution will have to be withheld. The plants can make little growth in dark weather, and can get along on the amount of nutrient material left from the last application.

It is helpful to use a nozzle or rose that gives a gentle spray for adding water to the pots between applications of nutrient solution. You can control the amount of water better this way than with an open hose.

Subirrigation

This method involves the use of specially constructed watertight benches, filled with Haydite, into which the nutrient solution is pumped, and from

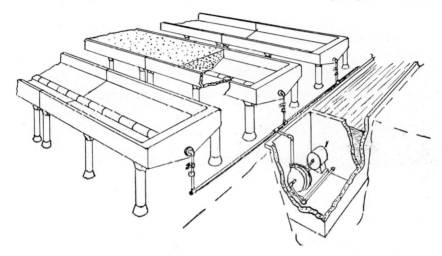

Fig. 1. V-bottom benches for subirrigation. Nutrient solution is pumped from the cistern to the benches, where it is distributed through the row of half-round tile in the bottom of each. After flooding, the solution drains back to the cistern. A valve on the pipe leading to each bench allows separate control. (Courtesy of Purdue University, Agricultural Experiment Station)

which it drains back into the storage tank. It saves a great deal of time, for a whole bench of plants is automatically watered at one time.

When subirrigation is used for orchids, the plants that are irrigated together must be all of the same variety. You cannot put plants together that have different blooming seasons and growth habits. For this reason subirrigation is more readily applicable to collections that include large blocks of species and hybrids whose seasonal behavior is similar. For instance, where there can be a bench of *Cattleya Trianaei* or other mid-winter blooming varieties, another for late winter and early spring flowering kinds, and so on. With some ingenuity, however, a small grower could divide one bench into sections that could be irrigated independently so that small groups of plants could be grown according to their needs. Since seedlings do not have rest periods, they can be grown together until they reach maturity when they can be sorted out.

A good strong wooden bench may be made over for subirrigation by coating it with horticultural asphalt (obtainable from Lord and Burnham, Des Plaines, Illinois). The horticultural asphalt is made especially for this purpose and is not toxic to plants. It comes as a solid, and when heated becomes fluid enough to be spread over the bottom and sides of the bench, filling all cracks. A hole is drilled in one end of the bench for connecting the pipe, and a row of half-round tile laid down the center of the bench for distributing the nutrient solution.

Cattleya plants in gravel, in concrete bench to which water and nutrients are supplied by subirrigation. (Courtesy of Floriculture Division, Ohio State University)

V-bottom concrete benches are fine for the purpose. Perhaps you can make the forms and pour them yourself, or have a contractor do the work. A steel bench made in sections to suit your purpose may be bought from Lord and Burnham. Both types must be coated inside with horticultural asphalt to prevent possible reaction with the mineral salts of the nutrient solution.

A set of V-bottom concrete benches with pipe lines connected to pump and storage tank is shown in Fig. 1. A valve on the pipe leading into each bench allows separate control. The nutrient solution is distributed throughout the bench by a line of half-round tile. All pipes and fittings, and the pump itself, should be made of iron. The time switch shown in connection with the pump may not be needed for your purposes.

The cistern to hold the nutrient solution should have a capacity of at least one-fourth, preferably one-third, of the volume of the benches. The amount of fluid necessary to flood the benches will depend partly on the size of the gravel used, since small particles have less space between them than large particles. The cistern should be of concrete, coated with horticultural asphalt as used in the benches. It is well to cover the cistern to prevent the growth of algae by eliminating light. The pump is placed in a pit next to the cistern. It should be far enough below the level of nutrient solution to insure priming.

There are two ways of placing orchids in the bench. One is to fill the bench with Haydite and plant the orchids directly into it. This method has such definite disadvantages that it is not recommended. For one thing, the roots become so entangled that it is difficult to remove the plants. A better method is to pot the plants separately in Haydite, and then plunge the pots into the Haydite in the bench. Even so, the surface roots grow around into the Haydite in the bench, but most of them are confined to the pot. With care, an individual plant may be removed from the bench for display purposes or for some other reason, and then returned to the bench.

It is customary to flood the benches with nutrient solution whenever the plants need watering. However, you may, if you choose, handle whole benches as you would single pots, and spray them lightly with water in between times if they need it more frequently than once a week. The valve between the bench and the cistern must always be left open after flooding, so that any excess water applied may drain out. And you must be cautious not to water so heavily that you dilute the nutrient solution.

The nutrient solution is allowed to rise in the benches to a level 1 inch below the surface of the gravel, and then to drain out immediately. The flooding will take between fifteen minutes and one hour, depending on the size of the bench and capacity of the pump. Drainage will take a comparable length of time. The surface of the gravel is kept on the dry side to discourage growth of algae. Other care of the plants, as to ventilation, humidity, light, and temperature, is the same as for orchids in general. Syringing the plants on warm, bright days is beneficial.

Chapter XVII

DIAGNOSING ORCHID AILMENTS

Orchid health depends on three fundamentals—good inheritance, proper environment, and freedom from disease and injury. Enough has been said previously about inheritance to emphasize the importance of selecting strong, free-growing, disease-free plants, whether you acquire them as small seedlings or as mature plants. Environmental conditions that contribute to the health of the plant are the right amount of light, temperature within the proper day-night range, humidity coupled with good air circulation, water to suit the needs of the plants, and proper nutrition combined with root aeration. Deviations from the optimal in any of these conditions may cause variations from the normal, thrifty condition of the plant. Diseases are caused by invading viruses, bacteria, or fungi, and, although orchids are remarkably free from such attacks, they do occur occasionally. Orchids are also rather immune to pests that plague most greenhouse crops, but prevention of insect injury is an absolute necessity.

AILMENTS ARISING FROM ENVIRONMENTAL CONDITIONS

LIGHT

When the light is too strong, chlorophyll (the green pigment) is destroyed faster than it is made, and leaves become yellow, or even white in young seedlings. Yellowed leaves cannot make as much food as leaves that have the normal amount of chlorophyll. If the condition is not corrected, the older leaves may fall before they should. The general result is a retarded plant.

Sudden exposure to too strong light may burn localized areas. Naturally, the efficiency of a leaf is decreased by the presence of a burned area. The sudden exposure may result from removing too much shading in the fall, from not applying it soon enough in the spring, or by allowing strong light to focus on a plant through a clear area on the glass, through an open ventilator, etc. Flowers are much more sensitive to light than the vegetative parts of a plant. Dried sepals are one of the first signs that the blooms may be exposed to too strong light.

Insufficient light causes the plants to become a darker green than normal. Even though the dark green plants are handsome to the eye, they are not as healthy as when the foliage is a lighter shade. The plants are usually soft and succulent, susceptible to disease, and their growths do not mature and harden as they should. Flower production is cut down or inhibited entirely.

TEMPERATURE

Each kind of orchid has its own temperature requirements. At temperatures too high for their kind, they will not flower. Growth is poor because food is used faster than it can be made. Often the leaves fall prematurely and death may result.

At temperatures below the specific requirement water and minerals are absorbed but slowly, and formation of chlorophyll is hindered. Yellow foliage and poor development result, and poor flowering is the logical sequel.

There is also an optimal difference between day and night temperatures. Too wide a gap, or not enough drop at night, retards growth.

Orchids can survive short spells of extremely hot weather if everything is done to aid them. The leaves absorb light with its associated heat, and their temperature is therefore usually warmer than the surrounding air. They do have some protection from heat in their evaporation of water (transpiration), which acts as a cooling system. For Cattleyas, it has been demonstrated that burning occurs if the temperature of the leaves remains at 110° F. for a few hours, or at 120°–125° F. for shorter periods. This means that during hot spells when the greenhouse temperature soars above 100° F., the temperature of the leaves may reach the danger point and sudden burning may occur. I know of a case where every plant in a small greenhouse was burned black when it was accidentally left unattended on a hot day. Under such conditions everything must be done to lower leaf temperatures. The plants should have cooling mists over the foliage, and proper attention to ventilation and shade.

Burning due to strong light would seem to be actually a heat effect. Concentration of light on one area of a leaf raises the temperature of that area to the burning point.

Flowers are even more sensitive to heat than plants. Flowering plants should therefore be kept as cool as possible under conditions of hot weather to prevent premature fading.

For regions where hot summers are a rule, varieties should be chosen with care as to their particular temperature requirements.

HUMIDITY

Insufficient humidity in the air makes it difficult to maintain an even water supply to the plants. The potting medium dries out quickly, and the plants lose water rapidly. This is especially critical for newly potted plants, whose root systems are temporarily non-functioning, and for young seedlings.

Excessive humidity is dangerous when coupled with low temperatures, which brings about susceptibility to certain diseases. Flowers may become spotted, either by simple engorgement with water or by fungous growths. From this fact comes the advice to water early in the day and to give the last syringing in time to let the plants dry off before night.

With under-bench sprayers, or by damping down by hand, it is easy enough to keep the daytime humidity up to 70%, the amount good for most orchids. Proper ventilation is a necessity, and Chapter XVIII gives suggestions on this matter.

WATERING

Enough has been said about the effects of overwatering on plants and flowers (see Chapters III and XVI) but one more suggestion might be helpful. If one plant turns yellow in the midst of others that are a good green, you might suspect overwatering as the cause. Evidently the light and temperature conditions are right, as evidenced by the good condition of the surrounding plants. Perhaps this one ailing plant is potted more tightly, or in softer osmundine, and retains water longer than the others. Knock it out of the pot and examine the roots. The chances are that the roots are rotten, in which case trim them off, remove all old fibre, and repot. Keep it on the dry side in a warm place for a while, with gentle syringings, until new root growth starts. A plant in very poor condition may lose a number of leaves before it regains healthy growth. Sometimes a plant with no living roots may be brought back to health by potting it in sphagnum moss until good root growth is established.

NUTRITION

Chapter XVI gives the symptoms of various nutritional deficiencies. It is not likely that plants potted in good osmundine will suffer any nutritional lack, provided they are potted firmly. Plants loosely potted will suffer from lack of minerals and perhaps water also. Some of the leaves will turn yellow and dry. It might be well to remember, however, that both over- and under-watering can produce the symptoms of mineral deficiencies. If such occur, and do not disappear in a reasonable length of time after the watering schedule has been corrected, it might be well to repot the plant.

AIR RELATIONS

Industrial regions may offer hazards to orchid growing, although the dangers are rapidly disappearing with modern methods of smoke control.

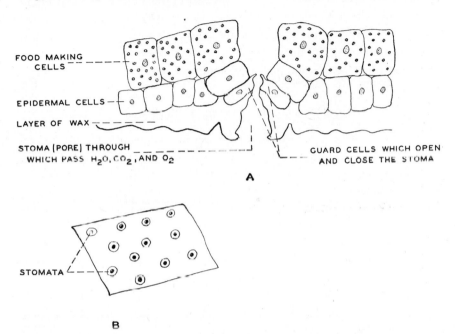

Fig. 1. A, a section of Cattleya leaf, showing the structure of a single stoma and the cells surrounding it. Note particularly the guard cells that regulate the opening and closing of the stoma, and the heavy layer of wax. B, a microscopic view of the under surface of a leaf showing how the stomata appear externally.

The presence of a large amount of sulfur dioxide in the air is hard on the plants, since the gas is poisonous. Soot is also a handicap, for it settles on the leaves and plugs up the stomata, the pores on the under side of the leaf through which transpiration takes place, and through which carbon dioxide and oxygen move. (Fig. 1 is a drawing of a section of a leaf showing the beautiful construction of a stoma.) Soot must be washed off if the leaves are to function properly. It is also a good practice to sponge the leaves when repotting to remove collections of dust and salts.

Some large collections of orchids have had to be moved out of smoky cities, for instance Low's of London. After moving, there was a tremendous improvement in the health of the plants and in their flower production. Perhaps as important as the freedom from soot was the improvement in light conditions when the collection was moved into the clean country air.

Artificial illuminating gas is disastrous to plant life. Even a small amount of the raw gas leaking into the greenhouse will quickly kill the plants. One grower lost a great many when the gas main in the street broke and the gas seeped through the earth into his orchid house. Artificial gas is not safe to use in open burners in the greenhouse, nor is gas that has the slightest amount of artificial gas mixed with it. On the other hand, absolutely pure natural gas is perfectly safe, provided combustion is complete.

PARASITIC DISEASES, BACTERIAL, FUNGOUS, AND VIRUS

Very little work has been done on diseases in orchids, possibly due to their rather infrequent occurrence in serious form. We do know of some general types of disease, and all orchid growers should be on the alert for them.

It is probable that in the best managed greenhouse there is an occasional diseased plant. Look over your own benches. You may have a plant with the tip of a leaf turning brown, or one with a few brown spots that you have either overlooked or attributed to sun burning. Perhaps you have had a seedling or two turn brown at the heart, where the leaves join the stem, with death soon following.

That a diseased plant has remained in your greenhouse without infecting other plants is a compliment to your management. Such a plant in a green-house where bad conditions exist can set off an epidemic and seriously injure a collection. By maintaining good, healthy growing conditions for your plants, you are unconsciously carrying on a program of disease prevention. Sometimes the elements conspire to spread infection, with long spells of cold, or warm, cloudy weather. Under these circumstances man's ingenuity must go to work.

Bacteria, fungi, and viruses are ever present. Many that attack common garden crops will also attack orchids. Some species of these organisms (we are including viruses as organisms merely for convenience) are parasites on plant tissue and digest the cells for their own food. They enter the plant through wounds, even through such a small injury as an insect puncture, or through the stomata of the leaves. Bacteria reproduce in the plant tissue and come to the surface in minute, oozing droplets. They are spread from plant to plant by contact, contaminated hands or instruments, insects, and splashing water. A fungus grows with its cobweb-like body (mycelium) inside of a leaf, pseudobulb, etc., destroying the tissues as it spreads. The only part of a fungus that appears on the surface is that which bears the spores, the reproductive cells. The spores are carried from plant to plant by the same means as bacteria.

As the orchids themselves require certain conditions for favorable growth, so also do the pathogenic organisms. Certainly many of the latter flourish when temperatures are low and humidity high, conditions that often plague European growers. So readily do diseases occur at such times that the earlier growers thought improper environment itself was the cause of disease. This idea prevailed until the last half of the nineteenth century, when it was demonstrated that plant infections were caused by bacteria and fungi, thriving and multiplying under these very conditions. Other pathogenic organisms thrive under conditions of warmer temperatures coupled with high humidity. Soft, succulent growth is particularly liable to infections.

A diseased plant cannot be cured by sprays, since these do not reach the organism within the plant tissue. Sprays and chemicals may be used successfully to protect healthy plants from attack and may arrest the disease in its very earliest stages. Surgery may save a plant in which infection has progressed. The best method of control is, of course, prevention, avoiding the conditions that favor the growth of pathogenic organisms.

Moisture is of the greatest significance in spread of disease. In order for a fungus spore to germinate, or for bacteria to enter a plant, water must be present on rhizome, pseudobulb, leaf, or sheath. Hence good orchid culture calls for watering and syringing early enough in the day to allow the plants to dry off before night. Then, when temperatures are lower and humidity runs up to the saturation point, the plant offers dry surfaces to the potential enemy. Luckily we do not have to go to the extreme of wiping each sheath by hand, as do some European growers. Avoid crowding the plants on the bench, as this cuts down air circulation and allows moisture to remain for long periods.

If infection gets a foothold in a greenhouse, the first steps in control are to isolate the diseased plants, cut down the humidity, dispense with syringing, and increase ventilation. This will not only reduce the spread of disease to healthy plants, but will help to check its spread in infected ones. If this is not effective, that is, if the disease continues to spread, the greenhouse may be sprayed with a fungicide.

Bordeaux mixture is an old and widely used fungicide. It may be purchased in powdered form, and consists of equal parts of copper sulfate and lime. It deteriorates if kept too long, so it is advisable to buy only a small quantity of it. The spray is made by adding the powder to water, according to directions. Never use Bordeaux mixture right before or after a nicotine spray.

Other sprays effective against fungous and bacterial diseases that have been tried on orchids are Cuprocide 54, Cuprocide 54-Y, Semesan, and Ceresan. Sprays should be used with caution. Fungicides sometimes cause plant injury as well as injury to the invading organisms. While the sprays given above have been used by occasional orchid growers, it would be wise to try them first on a few plants before running the risk of damaging a large number. They should always be used in the weakest dilution given in the directions, and the plants should be wet at the roots before application. Control of humidity is usually effective in stopping the spread of disease, and should be the first resort together with isolation and treatment of infected plants. The use of a spray should be a well considered, not a hasty, act.

Sanitation is important. Pathogenic organisms may be perpetuated on plant debris accumulated on or under the benches and may be spread from these sources by splashing water or by insects. All diseased parts of plants must be removed and burned, and all other debris must be cleared away. Insect control is related to sanitation, since insects play a dual role in plant infection. They inflict wounds through which pathogenic organisms can enter, and they sometimes place in the wound organisms which they have picked up by contact with infected material. Weeds should be removed from the pots.

If you can select your plants personally, choose those that are disease-free. Or, if you buy by mail, keep newly received plants separated from the others until you ascertain whether they are infected.

Bacterial diseases usually start with spots that appear semitransparent or water-soaked, becoming soft and brown, later turning darker brown or black. Spots may occur on leaf, pseudobulb, or rhizome, wherever water is present to aid their entrance. As the infection advances the spots increase in area and number. Many species of bacteria have been found to be the cause of disease in orchids. While some of these have been isolated from only one or two genera, it has been found experimentally that they may infect a long list of other genera.

Fungous diseases usually start with sunken spots, often yellow, red, or dark green, which may also have a water-soaked appearance, and which turn brown as the disease progresses.

It is often difficult to tell whether bacteria or fungi are the causal agents of disease, without the aid of a plant pathologist. Sometimes after one organism has produced lesions, other organisms will invade these areas. The treatment in both types of disease is similar.

The diseased areas must be removed by surgery. Cut away all spots on leaf, bulb, or rhizome, being sure to remove some of the clean tissue beyond the decayed area, where the disease may be spreading. Cover the wound with Bordeaux paste (available in prepared form), to prevent further spread of pathogenic organisms while the wound is healing. Badly diseased leaves and bulbs should be completely removed. All diseased parts of plants must be burned. Instruments must be sterilized after use, by soaking in alcohol, Clorox, or a solution of mercuric chloride (1 gram to 500 c.c. of water).

After the operation, sponge the rest of the plant with mercuric chloride solution, 1 gram to 1000 c.c. of water. Other plants that have the early symptoms of disease may be saved from infection by sponging with this same solution.

Soft rot caused by *Erwinia carotovora*. The affected leaf shows wrinkling due to collapse of internal tissues. (Courtesy of D. P. Limber and B. A. Friedman)

Sheaths require special treatment, discussed under fungous diseases, below.

Specific diseases that have been studied are given here, summarized from reports in scientific literature. For their control, refer to the methods just described, or follow special instructions for the particular disease.

Bacterial Diseases. A soft rot disease that frequently attacks Cattleya, Phalaenopsis, Paphiopedilum, Cymbidium is caused by *Erwinia carotovora* (probably the organism also called *Bacillus cypripedii* or *Erwinia cypripedii*). Infected areas show a dull, water-soaked condition, of a darker green than normal. The tissues become soft, and as the internal structure collapses, the epidermis becomes wrinkled, with blackened areas occurring. An exudate is often present. The disease usually enters through a wound, and rapidly spreads through the whole plant, causing death. Leaves that are inoculated experimentally show definite decay within twenty-four hours, with destruction of the whole leaf in four to seven days. Pseudobulbs and rhizome may also be the site of infection. Oncidium, Odontoglossum, Brassavola, and Lockhartia are also known to be susceptible to this organism, and others probably are too.

A bacterial leaf spot and bud rot is caused by *Phytomonas (Bacterium) cattleyae,* a disease that is particularly serious in Cattleya and Phalaenopsis, and that also may infect Epidendrum, Dendrobium, Paphiopedilum, and other genera. The disease first appears as small, dark, water-soaked spots, which rapidly increase in size, changing from light to dark brown with age. The spots may run together to form larger areas. When temperature and moisture conditions are favorable, the disease spreads rapidly through the plant, resulting in death. *Phytomonas cattleyae* usually enters the plant

A common bacterial disease is this leaf spot caused by *Phytomonas cattleyae.* (Courtesy of P. A. Ark and H. E. Thomas)

through a wound, but may attack a sound plant. New growths are sometimes destroyed by this disease. The eyes start, only to turn black and deteriorate before reaching any size.

A bacterial leaf rot has been reported in orchids sent to Java from the Philippines and India caused by *Phytomonas oncidii.* The infection may begin either at the tip or at the base, and affected tissues become yellow or grayish, finally presenting a completely translucent appearance. Diseased leaves are readily detachable and the petiole shrivels at the point of attachment. The disease does not appear to spread to the rest of the plant, and its effects are less serious than the two previously described. Phalaenopsis and Vanda are particularly susceptible.

Fungous Diseases. Fungous diseases are many. Anthracnose, a spot disease, is caused by at least thirty-six species of Gloeosporium and Colletotrichum. Other spot diseases are produced by species of Phoma, Macrophoma, Diplodia, Hendersonia, and Cercospora. Rusts are caused by species of Uredo and Puccinia. Rhizome infections are caused by Phytophthora and Fusarium, and a heart and leaf rot by Phytophthera. A root infection that causes wilt is produced by *Sclerotium rolfsii.*

The anthracnose of Gloeosporium and Colletotrichum are sometimes quite mild, affecting only a few plants or even just a leaf or two, but occasionally the infection assumes serious aspects. Cattleya, Paphiopedilum, Epidendrum, Cymbidium, Vanda, Coelogyne, Laelia, Odontoglossum, Phalaenopsis, and other genera are susceptible to this type of disease. Infection is favored by excessive moisture and temperature and insufficient light. The leaves develop circular or oval, sunken spots, that are reddish-brown at first, becoming dark brown or gray with age. The spots enlarge, taking on a crater-like appearance, and frequently coalesce. As the spots increase in number, they may kill the whole leaf. Pseudobulbs may be similarly infected, and destroyed in severe cases. Minute dark pustules exuding pink or yellowish oily droplets under damp conditions sometimes appear in concentric circles on old spots and give rise to spores.

A leaf die-back is caused by *Glomerella cincta.* The infection starts at the tip and spreads toward the base of the leaf, involving the whole width of the leaf. There is a marked line of distinction between the diseased and the healthy area. The infected area turns soft and brown, later drying.

Rhizome infections have been reported for many genera. One, called the "black rot" of orchids, is caused by a pythiaceous (soil dwelling) fungus that attacks the rhizome. It kills the tissues and spreads rapidly into the green parts of the plant. It has been found in Cattleya, Epidendrum, Oncidium, Laelia, Vanda, Stanhopea, and possibly others.

A serious rot that starts in the heart of the plant where the leaves join the stem, and spreads upward through the leaves, is caused by *Phytophthera omnivora.* This fungus is related to the one that infects the potato, and which ruined the potato crop in Ireland in 1845, causing the famine that killed some 250,000 people. *Phytophthera omnivora* infection of orchids begins with the appearance of dark, sharply delimited lesions in the very heart of the plant. The infected area spreads rapidly, until within a few days the entire leaf is discolored and falls off. In severe cases the infection spreads from the heart to new leaves formed after the older ones have fallen. In milder instances, the infection may be confined to one of the older leaves, especially if the plant is kept dry. The disease spreads rapidly from plant to plant, injuring especially the highly susceptible Vandas, but also infecting Cattleya and other genera. Young seedlings are very liable to infection. Moist, warm conditions favor its spread. Another species of fungus, *Phytophthera palmivora,* has been isolated from Dendrobium in Ceylon and Vanda and Cattleya in Java.

Orchid "wilt," caused by penetration of the root collar by *Sclerotium rolfsii,* has been reported a number of times. Under humid conditions it rapidly spreads to the leaves and kills them. Cymbidium, Paphiopedilum, and many other genera are affected. A good method of control is to immerse the diseased plants in 0.1% Ceresan for 15 minutes. Stronger solutions (even 0.25%) will injure the plant.

A disease that destroys young seedlings, particularly those just out of the flask, is produced by the "damping-off" fungus, various species of Pythium. If one plant in a community pot becomes infected (turns brown and dies) the disease may soon spread to the others. Removal of the diseased plant is the first step in control, followed by weekly spraying with a fungicide. One ounce of Cuprocide 54-Y to a gallon of water has been used with success at Ohio State University. Ventilating the seedling case is a good precaution.

A petal blight, or petal blotch, is caused by *Sclerotinia fuckeliana*. Transparent spots bordered with pink disfigure the flower. Control dictates cutting the flower immediately and burning it, lest the fungus produce spores to infect other flowers.

Rusts, caused by species of Puccinia and Uredo, are characterized by minute spots covered with an orange or yellowish powder, the spores of the causal fungus. If allowed to spread, they can cause damage to a wide variety of orchids, one result of which is failure to flower.

Under humid conditions green sheaths are sometimes attacked by a fungus that causes brown spots to appear, and eventually the whole sheath to decay. The fungus may also destroy the flower buds. The sheaths should be treated at the first appearance of spots in order to save the developing flowers. Dust the sheath with powdered sulfur, or sponge with mercuric chloride, 1 to 1000. Give close attention to ventilation, and cease syringing. Be sure that the sheath does not go into the night wet. If the sheath deteriorates, shine a flashlight behind it to see where the flower buds are and cut it off just above them. Dust buds and sheath with sulfur.

A sheath that simply dries without producing flowers should not be cut off, even if it acquires little black spots. Any dead plant tissue may be invaded by saprophytic fungi. These differ from parasitic fungi in that they do not harm living plants. They will develop on fallen leaves, or any parts of plants that are cut off and allowed to remain moist. They may also invade dead parts of a plant, for instance an area killed by sun burn, a dead pseudo-bulb that is not removed, or a sheath that dies from natural causes. The black mottling that appears on dried sheaths is a saprophytic fungus and will not harm any flower buds that may develop later.

Virus Disease. A mosaic disease caused by a virus has been reported on Cymbidiums in New South Wales, where it is called the "black disease." The younger leaves are flecked and streaked with yellow, followed by the development of black spots and streaks. Growth is retarded. A species of Dendrobium has been found to bear similar lesions, and other genera are undoubtedly susceptible to this virus. A virus infection is never localized, as are bacterial and fungous diseases. A virus affects the whole plant.

COLOR PLATE 9. Miltonia Marietta Armacost.

Any divisions of an infected plant will also carry the disease. Virus infection often shows up in streaked and mottled flowers. A virus mosaic disease has just been reported in Cattleyas. It causes mottling of the color in flowers and mosaic effects in leaves. Work is continuing on this disease but it has been found that the virus can be transmitted by aphids.

PESTS

Some of the insects that once were a nuisance in orchid houses are hardly ever seen nowadays. Routine quarantine, inspection, and fumigation at the port of entry have largely done away with the dread Cattleya fly and Dendrobium weevil. Before quarantine, these insects were imported with the plants, and growers used to fight a constant battle against them. It is wise to be on the lookout for them, since they have not been completely eradicated. We do not have to worry about them, however, for the DDT and Parathion sprays have proved completely effective against them.

DDT is also effective against other insect pests prevalent in a greenhouse— scale, sow bugs, cockroaches, thrips, and garden insects that gain access. DDT is not effective against red spider, Collembola, or slugs, and other methods must be used for their control.

The Cattleya fly, *Isosoma orchidearum,* is a minute black, wasp-like fly, about ⅛ of an inch long. It lays its eggs in new growths and sometimes in pseudobulbs, causing swollen places to appear. The larvae are protected within the plant and are not reached by ordinary sprays. DDT, by its residual effect, kills the new flies after they hatch out, but it is well to cut out the swollen places to get the larvae and prevent their destructive feasting.

The Dendrobium weevil, *Diorymerellus laevimargo,* also called the orchid beetle or the orchid weevil, is a very small, shiny black beetle that lays its eggs in root tips, particularly of Cattleyas. The developing larvae eat the root tissue, causing the root to die back. The adult beetles feed on leaves and flowers of any and all genera, seriously checking the growth of the plants and spoiling the blooms for enjoyment or sale. The beetle can slip into the opening sheath and do its work unseen. DDT kills prevalent adults and also the young beetles as they emerge.

Scale is a chronic enemy of orchids. The tiny, sucking insects cover them- selves with a shell-like secretion, similar to an oyster shell in appearance. The young scale insects hatch out in a fluffy deposit and then crawl around on the plant to find a permanent location, where they settle down and cover themselves with their shell. Since they suck the plant juice, large numbers of them can do serious harm. Yellow mottling appears where scale is at work, and even areas may be killed. Scale may attack any part of the plant, leaves, pseudobulbs, or dormant eyes. The thin coverings of pseudobulbs and rhizomes often harbor large colonies of scale insects, so that for the good of the plant it is well to remove these from mature bulbs. They also hide in the

Boisduval's scale on pseudobulbs of a Cattleya plant.
(Courtesy of University of Maryland)

axils of the leaves, and on their under sides. Most scales are whitish or brownish, and the insect itself is about ⅟₂₅ of an inch in diameter. Some are larger, and occasionally a soft black scale is found that is over a quarter of an inch long. The species of scale most commonly represented is *Diaspis*

Scale on the underside of a Paphiopedilum leaf. (Courtesy of University of Maryland)

Boisduvali. DDT is effective against all species of scale. It requires several treatments at three- to four-week intervals to kill all mature scale protected by shells, after which spraying at six-month intervals is sufficient. The young crawling stage is killed by the coating of DDT on the plant. The emulsion type of spray (see below) even penetrates the coverings of pseudobulbs to kill the scale beneath.

Thrips are extremely small, slender insects, wingless in some stages, varying in size from $\frac{1}{50}$ to $\frac{1}{16}$ of an inch in length. They move rapidly, and hide at the slightest jarring of the plant, so that often their presence is not suspected. They particularly damage young seedlings, flowers, and new growths. They tear the epidermis and suck the plant juices, and, working in

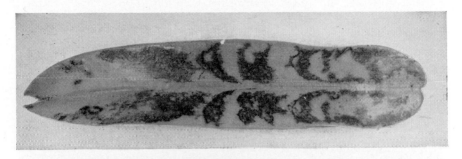

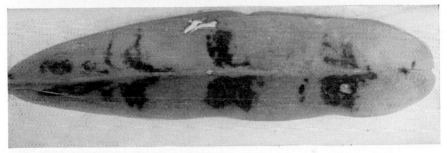

Thrip injury on Cattleya leaves. (Courtesy of University of Maryland)

a circular area, cause unsightly white or brown blotches. *Physothrips xanthius* and *Euthrips orchidii* are varieties that frequently occur. DDT is effective against thrips, but cannot be used on buds or flowers. Therefore, if thrip has not already been eradicated, the flower buds may be treated with a rotenone spray.

Sow bugs are prevalent in most large greenhouses and may be imported into yours. They are armadillo-like creatures that close end to end when disturbed. They feed on young root tips, and therefore check plant growth. Cockroaches, or any chewing beetles, do considerable damage. These are killed by DDT.

DDT may be used in plain water solution, or in water mixed with soap, or in an emulsion. The water solution is made by using 1 pound of 50%

wettable powder to 100 gallons of water, or 1 ounce to 6.25 gallons. If you desire, a small amount of soap may be added as a spreader.

The DDT emulsion is made up as a stock solution, a small amount of which is added to water for spraying. For 1 quart of stock solution, dissolve 189.25 grams of DDT (technical grade) in 567.75 c.c. of xylol (purified xylene) and shake thoroughly. Then add 189.25 c.c. of Triton B-1956 (a Rohm and Haas product) emulsifier, and stir thoroughly until mixed. For the first spraying, add 80 c.c. of this stock solution to one gallon of water, and cut this down to 40 c.c. to one gallon for subsequent spraying. The emulsion DDT spray has been thoroughly tested at the University of Maryland and by many growers. A satisfactory commercial preparation is put out by the Fennell Orchid Company.

When DDT is used, one spraying seems to check thrip, weevil, and other insects. However two or three applications may be necessary to eliminate scale. After the first course of spraying, it is not necessary or desirable to spray except at intervals of six months. Any new plants received should be isolated and sprayed before incorporating them in your collection.

DDT spraying should be done only when the plants have been recently watered.

There are many brands of DDT on the market. Unless they have been tried by orchid growers they should be used cautiously, in exact dilutions, and tried on a few plants first. Commercial products should always be used in the weakest dilutions recommended.

The older nicotine sprays have been used for years with a great deal of success, and, while they do not give complete eradication as does DDT, they are still recommended. Spraying must be done at more frequent intervals, possibly once a week or every ten days, certainly every two weeks. Caution: Cyanide fumigation is very injurious to orchids and therefore cannot be used.

Red spider (also called spider mite) an arachnoid, Tetranychus, is particularly troublesome on thin leaved orchids such as Cymbidiums. It thrives under warm, dry conditions and is almost automatically controlled by lower temperatures, higher humidity and frequent syringing. Red spider is very tiny, lives usually on the under side of leaves, and protects itself and its eggs by a fine web. It sucks the plant juice, producing little white spots, and undermines the normal activities of the leaf. Bad infestations may kill the leaves. Red spider will attack the flowers on plants, such as Cattleyas, whose leaves do not appeal to them. Where it is not possible to control red spider by lowering the temperature, they may be controlled by sprays containing rotenone or Parathion (see below), coupled with frequent syringing.

Collembola, the common springtail, can be injurious to orchids if present in any considerable numbers. It is a small wingless insect, with a segmented body and a forked appendage at its rear end by means of which it can jump several inches. It lives in the potting medium, on the benches, and on the ground. Its usual diet is decaying vegetable matter, but it will attack the tender parts of orchid plants. The injury consists of minute punctures on leaves, new growths, flower parts, and root tips. The latter may die back as a result. Collembola is not killed by DDT, and is only mildly sensitive to nicotine and rotenone. After the use of DDT in a greenhouse, the Collembola rapidly multiply, often literally into swarms. Their increase is possibly due to the extermination by DDT of some carnivorous insect that normally preys upon them.

The only truly effective method of control found so far is the extremely poisonous Parathion, which is so deadly to human beings and other warm-blooded animals that it must be used only with utmost caution. **Parathion is poisonous if inhaled, swallowed, or absorbed through the skin.** The user must wear a gas mask or some sort of respirator, fairly impenetrable clothing, rubber gloves, and a covering over head and neck. He must clean his equipment carefully after spraying, and wash himself thoroughly. House plants must be put out-of-doors for treatment. The residue of Parathion on the plants is effective for a week or more, and hands should be washed if plants are handled during this period.

A number of sprays containing Parathion are available under various trade names. Directions for dilution should be followed carefully. Parathion is also effective against red spider, thrip, and a host of other insects. Because of its effectiveness, Parathion need be used only at intervals of several months.

Slugs, naked or shell-less snails, cause a great deal of damage. Their mouth parts are composed of a series of rasps. They eat young leaves, flower buds, root tips, and the covering of young roots. One slug can mow down a whole pot of seedlings in an evening, or can destroy several flowers at a time. They leave a trail of slime, by which they can often be located. Although they usually work at night, they are often seen on the plants in the daytime. Their chief hiding places are just under the rim or on the bottom of the pot, or within the surface of the fibre. Hand picking at night with a flashlight is a good way for a hobbyist to net a few dozen and, incidentally, is one of the best means of control. Poison bait, commercial preparations containing a good proportion of metaldehyde, or made at home of bran, molasses and white arsenic or Paris green, should be scattered on the ground and on the benches. Paris green may be placed on slices of apple or sweet potato and laid on the fibre in the pots. These should be removed before watering. The slugs breed in the ground under the benches and if the ground can be kept dry for a few days, a sprinkling of lime will kill a large number of slugs. To protect flower buds, wrap cotton around the stem or the base of the pseudo-bulb.

Rats and mice can wreak havoc in a greenhouse. Mice can climb up a strong stem and eat flower buds, and both rats and mice will nibble on new growths and roots. A few traps set here and there are a good precaution, particularly when the nights get cold in the fall and field mice are seeking shelter.

Chapter XVIII

HOUSING YOUR ORCHIDS

Orchids are almost as adaptable as people. Under shelter, they may grow wherever human beings are comfortable. In gardens where there is no danger of freezing, they may camp out with your other garden plants. However, a family of people remains close to a certain number, between four and ten, we'll say. But your family of orchids will inevitably increase its numbers. For orchids are such intriguing plants that to grow a few usually creates the desire to have more.

A prospective orchid grower should be forewarned by the experience of many an amateur grower. The few plants on a window sill or in a glass case soon expand into a small lean-to greenhouse. This in time becomes crowded and has to have an addition. Again, cramped quarters lead to a regular greenhouse, and then, where first there was one there soon come to be two. Some of the present-day commercial growers expanded an original lean-to hobby greenhouse into a million square feet of glass.

This last is not necessarily the aim or fate of everyone who comes to love orchids. But it points to the suggestion that if your hobby reaches greenhouse proportions, build on the generous side. Compared to a window sill, a greenhouse that is six by six seems large and roomy at first. But if you acquire any number of seedlings, this space is soon filled to overflowing.

GREENHOUSES

The general impression that a greenhouse must be quite fancy to be suitable for orchids is entirely erroneous. Any glass enclosed area that is properly lighted, heated, and ventilated will do. Such an area may be simply table space with your other house plants, in which the orchids get along in the environment furnished for your African violets or begonias. Or it may be a glass case, of your own or of commercial design, with its climate automatically regulated. Or it may be a greenhouse, of simple home manufacture or commercially built.

Greenhouse manufacturers have responded to the appeal for home greenhouses with a variety of prefabricated models. These are usually obtainable in units so that you may start as small as you must and expand later to almost any length. Costs may be reduced by being your own plumber, by building your own foundation and walks, and by assembling the greenhouse yourself.

The advantages of a commercially built greenhouse are several, but are

A prefabricated greenhouse, simple to assemble. The removable slat shades can be used in combination with a light skim on the glass or with cheese cloth inside. (Courtesy of Lord and Burnham)

not necessarily advantages that you cannot emulate in building one of your own. Long-lasting materials are used, if wood it is usually cypress or redwood. Provision is made for carrying off water of condensation so that it does not drip on the plants. Ventilators are adequate to the volume of air, and advice is obtainable on methods of heating. The structure is strong, making it wind and weather resistant, and, with proper care, permanent.

A person who has patience, ingenuity, and a knack for picking up second-hand material can build his own greenhouse for very little cost. Greenhouses have been made from all sorts of things—old cold-frame sash, storm windows, windows from razed buildings, with ventilators made from single pane basement windows. Water supply may be furnished inexpensively by means of second-hand pipe attached to outdoor faucets. The hardest part of the installation is digging the ditch to take the pipe down below frost level. Warm water in the winter is obtained by connecting the greenhouse pipe with one from the hot water tank in the home, with a valve that can be turned on by hand when desired.

If you want to build your own greenhouse, it would pay to make a tour of the few home greenhouses in your vicinity, as well as those of professional growers. Study their systems of ventilating, heating, and bench planning, and then try to combine their best features in your own.

HINTS ON STRUCTURE AND PLANNING

Home built greenhouses exhibit such a wide variety of shapes, sizes, and materials that it is not possible to describe all the possibilities. There are, however, some ideals to strive for which should form a basis for your plans.

A lean-to should face the south. This will give the plants the longest pos-

Another prefabricated type of home greenhouse. (Courtesy of Lord and Burnham)

sible exposure to sunlight under the circumstances. An enclosed porch on the south side of the house can be made to substitute for a lean-to. Ideally, a regular greenhouse should run north and south, whether attached to an existing building or built separately. The north-south exposure gives the plants more even light from dawn to sunset. However, if your plans would be best suited by having the greenhouse run east-west, or at an angle, be assured that it will still function adequately.

The foundation may be of wood, brick, cinder blocks, or concrete, 2 or 3 feet high. Where wood other than cypress is used, it should be treated against decay with some such preparation as cuprinol. Do not use creosote in connection with a greenhouse.

The panes of glass should be separated by narrow bars to afford the maximum amount of light. In some types of wood construction, the necessarily wider bars are offset by wider panes. The beautiful curved-eave greenhouses associated with conservatories are expensive, not only in original cost, but in replacement. The less costly straight-eaved kind are simple to build and repair, and are almost as good looking.

The length and width of your greenhouse is a matter of choice. A very small greenhouse has certain disadvantages which are not present in slightly larger ones. One of these is the difficulty of maintaining an even temperature. The small volume of air changes temperature too quickly. A mere whiff of heat from the heaters, or the emergence of the sun from behind a cloud, sends the temperature up. Similarly, the air cools off rapidly. This should not discourage growers for whom a small greenhouse is the only possibility, but means that careful attention should be given it at all times.

Perhaps an ideal size for a home greenhouse would be 12 to 15 feet wide and 12 to 20 feet long. The 12-foot width allows two side benches and a center bench. In a narrower greenhouse, you might have a central walk with benches only at the sides. Watch out that you do not have the side benches so wide that you knock over plants trying to reach those in the back. The walks may be of concrete, brick, or cinders. The ground under the benches is left plain, or filled with gravel. A complete concrete floor is not recommended.

Heating Systems

The time tested method of heating greenhouses is the use of hot water circulating in pipes. An even temperature is maintained, with the warm pipes radiating some heat after the valve is closed and until it is opened again. Hot water may be brought to the greenhouse from the boiler used to heat your home. The pipes are best placed against the foundation walls, and the plants immediately above them protected by a deflecting board over the pipes. The greenhouse may be heated by an individual boiler if you do not have this system in your home, but this is rather expensive.

Natural gas heaters, although not as satisfactory as hot water, are used by many small growers. You must be sure that your supply of gas is 100% natural gas, as any admixture of artificial gas is fatal to plants. There is even the chance, with pure natural gas, that fumes, perhaps from incomplete combustion, may occasionally cause injury to flowers. This may show up during particularly bitter weather when the heaters are kept running full force in order to maintain the desired temperature. Under such conditions, watch the ventilation carefully, and check the flames to see that there is no yellow flame present (an indication of incomplete combustion). It may be necessary when ice seals up the greenhouse, to leave a ventilator open a crack. This is a real problem in windy weather, but one to which you should give careful attention.

Unless the gas heaters are carefully regulated, or have a sensitive thermostat, the temperature tends to fluctuate a bit too much. There is also the danger of unknowingly putting out a heater with the hose and incurring the danger of an explosion. Under-bench sprayers should be arranged so that the water will not be directed into the burner.

Oil burners come in the same class with gas heaters. They are cheaper than a separate boiler and stoker unit for the greenhouse, and may be used where natural gas is not available. Directions for their care should be followed for best results.

Where electric rates are cheap, electric heaters may be used, equipped with a fan to blow the air across the heating element. These would probably be most useful in mild climates, or as auxiliary heat, but might be too expensive in cold regions.

In all cases it is advantageous to have the heat thermostatically controlled. A high-low alarm is suggested, to warn the owner of a breakdown of the system on a cold night or of suddenly soaring temperatures. The mechanism is installed in the greenhouse and connected with a bell in the dwelling.

For advice on the amount of pipe or number of heaters necessary for the greenhouse you plan, consult a local heating expert. If you buy a prefabricated model, the manufacturer will advise you.

BENCHES

The pots must have free circulation of air around and under them. This may be achieved in a simple manner by making the bench of heavy hardware cloth (wire mesh) stretched over a strong frame. The wire mesh stays clean and is impervious to the growth of moss or fungi. Another method is to make the bench of narrow boards placed edgewise. Iron grill may also be used. Solid benches do not allow as good aeration of the bottoms of the pots. Growers who use solid benches usually raise the pots up from its surface. The pots stand on other pots turned upside down, or are held by wire frames.

For most purposes, flat benches are best for a small greenhouse. You will see another type frequently used, however—a bench built in steps. Those who like this kind feel that it gives each plant better aeration and more complete lighting. In large greenhouses, where stepped up benches are built quite high, special walks must be built at various levels in order to enable the workers to reach the plants. In a small greenhouse, however, the narrower benches might consist of three or four steps, and be quite easy to care for. If you are tempted to try this type of benching, be sure that one bench does not cut off the morning or afternoon light from the others.

For permanence, concrete posts or iron pipe make ideal bench supports.

But wood (cypress or treated two-by-fours) may certainly be used and is used widely. The height of your benches should be planned for your greatest convenience and for the benefit of the plants. A low bench, close to the ground, is usually a few degrees cooler than one twice its height. You may want to have one bench lower than the others for plants that require cooler temperatures. In any case, plan them so that you can water and weed with ease.

VENTILATORS

For most orchids, ridge ventilators are best. They allow exchange of air with a minimum amount of draft, and often need not be supplemented with additional openings. Side ventilators may be useful for some kinds of orchids, Cymbidiums, for instance, which can stand a good bit of air movement. Some experts advocate ventilators in the walls under the benches for use in very hot weather. The latter will admit the cooler ground air without bringing it directly into contact with the plants.

The top ventilators should be opened only on the lee side in windy weather. The air then passes across the opening, drawing out the air from the greenhouse. Either cold or hot air blowing directly on the plants through a windward ventilator is harmful. To keep the air in the greenhouse fresh and buoyant, the top ventilators should be open whenever possible, even if only a crack in cold weather.

In hot, dry weather, however, particular caution must be exercised. A check with the thermometer will show that having the ventilators open their full amount may not reduce the inside temperature any more than having them open only a few inches, or at best will give only 2 or 3 degrees of relief. At the same time, the greenhouse air may become dangerously dry. A compromise must be worked out, and for this it helps to have a humidity indicator as well as a thermometer. Find out what size opening gives the best temperature and humidity control. Frequent damping down will often accomplish more toward a cooler house than wide open ventilators. Syringing the glass directly also helps.

As the nights become cool, close the ventilators before the temperature drops to the night level. The greenhouse should cool off slowly. In some localities, the air cools off rapidly as soon as the sun sets. In these regions, the best method is to close the ventilators soon enough to retain some of the sun heat so that the greenhouse stays warm through the early evening hours. Then, as the greenhouse cools, turn on the heat when necessary to keep the temperature from falling too suddenly to the night level. Similarly, let the greenhouse warm up in the morning before turning off the heat and open-ing the ventilators.

HUMIDITY

Except perhaps in the very humid regions of this country, more atmos-pheric moisture must be provided than that contained naturally in the air. A light syringing of the plants on bright days is part of the control of humidity. But the plants must not be kept dangerously wet in order to keep the atmosphere damp. The air is better kept moist by wetting the walks, the ground under the benches, and the benches between the pots. This may be accomplished by going down the walks several times a day with a mist nozzle attached to the hose or by installing sprayers under the benches. The sprayers may be allowed to run as often and as long as necessary. The syring-ing of the plants may be accomplished by hand, or by a set of overhead sprayers. The latter should be turned on for only short intervals, once or twice a day. Over a long period of time they put out a considerable quantity of water and may actually soak your plants instead of just wetting the foliage.

As has been said many times, the plants should have dry foliage by evening. Also, since the atmospheric humidity rises naturally at night, sprayers must be turned off and hand damping discontinued at least by late afternoon.

In some greenhouses you will see other arrangements for supplying atmospheric moisture. Trays suspended 6 inches or a foot under the benches may contain water, or may be filled with coke or gravel which is dampened from time to time. On solid benches where the pots are raised in some manner, coke may be scattered to give additional evaporating surfaces. Adoption of such additional methods is a matter of personal choice.

SHADING

Most commercial growers shade their greenhouses by means of a white shading compound sprayed on the glass. This is entirely satisfactory and may be used for small greenhouses. White shading compounds are put out by many greenhouse suppliers, with directions for their use. A simple com-pound to make yourself is white lead mixed with gasoline to the desired consistency. Mix some and try it out on a section of glass, and modify it as you need. Whitewash is also usable. The shading must be heavier in the summer than in the winter, and modified for spring and fall. Often it can be removed entirely during December and January.

Roller blinds are highly recommended for small greenhouses. The slats allow a moving pattern of light to fall on the plants. Roller blinds may be particularly useful in areas that have long spells of dull weather where it would be desirable to have no white shading on the glass. The plants could then have all the light afforded them by clear glass in dull weather, and the

blinds could be lowered during occasional bright spells. During the summer in most regions it is necessary to have a thin skim of shading on the glass even when roller blinds are used.

Cloth shading inside of the greenhouse has many uses. It may be used as spot shading for groups of plants such as newly potted plants or young seedlings, or for genera that require less light. Some growers use cloth shading entirely. A cheap grade of muslin is perhaps the best. Cheesecloth is useful in some cases, but several layers are necessary during the summer. Wires may be stretched from eave to eave and the cloth laid upon them, with curtains of muslin that may be rolled up or down at the sides.

Roller blinds are used to shade this prefabricated lean-to greenhouse. (Courtesy of Lord and Burnham)

ADDITIONAL SPACE

Some kinds of orchids should be grown in suspended pots or baskets. Pot hangers may be bought or can be made simply by bending a loop in one end of a piece of heavy wire to fit around the pot and curving the other end into a hook.

When the benches become too crowded, Cattleyas and many other kinds may be suspended. The hangers may be hooked over the greenhouse braces, or a pipe may be run the length of the greenhouse for the purpose. Chicken wire stretched across the end walls makes this space available, and the resulting display of plants is quite decorative.

Hanging plants dry out faster than those on the bench, due partly to the somewhat higher temperature in the upper part of the greenhouse and partly to the freer circulation of air. Therefore, they must be watered more frequently, perhaps every day in bright weather. If they are placed directly above the benches, care must be exercised so that the plants under them do not receive too much water in the process.

Shelves may be run the length of the greenhouse near the glass for kinds that like warm sunny positions. Here again care must be taken to see that in watering these plants you do not give an overdose to those below them.

Water

Rain water is considered ideal for orchids. It can be collected from the roof of the dwelling (not from the greenhouse if whitewash is used), and stored in vats. This is reserved for the plants, and tap water is used for damping down.

Most city water is entirely satisfactory for orchids. It is said that water with a *p*H of over 7.3 is not good. This cannot be the only standard, for water with the same *p*H in different regions may have quite different chemical content. In the region from which the author writes, the tap water has a *p*H of 7.4, due to a high calcium and magnesium content, and the orchids thrive on it. If you are in doubt about your city water, you might visit local greenhouses and see how they manage the problem.

Orchids should not be soaked with cold water. The temperature of the water should always be that of the greenhouse air. It is advisable in the winter to have a mixing arrangement so that hot water may be added to bring the temperature of the water to between 50° and 60° F. Or, the water should be stored in a tank in the greenhouse so that it is warm when used.

Automatic Greenhouses

Most of us like to putter around in our greenhouses. The more time we spend with our plants, the better we come to know them. We take a minute while turning on the sprayers or lighting the heaters to glance at the plants and often discover something exciting that had escaped our notice. It is a joy just to take into our lungs the good damp earthy air, and even a greater joy if something fragrant is flowering. We relish the necessity of going out to the greenhouse several times a day, and take pleasure in the hose work and ventilator adjustment.

But there are times when even a housewife, who is supposedly at home all day, cannot give the needed attention to the greenhouse. And if the greenhouse belongs to someone who is gone during the day, it must get along regularly without care for 8 or 9 hours. Occasionally the family wants to take a little vacation, and a willing neighbor is found to officiate at the sprayers and the ventilators. In the absence of a willing neighbor, the family must just stay at home.

On the market today are various kinds of equipment for automatic control of ventilation and humidity, in addition to the usual temperature regulators.

These will, of course, add to the expense of the greenhouse and may not be afforded by all would-be orchid growers. But surely they are a great comfort to greenhouse owners, and merit the consideration of all who need them.

The ventilator controls are thermostatically operated. When the greenhouse temperature goes above a certain point, the ventilators open, and stay

Many features of construction shown in this large greenhouse are adaptable for home greenhouses: the benches built of strips to allow free air circulation; the iron bench supports; the tray of coke under the bench, kept damp to increase humidity; roller blinds combined with white shading on the glass. (Courtesy of Lord and Burnham)

open until the temperature drops back. The size of the opening is pre-set, so that the ventilators respond to the thermostat by opening only to the desired height.

Fairly good humidity control may be had by rigging a time clock to the under-bench sprayer system. You may have the sprayers turned on at certain intervals to run for any length of time you desire, say from 10:00 A.M. to 4:00 P.M., or for half-hour intervals between those hours. You will have to judge what kind of a day it is going to be, and trust that it won't turn cold and rainy while you are gone.

Better humidity control is by means of a humidistat. This may be connected to an existing line of sprayers, to turn them on or off as the humidity rises

COLOR PLATE 10. Orchids in Their Native Habitat.

and falls. Then you may be assured that the atmospheric moisture in the greenhouse will be kept where you want it, and that the sprayers will not run when the weather is not favorable. Available on the market is a handy but more expensive method in the form of a moist air blower run by a humidistat.

ORCHIDS IN YOUR HOME

For all of the pleasure and ease in the possession of a greenhouse, there is nothing quite like having orchids in your home. Those who would experience the thrill of growing orchids, but for whom a greenhouse is out of the question, should certainly try a few along with other house plants.

English, French, and German flower lovers of fifty years ago found no mystery attached to growing orchids in their homes. Somehow in this country the orchid was pigeonholed as a fancier's flower, and since it found a natural place in the conservatories of the wealthy it was assumed that it belonged only there. In the last decade or so, however, people have expressed an unwillingness to leave anything as lovely as orchids to the pleasure of a few. Little greenhouses have sprung up everywhere in the small backyards of the average home owner, witness to the spread of orchid growing across the United States. And apartment dwellers, or people who do not have or want a greenhouse, are not content to leave orchids only to those who do. Orchids are appearing more and more frequently in homes, along with the more familiar house plants. Bay window collections number any where from two or three to twenty-five or more plants.

Often orchids thrive in the same environment as other plants, with only the bare precautions of supplying them with extra humidity and with the proper light. By watching the foliage, you can tell whether the plant has enough, too much, or too little light. A little patience will find the right location for the plant, even though it may have to live in a bedroom. In general, a south window should do, with the plant placed far enough from the glass so as not to get the intense solar heat. An east window is perhaps ideal for young seedlings, which would then receive the cool morning sun, and subdued light for the rest of the day.

Extra humidity may be furnished partly by a gentle syringing of the foliage once or twice a day. The pot itself may be placed over (not in) water in a saucer. A wire frame might be made as a stand for the plant by bending down the edges of a piece of hardware cloth. Hardware cloth might be fastened over a large pan of water on which several pots could sit. The pots should not be plunged in wet gravel, as there is a tendency for water to collect in the gravel without being noticed. Also aeration is less complete.

The care of orchids in the home follows the general rules described for greenhouse plants. Watering may have to be more frequent in the drier atmosphere. Keep them free from pests by an occasional nicotine spray, or by a DDT spray twice a year.

There are many kinds that you might try in your home. Choose those that thrive with moderate temperature and humidity, not the cool or the very warm growing ones. Paphiopedilums are well suited to home culture, as are Cattleyas and Laelias and the smaller Epidendrums, Dendrobiums, and Oncidiums. Variety may be added by selections from such genera as Brassia, Coelogyne, Lycaste, and from many of the botanicals whose size and requirements fit them for your purpose.

An orchid case gives the plants a humid environment. Top and bottom ventilators prevent air stagnation. A pan of water under the grill supplies humidity. (Courtesy of Clint McDade and Sons)

Orchid Cases

In a home where the atmosphere is particularly hot and dry, such as it is in many apartments, it might be well to protect orchid plants by enclosing them in a ventilated case that has added humidity. Such a case is not limited to the home, for men who hate to part from their orchids every day often keep a few plants in cases in their offices.

Cases for orchids are descended from the famous Wardian case, invented by N. B. Ward in about 1836. Its purpose was for the safe transportation of living plants on ocean voyages. It was nearly airtight, and literally sealed the plants in a humid atmosphere, safe from salt spray and foul gases. Many a sea captain of those days carried a garden with him in his cabin in a Wardian case.

The cases of today, familiarly called Wardian cases, are equipped with ventilation. The orchid case pictured is put out by a leading orchid grower and is an excellent type. It has top and bottom ventilators, and the sliding front section may be opened when desired. The plants stand on a grill over a pan of water. The population in this case can be varied. Seedlings may be added and other plants of a suitable size. A selection can be made from the list given above. Choose plants of like requirements so that they will live together well in the same case.

Ventilation is as important with an orchid case as with a greenhouse. This is particularly true when sheaths appear and flowers are formed. Some of the troubles reported by people who have orchid cases are traceable to too much humidity and too close an atmosphere. Such troubles are usually in the form of sheaths turning black, and flowers becoming spotted and spoiling rapidly. Open the ventilators for a while each day, during the warmest part or when the orchids are receiving the most light.

Home orchid growers are as handy at inventing cases as they are at building their own greenhouses. An old-fashioned glass-front china cabinet with its back replaced with glass makes a good case. By adjusting the shelves, you can have some tall and some short plants in it. I have even seen a store showcase converted for orchids. With a little paint to cover its sanitary white, a doctor's instrument cabinet may be made into an orchid case. In all of these, it is necessary to add some sort of pan to hold water.

Orchids in a Florida garden. The plants are grown in coconut shells or baskets fastened to the trees. In this group are Cattleyas, Phalaenopsis, Dendrobiums, Oncidiums, *Renanthera coccinea* and *Vanda caerulea*. (Courtesy of H. F. Loomis)

Flasks of seedlings, sown in the kitchen, will thrive in an orchid case. They should not have as bright light as older plants, so perhaps might need a separate case. Humidity is important to prevent the agar from drying out. When the seedlings are ready to be transplanted, community pots may take the place of the flasks, and the seedlings may be grown on to flowering size in the same case. As the seedlings require more light, move the case to a brighter spot, and adjust the ventilation to the needs of the maturing plants.

Orchids in Your Garden

Here and there throughout the descriptions of the genera you will come across kinds that may be grown out-of-doors or that may be moved into your garden in the summertime. Not all of us are as fortunate in our climate as those who live in Florida and parts of California, where orchids may be fastened into the trees, or grown among other plants on the ground. But there is no reason why some of us should not hang a few plants in the trees at least for part of the year. And it is even necessary to do so with some of the cooler growing kinds.

Our native orchids, of course, can be a regular part of the garden. There are numerous genera of these which will be found in the key in the Appendix. Catalogues of hardy orchids are obtainable from nursery specialists and often these contain growing suggestions.

In climates that are warm and humid all year round, gardens may be decorated with Laelias, Vandas, Phalaenopsis, Dendrobiums, Epidendrums, Cattleyas, Oncidiums, and many other genera. Cymbidiums require uniformly temperate weather but cannot stand as high temperatures as the foregoing.

The many ways in which orchids can be grown in this country suggest that we forget our former shyness of this wonderful plant family and grow them with the same abandon that we do geraniums. The marvelous variety offers an endlessly interesting hobby. And if we do not go as far as to make them a hobby in themselves, a few orchids among our house plants increase the thrill of growing green things in the home. A little love, a little care, and the orchids almost seem to grow themselves. Their reward to you for that little attention is some of the finest, the most delicately contrived and beautifully formed, and the most unusually colored flowers known in this world. What more could you ask for the expenditure of a few dollars and a few hours?

Chapter XIX

THE CARE AND USE OF CUT FLOWERS

Even if at first you cannot bear to cut an orchid while it is still fresh, there will come a time when you will want some to wear, to use in a bouquet, to give to a friend, or even to sell. Because of their good keeping qualities, orchids make wonderful corsages that can be worn to one event after another. And because they are in demand commercially, most small growers can find a florist who will be glad to buy an occasional few. Thus an amateur can enjoy his flowers for a few days and then turn them into dollars for the support or expansion of his hobby.

The beauty of growing your own orchids lies in the possibility of having the plants to cherish and the flowers to enjoy in any number of ways.

MAKING CORSAGES

The larger orchids make attractive corsages when only one is used at a time. The smaller ones may be used in groups of two or three, or as a dainty spray if they are very tiny. A single large Cattleya is about as much as most women can wear without seeming to be overdressed, but for special occasions, two medium sized ones make an elegant corsage. A single Cymbidium or Cypripedium makes a neat, tailored corsage that can be worn with a suit or other daytime attire and is no less lovely when worn with an evening gown. For more elaborate corsages, Cymbidiums and Cypripediums may be made up two or three together. Among the dozens of orchids described in this book, there are many that would make outstanding corsages, all the more desirable for being unusual. Imagine the comment of your friends if you appeared wearing a *Peristeria elata,* an *Oncidium splendidum,* or a *Diacrium bicornutum,* or their wonder at a few velvety Miltonias or lacy Odontoglossums.

When you grow your own orchids, you can design the corsages according to your own whims and fancies.

The flowers should be cut only after they have been open 48 hours or so. Colored blooms should reach their richest hue, white ones should have lost all traces of their early green or creamy tinge. At the peak of perfection the

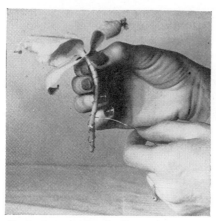

Beginning at the back of the flower, wrap the stem to the end with pliable wire. Then wrap it back in spiral fashion.

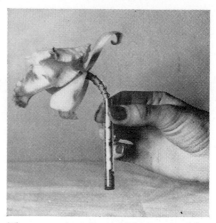

The novocain tube used here to supply water to the flower may be replaced with damp cotton if necessary, or wet chenille wire could have been used.

Wrap the stem and tube with Flora-tape.

Form the bow in your fingers. Twist the ribbon between thumb and forefinger to make the loops keep their position.

fragrant ones will smell their sweetest. With a razor blade, cut the flower from the plant, leaving as long a stem as possible. Bring it into the house and, holding the stem under water, cut off a tiny slice from the end. This prevents air bubbles from entering the cells, and enables the stem to take up water more efficiently. Then put the flower in water in a narrow necked vase so

Gather the loops in the center in a twist of fine wire. Leave enough wire to fasten the bow to the orchid.

Before fastening the bow to the stem, tie a bit of ribbon around the tube with a firm knot at the back. This will give something through which to put the corsage pin. Then fasten on the bow, and your corsage is complete.

Ready for wearing, each with bow designed to suit its proportions, are, left to right, *Cattleya Trianaei, Odontoglossum grande,* a hybrid Cymbidium, and the hybrid *Paphiopedilum Leander.*

that the water does not touch the flower itself. Set it in a cool (50° F.), shaded place until you are ready for it. A pop bottle is a good container, in lieu of a vase.

A tiny glass tube of water may be placed on the stem to keep the flower fresh while it is being worn. Any small tube will do, a novocain tube from

your dentist, a tiny medicine bottle, or a piece of glass tubing sealed at one
end. If the tube is obviously not decorative it may be covered with ribbon,
but a plain little tube is often no detriment to the appearance of a corsage.
Orchid shipping tubes are too large, but some companies put out small wearing tubes, which have a rubber stopper pierced with a hole for the stem.

Corsage-making kits are available from supply houses. They contain wires
of various thickness, ribbons, pins, and the all-important Flora-tape. This is
waxed crepe paper that is sticky and elastic, used for winding around the
stem and for covering the top of the water tube to prevent spilling.

There are a number of ways to make up a corsage. The brittle stem must
be reinforced with wire unless a wearing tube is to be used. Wrap the wire
around the stem in a spiral manner. In lieu of a water tube a thin layer of
damp cotton placed around the stem helps keep the flower fresh, or wet
chenille-covered wire (a pipe cleaner if you do not have the florist's product).
If a tube is used, the stem is placed in it as far as it will go, being certain
that the top of the tube does not pinch the stem.

Now stem and wire, or stem and tube, are covered with Flora-tape. Place
one end of the tape on the back of the stem just where it joins the flower.
Now turn the flower with one hand, and with the other press the tape to
the stem and pull on it at the same time to make it stick tightly. Wind
several thicknesses at the point where flower joins stem, and then wrap it in
spiral manner to the end of the stem or tube, turn, and wrap it back up the
length of the stem. This gives a waterproof coating to the stem, and at the
same time covers the unsightly wire.

An orchid really needs no decoration, but most people feel that the addition of a bit of ribbon completes the dressing of the flower. A very simple
bow of only two, possibly three or four, double loops of ribbon is enough.
It is a shame to see an orchid so highly dressed that the ribbon is more
conspicuous than the flower. The ribbon may blend with the tones of the
flower, or perhaps a happy contrast in color may be found. The bow is made
by forming the loops over your fingers and then gathering the ribbon in
tightly with a fine wire. The ends of the wire serve to fasten the bow to the
stem.

When a corsage is to be made of several small flowers, it is usually best to
separate them and wrap each stem individually. Delicate stems are likely to
break at the back of the flower and should have a wire forced up through
the stem and into the column. The ends of the wrapping wire are allowed
to extend longer than the stem, and then stem and wire are wrapped with
Flora-tape. The flowers are then arranged in whatever way you wish, each

facing front, and the stems are wired together. After they have been joined, the individual flowers may be turned to give the most effective design. Perhaps a group of small flowers may be made to follow the neckline of a dress, or one flower may stand on the shoulder while the others descend in a graceful curve. There is no limit to what can be done with a spray corsage, and your own ingenuity will produce many lovely arrangements. A spray to be worn in the hair should be light as a feather and may be wired to a comb or a barette to make it secure. Any group of small orchids is more effective when each flower stands alone in airy grace. A jammed up bunch looks awkward and hides the beauty of the flowers.

A single flower is most attractive worn right side up, as it grows. When several blooms are used in a corsage, the central one should be right side up, and the others may be turned to make a tasteful design. When you put on the corsage, let the pin go through the ribbon, not through the stem.

KEEPING THE CORSAGE

After you have worn your corsage, you will want to keep it fresh for another time. The flowers should be kept in a refrigerator, at a temperature not lower than 45° F. Cattleyas keep beautifully in an airtight container, without being placed in water. The whole corsage may be laid on a bed of wax paper in a large-mouthed jar with a tight lid. A good procedure is to put the jar in the refrigerator when you put on your orchid, so that it will be cool when you are ready for it. As you put your corsage in it, take off the lid and blow into the jar, so that a film of water vapor covers its sides. Then quickly lay the corsage on the shredded wax paper (to prevent contact with the cold glass), replace the lid, and return the jar to the refrigerator. The moisture retained in the jar is enough to keep the flower fresh for ten days to two weeks. It must be remembered that some individual flowers keep longer than others, so if you have one that lasts only a few days, perhaps the next one will keep better. I have seen a friend wearing an orchid in pretty fair shape as long as a month after I had given it to her.

Cymbidiums, and perhaps some other kinds, seem to keep better if they are allowed to stand in water in the refrigerator. From time to time a thin slice should be removed from the end of the stem and the water changed. This necessitates removing the trimmings of the corsage. It is better to let the orchid stand free in the water than to leave the wearing tube on it.

A flower that is a little wilted can sometimes be revived by tying a wire to its water tube and suspending tube and orchid upside down in the refrigerator. Do not allow the flower to touch any object in the refrigerator.

Orchids as Decorations

A flowering plant commands attention, even in its red clay pot, and a plant set temporarily in a pretty jardiniere is an addition to any room. Flowering plants like to be kept somewhat dry, so there is no danger to the flowers in moving them from the damp greenhouse into the living room. A flowering

plant may even be transported to a hospital room for the pleasure of a sick friend without injury.

But many orchid plants are stiff and ungraceful, and their flowers may be used in a more decorative manner if they are cut. A fine hand with flowers can turn out beautiful things. One orchid in a simple little vase is a spot of beauty for table or mantel. One of my favorite arrangements was a single yellow Cymbidium with three Columbine blossoms in a tiny piece of brown and green Mexican pottery. From there you may go to any lengths. Grand, impressive arrangements using whole sprays of Cymbidiums with other flowers, low settings for a few Cat-

Orchids lend themselves to cut flower arrangements. Here are three hybrid *Paphiopedilums* and *Odontoglossum grande* arranged with leaves of Strelitzia and Philodendron.

tleyas, stunning combinations of Cypripediums with unusual foliage, arrangements of Oncidiums with Delphinium that are all blue and gold lace, and so on ad infinitum. The flowers used with orchids will have to be renewed from time to time, for the orchids will far outlast them in freshness.

To keep the cut orchids for as long as possible, remove them to a cool place at night. And trim the stems from time to time, holding the tip under water as described above.

Selling and Shipping Blooms

Orchid flowers must be carefully packed in order to arrive at their destination in perfection. Whether you send a corsage to a faraway friend or blooms to a wholesaler in the next town, the same packing method is used. Shredded wax paper is obtainable at any wholesale florist house, or possibly from your local florist. This springy, non-absorbent stuff protects the flowers from jostling and keeps the flower parts from rubbing and bruising each other.

A few shreds of the wax paper are woven between sepals and petals and around the lip. The flower in its tube of water is then laid on a bed of shredded wax paper in a strong box. The tube must be fastened firmly to

Preparing a flower for shipping. The stem is placed in water in the tube. Shredded wax paper is then woven between the flower parts and around the lip. (*Cattleya labiata*)

A box of orchids ready for shipping, except for some additional wax paper around each flower. Each tube has been fastened tightly to the bottom of the box.

the bottom of the box so that the flower will not move from its position. Holes punched in the box on either side of the tube allow wire or string to be tied around the tube, or it may be fastened down with Scotch tape. More shredded wax paper is tucked under the large parts of the flower, and a little put on top to keep them firm.

In moderate weather, the box need be wrapped in only one thickness of paper. But in cold weather, the box is wrapped in layer after layer of newspaper to insulate it. The insulation retains the inside warmth for an hour or two, possibly longer depending on the number of layers. Railway and Air Express are recommended as the best shipping methods, the extra expense being worth the care in handling. A label on the box stating that it contains cut flowers to be protected from heat and cold will insure its being properly cared for.

If you have only two or three cut flowers to market at a time you will do better to sell them to a local florist rather than to a wholesaler. The latter buys flowers either on a commission basis, or pays you a price within the range of their market value. He must make a profit on them, above his cost of handling and bookkeeping. The trouble of opening your small shipment, grading your flowers, and keeping track of their sale is really not a profitable venture for him, compared to what he can make on a shipment of a hundred blooms. Nor is it profitable for you to pay shipping expenses and the sales commission. When you have a steady supply of good quality flowers, and the wholesale florist can count on you for a certain number a week, then it becomes profitable for both of you.

Orchid prices vary according to the season, often being higher at holiday times, and lower when the market is full of blooms and the demand is slow. It is therefore difficult to give definite prices that can be counted upon in the future. At present, when you see an orchid corsage selling for $6 you may know that the florist paid about a third of that for the flower. If it came from a wholesaler, that means that the grower received about $1.50 for it. In other words, when you market your flowers, you must be prepared to accept for them approximately one-third of their retail value.

The ups and downs of the market are sometimes disconcerting. Perhaps you ship a box of nice blooms, only to receive 50 cents apiece for them because your contribution arrived at the wholesale house along with several thousand flowers from one of the big growers. Another time you may send a box of the same quality blooms and receive three times that price, because at that particular moment orchids were scarce.

In general, good Cattleya species wholesale for $1 to $2, depending on their size and quality. Poor samples often go begging at 50 cents apiece. Hybrids that are no better than the species come in the same range, while species that are superior in every way often sell along with good hybrids. An average price range for colored hybrids is $2 to $3. When white orchids are in abundance they go in the colored hybrid price range, as do white with purple lip. When whites are scarce, they may sell for more.

Cypripediums and Cymbidiums, and perhaps large, choice specimens of some other genera, range between $1 and $2, depending on size and quality. Small ones go for around 50 cents. Here again, the locality, the numbers available, and the season regulate the price.

With these prices in mind, you can approach a florist you know on the subject of buying your orchids. He will probably be glad to have them, for two reasons. They will come to him fresher than those he ships in, and he will not have the transportation cost. You can work out some arrangement with him whereby you let him know early in the week just what you will have, so that he can make his plans. Sometimes he will not be able to take all you have, and at other times you will probably not have enough for him. Remember that you are competing with large outfits, from whom he can get what he orders. Grade your flowers dispassionately, on the basis of their actual quality rather than on how proud you are of them. Offer him a fair price, be sure that you take him good flowers, and he will be a steady customer.

BIBLIOGRAPHY

AMES, OAKES. *An Enumeration of the Orchids of the United States and Canada*. Boston. 1924.

——. *Orchids in Retrospect*. Cambridge. 1948.

BAILEY, L. H. *Standard Cyclopedia of Horticulture*. New York. 1928.

BOYLE, FREDERICK. *The Culture of Greenhouse Orchids, Old System and New*. London. 1902.

BRUHL, PAUL. *A Guide to the Orchids of Sikkim*. Calcutta. 1926.

BURGEFF, HANS. *Die Samenkeimung die Orchideen*. Jena. 1936.

COSTANTIN, J. *Atlas en Couleurs des Orchidées Cultivées*. Paris.

COX, J. M. *Cultural Table of Orchidaceous Plants*. Sydney. 1946.

CURTIS, C. H. *Orchids for Everyone*. New York. 1910.

DARWIN, CHARLES. *On the Fertilisation of Orchids by Insects*. New York. 1889.

DUVAL, L. *Les Cattleya*. Traité de culture pratique. Paris. 1907.

——. *Les Odontoglossum*. Leur histoire, leur description, leur culture. Paris. 1900.

——. *Les Orchidées*. Paris. 1905.

GRATIOT, J. *Les Orchidées, Leur Culture*. Paris. 1934.

HARRISON, C. ALWYN. *Commercial Orchid Growing*. London. 1914.

. *Orchids for Amateurs*. A Practical Guide to the cultivation of sixty easily grown, cool, and fifty warm house kinds, adapted for small mixed greenhouses. London. 1911.

HOGG, R. BRUCE. *Orchids for Everybody*. Abbotsford, N.S.W. 1946.

HURST, CHARLES C. *Experiments in Genetics*. Cambridge. 1925.

LOGAN, H. B., and L. C. COSPER. *Orchids Are Easy to Grow*. Chicago. 1949.

KRÄNZLIN, F. *Beiträge zu Orchideenflora Sudamerikas*. Upsala and Stockholm. 1911.

MILLICAN, ALBERT. *Travels and Adventures of an Orchid Hunter*. An account of canoe and camp life in Colombia while collecting orchids in the northern Andes. London. 1891.

MORRIS, F., and E. EAMES. *Our Wild Orchids*. New York. 1929.

NICOLAI, W. *Orchideen*. Frankfurt (Oder). 1939.

O'BRIEN, JAMES. *Orchids*. London. 1890.

OSORIO, L. F. *Colombian Orchids*. Medellin. 1941.

SANDER, F. K. *Sander's Complete List of Orchid Hybrids*. St. Albans. 1947.

——. *Sander's Orchid Guide*. St. Albans. 1927.

SCHLECHTER, R. *Die Orchideen. Ihre Beschreibung, Kultur und Zuchtung.* Berlin. 1915.

WATKINS, J. V. *ABC of Orchid Growing.* Chicago. 1948.

WATSON, W., and W. BEAN. *Orchids: Their Culture and Management.* London. 1890.

WATSON, W., and H. J. CHAPMAN. *Orchids: Their Culture and Management.* London. 1903.

WHITE, E. A. *American Orchid Culture.* New York. 1942.

WILLIAMS, B. S. *The Orchid Grower's Manual.* London. 1894.

JOURNALS AND MAGAZINES OF INTEREST TO ORCHID GROWERS

The American Orchid Society Bulletin. Botanical Museum, Cambridge, Mass.

The Orchid Digest, published by the Orchid Society of California.

Orchid Lore, published by the Houston Orchid Society.

The Orchid Review, an English publication.

My Garden, an English gardening magazine.

Australian Orchid Review, published by the Orchid Society of New South Wales.

Bulletin, Pacific Orchid Society of Hawaii.

Cymbidium News, published in Los Angeles, California.

Flower Grower, a gardening magazine published in New York.

APPENDIX A

Key to the tribes and genera of the orchid family (Orchidaceae). (Note: This key is reproduced from the *Standard Cyclopedia of Horticulture* with the kind permission of The Macmillan Company (copyright 1900 and 1914) and its author, Liberty Hyde Bailey, copyright 1928. A few notes have been added (given in parentheses) as explanation to those tribes not described in the text of this book.)

I. SUMMARY OF TRIBES

A. Fertile stamens 2, with a broad shield-shaped sterile one (stami-
   nodium)... 1. CYPRIPEDIUM TRIBE
AA. Fertile stamen 1, with no staminodium.
   B. Anther persistent; pollinia with basal appendages.
      C. The anther erect.
         D. Stigma flat, unappendaged..................... 2. SERAPIAS TRIBE
         DD. Stigma with appendages...................... 3. HABENARIA TRIBE
      CC. The anthers placed obliquely..................... 4. SATYRIUM TRIBE
   BB. Anther usually readily deciduous; pollinia not appendaged
       or with terminal ones.
      C. Infl. terminal.
         D. Lf.-buds convolute.
            E. Lf.-blade not jointed to stalk.
               F. The anther commonly much exceeding the
                  beak of the column which is not distinctly
                  cut.
                  G. Lip without hypochil, usually spur-
                     less.
                     H. St. short, with only 1 or 2 lvs.. 5. POGONIA TRIBE
                     HH. St. long, with many lvs........ 6. VANILLA TRIBE
                  GG. Lip with distinct hypochil, which is
                      often spurred.................... 7. CEPHALANTHERA TRIBE
               FF. The anther commonly about as long as the
                   beak of the column which usually bears a
                   sharp cut or groove.
                  G. Pollinia waxy or powdery, not divided.
                     H. Lip turned down............. 8. SPIRANTHES TRIBE
                     HH. Lip turned up.............. 9. CRANICHIS TRIBE
                  GG. Pollinia divided into distinct masses. 10. PHYSURUS TRIBE
            EE. Lf.-blade distinctly jointed to the petiole.
               F. Pollinia 8: st. slender: fls. usually with
                  spurs or chins....................... 11. THUNIA TRIBE
               FF. Pollinia 4: st. a short pseudobulb: fls. with-
                   out spurs or chins.................. 12. COELOGYNE TRIBE

DD. Lf.-buds conduplicate.

    E. Sepals and petals about equally developed, the lip usually very conspicuous.

        F. Lvs. usually not jointed: column footless.   13. LIPARIS TRIBE

        FF. Lvs. usually jointed.

            G. Nerves of lvs. 1.

                H. Pollinia 2–4, with very short stalks. . . . . 14. POLYSTACHYA TRIBE

                HH. Pollinia 4–8, with distinct caudicles.

                    I. Column-foot forming a chin with the lateral sepals or a short sac with the lip. . . . . . 15. PONERA TRIBE

                    II. Column footless. . . . . 16. CATTLEYA TRIBE

            GG. Nerves of lvs. several. . . . . 17. SOBRALIA TRIBE

    EE. Sepals much more developed than the petals and lip. . . . . 18. PLEUROTHALLIS TRIBE

CC. Infl. lateral, or on separate shoot.

    D. Lf.-buds convolute.

        E. St. slender or gradually swollen.

            F. Pollinia with caudicles but without stalks   19. PHAIUS TRIBE

            FF. Pollinia without caudicles but with stalks.

                G. Lip jointed to column-foot or forming a spur with it. 20. CYRTOPODIUM TRIBE

                GG. Lip not jointed, often with a distinct hypochil. . . . . 21. CATASETUM TRIBE

        EE. St. a short distinct pseudobulb.

            F. Lip jointed to the column-foot.

                G. Callus-ridges lengthwise. . . . . 22. LYCASTE TRIBE

                GG. Callus-ridges transverse. . . . . 23. ZYGOPETALUM TRIBE

            FF. Lip continuous with column-foot. . . . . 24. GONGORA TRIBE

DD. Lf.-buds conduplicate.

    E. St. terminating its growth in 1 year.

        F. Lip movably jointed to foot of column.

            G. Lvs. not strap-shaped: pollinia unappendaged or with either caudicles or stipes, but not with both.

                H. Flowering st. arising from near the apex of the slender st. or from the pseudobulb. . . . . 25. DENDROBIUM TRIBE

                HH. Flowering st. arising under the pesudobulb or at the base of the st.

                    I. Pollinia without appendages 26. BULBOPHYLLUM TRIBE

                    II. Pollinia with distinct stalks.

                        J. Pseudobulbs usually present: flowering st. arising lower than new growth. . 27. MAXILLARIA TRIBE

                        JJ. Pseudobulbs usually wanting: flowering st. arising higher than new growth. 28. HUNTLEYA TRIBE

GG. Lvs. strap-shaped: pollinia with broad
    caudicles and stipes.............   29. CYMBIDIUM TRIBE
FF. Lip immovably united to foot of column.
    G. Fls. with spurs..................   30. IONOPSIS TRIBE
    GG. Fls. without spurs.
        H. The fls. narrow, not open......   31. ADA TRIBE
        HH. The fls. wide open.
            I. Lip   enrolled   around   the
               column..................   32. TRICHOPILIA TRIBE
            II. Lip not enrolled.
               J. The lip united to column
                  to the middle..........   33. ASPASIA TRIBE
               JJ. The lip united only to the
                  base of the column.....   34. ODONTOGLOSSUM TRIBE
EE. St. increasing in length from year to year....   35. AERIDES TRIBE

II. Key to the Tribes

1. Cypripedium Tribe (See text)

A. Fl. persistent, withering on the ovary: Lf.-buds convolute...............   1. *Cypripedium*
AA. Fl. soon deciduous: Lf.-buds conduplicate.
  B. Ovary 3-celled, the placentae central; mouth of lip with broad inturned
    margin..   2. *Phragmopediium*
  BB. Ovary 1-celled, the placentae parietal; mouth of lip usually with no
    broad inturned margins..   3. *Paphiopedilum*

2. Serapias Tribe

(Terrestrial, North Temperate Zone, not showy. *Orchis* is the type genus of
the orchid family.)
A. Lip spurred.
  B. Sepals free...   4. *Orchis*
  BB. Sepals united into an arching hood............................   5. *Galeorchis*
AA. Lip spurless.
  B. Pollinia glands in a single sac..................................   6. *Serapias*
  BB. Pollinia glands separate, in 2 distinct sacs......................   7. *Ophrys*

3. Habenaria Tribe

(Terrestrial, temperate and tropical regions, not showy but includes some of
our finest native orchids.)
A. Lip adnate to column at base; stigma broad..........................   8. *Cynorchis*
AA. Lip free; stigma slender...   9. *Habenaria*

4. Satyrium Tribe

(Terrestrial, South Africa, pretty, but hard to grow.)
Dorsal sepal helmet shaped..   10. *Disa*

5. Pogonia Tribe

(Terrestrial, mostly North and South America. A few can be grown in
gardens.)
A. Fls. on a scape with a terminal whorl of lf.-like bracts.................   11. *Isotria*
AA. Fls. on a leafy st.
  B. Lip crested...   12. *Pogonia*
  BB. Lip not crested...   13. *Triphora*

6. Vanilla Tribe (See text)

Sts. rooting at nodes.. 14. *Vanilla*

7. Cephalanthera Tribe

(Terrestrial, North Temperate Zone, of minor interest.)
A. Fls. with a chin; lip long.. 15. *Cephalanthera*
AA. Fls. chinless; lip round... 16. *Epipactis*

8. Spiranthes Tribe

(Terrestrial, mostly tropical, but with a few native species adaptable to gardens.)
A. Dorsal sepal forming a hood with the petals.
    B. Infl. 1-sided; fls. without a chin.............................. 17. *Spiranthes*
    BB. Infl. not 1-sided; fls. with a chin............................ 18. *Stenorrhynchus*
AA. Sepals and petals spreading.. 19. *Listera*

9. Cranichis Tribe

(Terrestrial, native to tropical America, of minor interest.)
Lip and petals inserted upon the elongated column........................ 20. *Ponihieva*

10. Physurus Tribe

(Terrestrial, widely distributed in temperate and tropical Asia and America. Of interest for their variegated foliage. The flowers are insignificant, the whole plant having the shape of a plantain weed. *Goodyera* and *Physurus* are fairly well known.)
A. Lip with a distinct spur.
    B. Lvs. green: lip concave above the spur......................... 21. *Physurus*
    BB. Lvs. usually variegated: lip with a long fimbriate claw........ 22. *Anoectochilus*
AA. Lip spurless or nearly so.
    B. Column straight; fls. symmetric.
        C. The lip not clawed...................................... 23. *Goodyera*
        CC. The lip clawed.. 24. *Dossinia*
    BB. Column twisted; fls. not symmetric.
        C. The column with 2 upright appendages in front............ 25. *Macodes*
        CC. The column without appendages......................... 26. *Haemaria*

11. Thunia Tribe

(Terrestrial, Asia. *Thunia* and *Bletilla* are seen in collections, the latter adaptable to gardens in some regions.)
A. Fls. without chin.
    B. Sts. without basal pseudobulbs................................. 27. *Thunia*
    BB. Sts. with basal pseudobulbs.................................. 28. *Bletilla*
AA. Fls. with a distinct chin, formed of lateral sepals and column-foot......... 29. *Trichosma*

12. Coelogyne Tribe (See text)

A. Base of lip with sac-like hollow.
    B. Column short, winged above; sepals flat........................ 30. *Pholidota*
    BB. Column slender; sepals sac-like, concave...................... 31. *Neogyne*
AA. Base of lip flat.
    B. Column slender, without horns.
        C. Lvs. and pseudobulbs perennial.......................... 32. *Coelogyne*

CC. Lvs. and pseudobulbs annual................................. 33. *Pleione*
BB. Column short, with 2 horns................................... 34. *Platyclinis*

13. Liparis Tribe

(Terrestrial, North Temperate Zone, many in North America. Best known is
Calypso, one of our native orchids.)
A. Lvs. green: fls. without chin.
B. Lip shoe-shaped... 35. *Calypso*
BB. Lip not shoe-shaped.
C. Column short; lip turned upward............................ 36. *Microstylis*
CC. Column slender; lip turned downward....................... 37. *Liparis*
AA. Lvs. wanting: fls. with chin.. 38. *Corallorrhiza*

14. Polystachya Tribe

(Mostly epiphytic, tropical except for one rare North American species.
Seldom grown.)
A. Lip spurred.
B. Plant tuberous: spur slender................................... 39. *Tipularia*
BB. Plant not tuberous: spur funnel-shaped......................... 40. *Galeandra*
AA. Lip not spurred.
B. The lip 3-lobed.
C. Column short; chin distinct.............................. 41. *Polystachya*
CC. Column slender, curved; chin indistinct..................... 42. *Ansellia*
BB. The lip entire... 43. *Neobenthamia*

15. Ponera Tribe

(Epiphytic, Central America, seldom grown.)
A. Lip normal.
B. St. slender, leafy; no pseudobulbs; pollinia 4...................... 44. *Isochilus*
BB. St. a pseudobulb; pollinia 8................................... 45. *Coelia*
AA. Lip forming a beaker-like cavity, with the column, or the former hollow at
base.
B. Young shoots at the apex of the old........................... 46. *Hexisea*
BB. Young shoots from base of old.
C. Fls. in dense spikes; pollinia 8............................. 47. *Arpophyllum*
CC. Fls. in short clusters; pollinia 4............................ 48. *Hartwegia*

16. Cattleya Tribe (See text)

A. Anther not toothed, nor in an excavation.
B. Pollinia 4.
C. Lip adnate to the column, at least at its base.
D. Ovary produced into a hollow neck...................... 49. *Broughtonia*
DD. Ovary not so produced............................... 50. *Epidendrum*
CC. Lip free.
D. The lip flat, with 2 elevations on upper side.............. 51. *Diacrium*
DD. The lip enrolled about column, with no elevations......... 52. *Cattleya*
BB. Pollinia 5–7, some of them often abortive....................... 53. *Laelio-cattleya*
BBB. Pollinia 8.
C. Stigma pitted upon the front of the column; anther inclined.
D. Base of lip gradually merging into blade.
E. Lip distinctly surrounding the column; sepals and petals
not wavy.. 54. *Laelia*

EE. Lip not as above; sepals and petals distinctly wavy.... 55. *Schomburgkia*
DD. Base of lip tightly encompassing column, suddenly broadened into the broad blade.................................... 56. *Brassavola*
CC. Stigma running up on 2 extensions of the column-apex; anther erect... 57. *Sophronitis*
AA. Anther 2-toothed below, in an excavation in the column................. 58. *Leptotes*

17. Sobralia Tribe (See text)

A. St. many-lvd., not bulbous at base: lip not bearded...................... 59. *Sobralia*
AA. St. 1- or 2-lvd., bulbous at base: lip bearded........................... 60. *Calopogon*

18. Pleurothallis Tribe (See text)

A. Lip turned upward; lateral sepals united into a boat-shaped hood......... 61. *Scaphosepalum*
AA. Lip turned down.
    B. Sepals united... 62. *Masdevallia*
    BB. Sepals free, or the lateral only united.
        C. Dorsal sepal and petals attenuated into a club-shaped apex..... 63. *Restrepia*
        CC. Dorsal sepal and petals not as above....................... 64. *Pleurothallis*

19. Phaius Tribe (See text)

A. Lvs. not articulated to petiole.
    B. Lip free, encompassing the column.............................. 65. *Phaius*
    BB. Lip adnate to column, the blade spreading....................... 66. *Calanthe*
AA. Lvs. articulated to petiole.
    B. Sepals and petals spreading.
        C. Lip with its base tightly inclosing the column, the blade spreading 67. *Limatodes*
        CC. Lip not inclosing column.
            D. Fls. with distinct chin................................. 68. *Chysis*
          DD. Fls. without chin.
              E. Pollinia 8.
                F. Middle lobe of lip not clawed.................... 69. *Bletia*
                FF. Middle lobe of lip clawed....................... 70. *Spathoglottis*
              EE. Pollinia 4... 71. *Aplectrum*
    BB. Sepals and petals erect.. 72. *Acanthophippium*

20. Cyrtopodium Tribe

(Both epiphytic and terrestrial, tropical, seldom grown.)
A. Fls. spurred or with sac-like base.
    B. Sepals narrower and less colored than petals...................... 73. *Lissochilus*
    BB. Sepals and petals alike or nearly so............................ 74. *Eulophia*
AA. Fls. not spurred nor saccate.
    B. Lip only inserted on column-foot............................... 75. *Cyrtopodium*
    BB. Lip and lateral sepals inserted on column-foot.
        C. Chin distinct, rectangular.................................. 76. *Warrea*
        CC. Chin indistinct, round.................................... 77. *Eulophiella*

21. Catasetum Tribe (See text)

A. Fls. perfect; column twisted... 78. *Mormodes*
AA. Fls. of 2 or 3 forms; column not twisted.
    B. Column stout, straight; fls. with antennae....................... 79. *Catasetum*
    BB. Column slender, curved; fls. without antennae.................... 80. *Cycnoches*

22. Lycaste Tribe (See text)

A. Pollinia upon a single stalk.
    B. Fls. globose...   81. *Anguloa*
    BB. Fls. with spreading sepals and petals.
        C. Stalk of pollinia long and narrow; fls. 1 to few.
            D. Infl. of a single erect fl.; lip turned down.................   82. *Lycaste*
            DD. Infl. of 2 to few drooping fls.; lip turned upward..........   83. *Paphinia*
        CC. Stalk of pollinia short; fls. many............................   84. *Batemannia*
AA. Pollinia upon 2 separate stalks..   85. *Bifrenaria*

23. Zygopetalum Tribe (See text)

A. Lip clawed distinctly...   86. *Colax*
AA. Lip not distinctly clawed.
    B. The lip with horseshoe-shaped callus............................   87. *Zygopetalum*
    BB. The lip with few longitudinal lamellae...........................   88. *Eriopsis*

24. Gongora Tribe (See text)

A. Lip turned downward.
    B. Fls. with sepals and petals erect or incurved.
        C. Hypochil separated from column by a strong stricture; no
            pleuridia..   89. *Lacaena*
        CC. Hypochil united with column by a broad base: pleuridia present.
            D. Epichil movably attached to hypochil; pollinia with short
                stalk at most.......................................   90. *Peristeria*
            DD. Epichil immovably attached to hypochil; pollinia with
                elongated stalk.....................................   91. *Acineta*
    BB. Fls. with sepals and petals spreading or reflexed.
        C. Lateral sepals much larger than the dorsal sepal and petals.....   92. *Coryanthes*
        CC. Sepals and petals nearly alike.
            D. Hypochil concave; epichil flat.
                E. Pollinia 2...   93. *Stanhopea*
                EE. Pollinia 4..   94. *Aganisia*
            DD. Hypochil not concave.................................   95. *Houlletia*
AA. Lip turned upward...   96. *Gongora*

25. Dendrobium Tribe (See text)

A. Sts. many-jointed; rhizome short.
    B. Lip without callus, or with lamellate or elevated lines..............   97. *Dendrobium*
    BB. Lip with basal callus; joints of st. long-filamentose................   98. *Inobulbon*
AA. Sts. 1- or rarely 2-jointed; rhizome long-creeping.......................   99. *Sarcopodium*

26. Bulbophyllum Tribe (See text)

A. Lateral sepals with their outer margins adhering, except at the free base.   100. *Cirrhopetalum*
AA. Lateral sepals free..   101. *Bulbophyllum*

27. Maxillaria Tribe (See text)

A. Lip without claw, movable: lvs. normal.................................   102. *Maxillaria*
AA. Lip clawed, or adnate to column-base: lvs. whip-shaped.................   103. *Scuticaria*

28. Huntleya Tribe

(Epiphytic, Central and South America. Similar to *Zygopetalum*.)
A. Pseudobulbs distinct... 104. *Promenaea*
AA. Pseudobulbs wanting or rudimentary.
    B. Lip entire... 105. *Chondrorrhyncha*
    BB. Lip lobed.
        C. Callus of lip fringed....................................... 106. *Huntleya*
        CC. Callus not fringed.
            D. Column boat-shaped, concave.......................... 107. *Bollea*
            DD. Column slender, not concave.
                E. Claw very short: callus free in front and resting upon the
                lip... 108. *Warscewiczella*
                EE. Claw distinct: callus not free in front............... 109. *Pescatorea*

29. Cymbidium Tribe (See text)

A. Lvs. many: sts. elongated... 110. *Grammatophyllum*
AA. Lvs. few: sts. short.
    B. Sts. concealed by the lf.-sheaths.
        C. Pollinia pear-shaped, upon a quadrate stalk: st. not bulbous..... 111. *Cyperorchis*
        CC. Pollinia round, upon a stalk much broader than high: st. bulbous 112. *Cymbidium*
    BB. Sts. naked: lvs. only at its apex................................ 113. *Grammangis*

30. Ionopsis Tribe (See text)

A. Sepals free.. 114. *Trichocentrum*
AA. Sepals, the lateral ones, united, at least below.
    B. The lip spurred... 115. *Rodriguezia*
    BB. The sepals spurred.
        C. Spur short.. 116. *Ionopsis*
        CC. Spur long and slender.................................... 117. *Comparettia*

31. Ada Tribe (See text)

A. Lvs. flat.
    B. Sepals free.. 118. *Ada*
    BB. Lateral sepals united....................................... 119. *Mesospinidium*
AA. Lvs. cylindric.. 120. *Quekettia*

32. Trichopilia Tribe (See text)

Lip rolled around the column.. 121. *Trichopilia*

33. Aspasia Tribe (See text, with *Odontoglossum* Tribe)

A. Middle lobe of lip broad.. 122. *Aspasia*
AA. Middle lobe of lip narrow.. 123. *Cochlioda*

34. Odontoglossum Tribe (See text)

A. Lip surrounding column with 2 longitudinal calluses: blade reflexed........ 124. *Gomeza*
AA. Lip not as above.
    B. Base of lip parallel to column and sometimes adnate to it.......... 125. *Odontoglossum*
    BB. Lip spreading from base of column.
        C. Lateral sepals united entirely; lip like dorsal sepal............. 126. *Palumbina*

CC. Lateral sepals free or only partly united; lip unlike dorsal sepal.
    D. Sepals and petals long and much attenuated; lip entire or fiddle-shaped...................................... 127. *Brassia*
    DD. Sepals and petals not much attenuated.
        E. The lip entire, flat, broad........................ 128. *Miltonia*
        EE. The lip mostly 3-lobed, with warts or a cushion at base. 129. *Oncidium*

35. Aerides Tribe (See text)

A. Lip movably jointed to column.
    B. Middle lobe of spurless lip flat.................................. 130. *Renanthera*
    BB. Middle lobe of spurred lip compressed........................... 131. *Arachnanthe*
AA. Lip immovably united with column.
    B. Spurless.
        C. Column without a foot.
            D. Summit of lip laterally compressed..................... 132. *Vandopsis*
            DD. Summit of lip not compressed......................... 133. *Luisia*
        CC. Column with a foot, the lateral sepals attached to it........... 134. *Phalaenopsis*
    BB. Spurred.
        C. Column without a foot.
            D. Pollinia upon a single stalk.
                E. Spur appendaged.
                    F. With a longitudinal septum..................... 135. *Sarcanthus*
                    FF. With the mouth covered with a plate............ 136. *Cleisostoma*
                EE. Spur not appendaged.
                    F. Stalk of the pollinia filiform.
                        G. Fls. firm; lip turned downward............. 137. *Saccolabium*
                        GG. Fls. fragile; lip turned upward............. 138. *Acampe*
                    FF. Stalk of the pollinia broadened upward or throughout.
                        G. Spur short and broad..................... 139. *Vanda*
                        GG. Spur long and slender..................... 140. *Angraecum*
             DD. Pollinia on 2 separate stalks, or these united by the gland.
                E. Stalks membranous, the pollinia attached to the face.
                    F. Plants leafy: lip entire........................ 141. *Macroplectrum*
                    FF. Plants without lvs.: lip 3-lobed................. 142. *Polyrrhiza*
                EE. Stalks slender.
                    F. Column bent toward the dorsal sepal............. 143. *Listrostachys*
                    FF. Column straight............................. 144. *Mystacidium*
         CC. Column with a foot, the lateral sepals attached to it.
            D. Spur curved upward against the lip-blade................ 145. *Aërides*
             DD. Spur straight or reflexed.
                E. Lip 3-lobed..................................... 146. *Camarotis*
                EE. Lip entire....................................... 147. *Rhynchostylis*

APPENDIX B.

(Compiled from advertisements. This list is for information only
and no endorsement of the companies is implied.)

AGAR

Difco Laboratories, 920 Henry Street, Detroit 1, Mich.

CHEMICALS, GLASSWARE, pH METERS, ETC.

Eimer and Amend, 655 Greenwich Street, New York 14, N.Y.

CUSTOM HOUSE BROKERS

H. W. St. John and Co., 18 Pearl Street, New York 4, N.Y.

GREENHOUSES AND GREENHOUSE SUPPLIES

American Moninger Greenhouse Mfg. Corp., 1820 Flushing Ave., Brooklyn 6, N.Y.
Lord and Burnham, Irvington, N.Y.; Des Plaines, Ill.
Metropolitan Greenhouse Mfg. Corp., 1859 Flushing Avenue, Brooklyn 6, N.Y.
National Greenhouse Co., Pana, Ill.

INSECTICIDES

Botany Chemical Co., P. O. Box 20, Middle Village, N.Y.
Doggett-Pfeil Co., Springfield 9, N.J.
Fennell Orchid Co., Route 1, Box 230, Homestead, Fla.
Andrew Wilson Inc., Springfield, N.J.

ORCHID PLANTS (In addition to these there may be local growers who can furnish plants.)

L. Sherman Adams Co., Wellesley 81, Mass.
Alberts and Merkel Bros., Inc., P. O. Box 77, Route 6, South Jacksonville, Fla.
H. G. Alexander, Ltd., Westonbirt, Tetsbury, Glos., England
Armacost and Royston, Inc., Los Angeles 25, Calif.
George E. Baldwin, Inc., Mamaroneck, N.Y.
Black and Flory, Ltd., Slough, Bucks, England
Brookville Orchids, 465 E. 57th Street, New York 22, N.Y.
Butterworths, Framingham, Mass.
Carolina Orchid Growers, Inc., Southern Pines, N.C.
Carr's Orchid Laboratory, Bedminister, N.J.
Pierre Cholet and Cie. s.a. Chateau d'Achtendries, Oostaker, Belgium
Clarelen Orchids, Fox Bluffs on Lake Mendota, Madison, Wis.
N. W. Curson, 2246 96th Avenue, Oakland 5, Calif.
H. A. Dunn, Box "0", Ancon, Canal Zone
Fennell Orchid Co., Route 1, Box 230, Homestead, Fla.
Jan Goo's, 2533 Coyne St., Honolulu, T.H.
R. H. Gore, Box 211, Fort Lauderdale, Fla.
Firme Louis Hoornaert, St. Nicolas (Waes), Belgium
Mable B. Ingham, Walkley Hill Road, Haddam, Conn.
Jones and Scully, Inc., 2154 N. W. 33rd Ave., Miami 35, Fla.

A. J. Keeling and Sons, Westgate Hill, Bradford, Yorks, England
Kiesewetter, R. F. D. Roslyn, Long Island, N.Y.
C. M. Kilian, 210 Yorkshire Drive, Birmingham 9, Ala.
Lager and Hurrell, Summit, N.J.
Lines Orchids, Taft Highway, Signal Mountain, Tenn.
Stuart Low Co.'s, Jarvisbrook (Crowborough), Sussex, England
Edward A. Manda, Inc., 130 Main St., West Orange, N.J.
Mansell and Hatcher, Ltd., Rawdon, Leeds, Yorks, England
McBean's Orchids, Ltd., Cooksbridge, Sussex, England
Clint McDade and Sons (Rivermont Orchids), Signal Mountain, Tenn.
Orchidwood, 52 Askins Place, New Rochelle, N.Y.
Orquideas, S. A., Monte Himalaya 520, Mexico City, Mexico
H. Patterson and Sons, Bergenfield, N.J.
Riverview Orchids, Anderson Blvd., East Liverpool, Ohio
Manoel Roxo, Av. Almirante Cocrane, 96, Santos, Brazil
Daniel Ryerson, P. O. Box 805, Homestead, Fla.
Sanders, Ltd., St. Albans, Herts., England
Earl J. Small Orchids, Inc., 2235 Central Ave., St. Petersburg, Fla.
Julio C. Urbano, Granja Santa Eduviges, Los Dos Caminos, Caracas, Venezuela
Vacherot-Lecoufle, Seine et Oise, France

OSMUNDA FIBRE (Osmunda fibre can be purchased from most companies which sell orchid plants in addition
to the companies listed below.)
Julius Loewith, Inc., 120 E. 16th St., New York 3, N.Y.
Mercer and Phipps, Route 1, Box 504, Auburndale, Fla.
Sussex Peat Co., 20 Diller Ave., Newton, N.J.
H. L. Weisner, 939 Odd Fellow St., Gainesville, Fla.
Van Hyning Bros., P. O. Box 509, Sebring, Fla.

SUPPLIES, ORCHID TUBES, INSECTICIDES, LABELS, RIBBON, OSMUNDA FIBRE, SHREDDED WAX PAPER, ETC.
Fight Floral Co., Inc., 22 West 26th St., New York 10, N.Y.
McHutchison and Co., 95 Chambers St., New York 7, N.Y.
Nurserymen's Exchange, 938 Howard St., San Francisco 3, Calif.
Schupp Florist Supply Co., 1143 Greenleaf Ave., Wilmette, Ill.
Wrightwood Floral Co., 2407 N. Main St., Houston 9, Tex.

INDEX

Acampe, 134
Acanthophippium javanicum, 205
Acineta, 196
Ada aurantiaca, 189
Ada Tribe, 189
Aerides odoratum, 133
  A. Fieldingii, 133
Aerides Tribe, 122–134
Aganisia, 197
air relations, 227–228
Angraecum sesquipedale, 133
Anguloa Clowesii, 200
  A. Ruckeri, 200
  A. uniflora, 200
anther, 100–102
anthocyanin, 20
anthracnose, 232–233
Aplectrum hyemale, 205
Aspasia Tribe, 187

Bacillus cypripedii, 231
Bailey, L. H., 120
Batemannia Colleyi, 200
Bifrenaria aurantica, 200
Black Leaf, 10, 27
Bletia verecunda, 204
  B. Shepherdii, 204
  B. Sherrattiana, 204
blind growths, 20
Brassavola
  characteristics and culture, 58
  B. Digbyana, 58
  in hybrids, 71–72
Brassia verrucosa, 188
  B. longissima, 188
Brassocattleya
  characteristics, 71–72
  Bc. Mrs. J. H. Leeman, 71
  original cross, 52
Brassolaeliocattleya
  characteristics, 72
  first tri-generic cross, 52
Bulbophyllum Careyanum, 190
  B. grandiflorum, 190
Bulbophyllum Tribe, 189–190

Calanthe
  characteristics and culture, 203–204
  species
    C. furcata, 204
    C. masuca, 204
    C. vestita, 204
  hybrids
    C. Dominii, 203
    C. Veitchii, 204
calcium chloride, 106
calcium hypochlorite, 110
Calopogon pulchellus, 207–208
Camarotis, 134
Catasetum
  characteristics and culture, 191
  species
    C. bicolor, 191
    C. Oerstedii, 191
    C. viridiflavum, 191
Catasetum Tribe, 191–192
Cattley, William, 36
Cattleya
  adult plants, structure and culture, 12–35
  agar-nutrient medium, 80, 108–109, 116–117
  community pot to first bloom, 89–97
  development of seed pod, 104–106
  development of seedlings, 114–116
  establishment of genus, 36
  first bi-generic cross, 52
  flask culture, 108–109, 114, 116–117
  flask to community pot, 81–88
  general information, 2–11
  hand pollination, 101–103
  history of seed germination, 78–80
  hybrids (see also genetics)
    C. Ballantineana, 8
    C. Fabia, 53
    C. Hardyana, 53
    C. Princess Royal, 53
    C. Princess Royal alba, 53
    C. Trimos, 8
  influence of day length on flowering, 41
  inheritance (see also genetics)

Cattleya, inheritance, Brassocattleya, 71–72
   Brassolaeliocattleya, 72
   color in Cattleya hybrids, 62–63, 65–66
   color in Laeliocattleya hybrids, 63, 66, 68–71
   Potinara, quadrigeneric hybrids, 73
   size, 63–64
   Sophrolaeliocattleya, 72
   white, 66–68
   white with purple lip, 68
  jungle plants, 31–33
  Knudson's discovery, 79–80
  labiata group, 37–39
  pollination in nature, 99–101
  seasonal habits, 39–42
  selection for quality, 38–39
  special techniques, 117–119
  species
    C. Aclandiae, 48–49
    C. amethystoglossa, 49
    C. bicolor, 49
    C. Bowringiana, 49
    C. citrina, 49
    C. dolosa, 49
    C. Dowiana, 37, 42–43, 53, 62
    C. Dowiana, aurea, 43, 53
    C. Eldorado, 43
    C. Forbesii, 49–50
    C. Gaskelliana, 43
    C. gigas, 8, 37, 38, 43–44, 53, 62–63, 65
    C. granulosa, 50
    C. guttata, 50
    C. Harrisoniana, 50
    C. intermedia, 50
    C. labiata, 36, 37–39, 44, **53**
    C. Lawrenceana, 44
    C. Leopoldii, 50
    C. Loddigesii, 50
    C. Lueddemanniana, 44–45
    C. luteola, 45
    C. maxima, 45
    C. Mendelii, 37, 45
    C. Mossiae, 8, 37, 42, 45–46
    C. nobilior, 50–51
    C. Percivaliana, 37, 38, 46
    C. Rex, 46
    C. Schilleriana, 51
    C. Schroederae, 46–47

    C. Skinneri, 51
    C. speciosissima (see *C. Lueddemanniana*)
    C. Trianaei, 8, 37, 38, 47, 60, 64, 73
    C. Victoria Regina, 51
    C. violacea, 51
    C. Warneri, 47–48
    C. Walkeriana, 48
  storing seed and pollen, 107
  viability tests, 107–108
Cattleya fly, 235
Cattleya Tribe
  characteristics, 135
  genera, 42–51, 55–59, 135–140
caudicle, 100
Cercospora, 232
chromosomes (see genetics)
Chysis aurea, 204
  C. bractescens, 204
  C. Chelsonii, 204
  C. laevis, 204
  C. Limminghei, 204
  C. Sedenii, 204
Cirrhopetalum medusae, 190
  C. picturatum, 190
cirri, definition, 127
Cleisostoma, 134
Clorox, 114, 118
Cochlioda, 187
Coelogyne
  characteristics and culture, 193
  species
    C. cristata, 193
    C. Dayana, 194
    C. pandurata, 193
    C. tomentosa, 194
Coelogyne Tribe, 193–194
Colax jugosus, 211
colchicine,
  action of, 75
  methods of use, 75–76
  mitosis and, 74
  polyploidy, 73
  tetraploids, 74–77
  triploids, 74
collecting orchids, 4–7
Collembola, 239
Colletotrichum, 232
column, 100
community pots, 82–88

Comparettia coccinea, 198
  C. falcata, 198
corsage making, 255–259
Coryanthes, 196
Cycnoches chlorochilon, 192
  C. pentadactylon, 192
Cymbidium
  characteristics, 141–143
  flowering, 143, 147
  garden culture, 147
  greenhouse culture, 143–148
  hybrids
    C. Alexanderi Westonbirt variety, 151
    C. eburneo-Lowianum, 150
    C. Pauwelsii, var. *Compte de Hemptinne,* 151
  species
    C. eburneum, 149–150
    C. erythrostylum, 150
    C. giganteum, 150
    C. grandiflorum, 150–151
    C. insigni, 149, 151
    C. l'Ansoni, 151
    C. Lowianum, 149, 151
    C. Parishii, 151–152
    C. Schroederi, 152
    C. Tracyanum, 149, 152
Cymbidium Tribe, 141–153
Cyperorchis, 152
Cypripedium (see also Paphiopedilum)
  characteristics, 167
  species
    C. acaule, 167
    C. californicum, 167
    C. candidum, 168
    C. montanum, 168
    C. parviflorum, 168
    C. pubescens, 168
    C. reginae, 168
    C. spectabile, 168
Cypripedium Tribe, 154–168

damping off, 234
Darwin, Charles, 133
day length, influence on flowering, 41
DDT, 235–239
decorative use of orchids, 260
Dendrobium
  characteristics and culture, 169–171

species
    D. aggregatum, 172
    D. aureum, 172
    D. bigibbum, 172–173
    D. Dearii, 173
    D. fimbriatum, 173
    D. Findlayanum, 171
    D. formosum, 173
    D. heterocarpum (see *D. aureum*)
    D. nobile, 171
    D. Phalaenopsis, 173
    D. Pierardii, 171–172
    D. superbum, 172
    D. Thyrsiflorum, 173
    D. Wardianum, 172
Dendrobium Tribe, 169–174
Dendrobium weevil, 235
desiccator, 106
Diacattleya, 140
Diacrium bicornutum, 140
Dialaelia, 140
Diaspis Boisduvali, 236
Difco bacto agar, 116
Difco orchid agar, 108
Diorymerellus laevimargo, 235
Diplodia, 232
Diseases (see also under name of disease)
  bacterial, 231–232
  control, 229, 231
  environmental, 224–228
  fungous, 232–234
  general information, 228–229
  virus, 234–235
Dominy, J., 52
Dove Orchid (see *Peristeria elata*)
Dow, Captain, 43
Duval, Léon, 39

embryo, 107, 115
Epicattleya, 140
Epidendrum
  characteristics and culture, 135
  species
    E. atropurpureum, 136
    E. aurantiacum, 136
    E. ciliare, 136
    E. cochleatum, 135, 136–137
    E. fragrans, 137
    E. prismatocarpum, 137
    E. radicans, 137

Epidendrum, species, *E. Stamfordianum,*
138
E. vitellinum, 138
Epidiacrium, 140
Epilaelia, 140
Epiphronitis, 140
epiphyte, definition, 3
Eriopsis, 211
Erwinia carotovora, 231
Erwinia cypripedii, 231
Euthrips orchidii, 237
eye, definition, 12

Fennell Orchid Company, 238
flask culture
history, 9, 79–80
seedlings, 81–82
sowing, 108–114
flowering
carbohydrate-nitrogen balance in, 98
influence of day length upon, 41
opening of a flower, 9
fungicides
Bordeaux mixture, 229
Bordeaux paste, 230
Ceresan, 230, 233
Cuprocide 54 and 54Y, 230, 234
mercuric chloride, 231
Semesan, 230

Gaskell, Mr., 43
genes (see genetics)
genetics
characteristics influenced by genes, 59
chromosomes, 59–61, 73–77
colchicine, 73–77
diploid, 61
dominant, 62
fertilization, 61
F_1 and F_2, 65
genes, 59–71
haploid, 60
heterozygous, 64
homozygous, 64
incomplete dominance, 63
mitosis, 74
recessive, 62
reduction division, 60–61
stud, 64
Gloeosporium, 232

Glomerella cincta, 233
Gomesa, 188
Gongora, 197
Gongora Tribe, 194–197
Grammangis, 152
Grammatophyllum Fenzlianum, 153
G. speciosum, 153
gravel culture
introduction, 216–217
nutrient solutions, 217–218
Ohio W. P. solution, 218
pot method, 218–220
subirrigation, 221–223
green seed
Cattleya, 118–119
Paphiopedilum, 163
Phalaenopsis, 126
greenhouses
automatic control, 249–251
benches, 245–246
heating, 244–245
humidity, 247–250
planning and structure, 242–244
shading, 247
ventilators, 246
water, 249

Harris, Dr., 52
Haydite, 218–223
heart rot, 233
Hendersonia, 232
Hernandez, 49
Holy Ghost flower (see *Peristeria elata*)
horticultural asphalt, 222
Houlletia, 197
humidity
automatic control of, 250–251
influence in disease, 226–229
mist sprayers for, 19, 247
relative, 18–19
Hurst, Charles, 67–68
hybrids, 8–11, 52–55 (see also genetics, and
see also hybrids under each genus)
Hyponex, 215, 217

inheritance (see genetics)
Inobulbon munificum, 174
insect control, 235–239
insecticides
DDT, 235–239

insecticides, nicotine, 27, 238
  Parathion, 238–239
  rotenone, 35, 238
insects, 235–239
Ionopsis paniculata, 198
Ionopsis Tribe, 197–198
Isosoma orchidearum, 235

jungle orchids
  care of imported plants, 31–33
  condition of imported plants, 15–16
  in native habitat, 3, 39–42

Knudson, Lewis, 79–80
Knudson's formula "C," 116

Lacaena, 197
ladyslipper (see Paphiopedilum)
Laelia
  characteristics and culture, 55
  first bi-generic cross, 52
  inheritance, 63–64, 66, 68–71
  species
    L. albida, 55
    L. anceps, 56
    L. autumnalis, 56
    L. cinnebarina, 58
    L. crispa, 57
    L. flava, 56
    L. monophylla, 58
    L. pumila, 57
    L. purpurata, 57
    L. Sawyeri, 57
    L. superbiens, 57
    L. tenebrosa, 57
  hybrids (see Brassolaeliocattleya, Laelio-
    cattleya, Potinara, and Sophrolaelio-
    cattleya)
Laeliocattleya
  characteristics, 68–69
  inheritance, 63–64, 66, 68–71
  Lc. Exoniensis, 52
lead, definition, 12
leaf die-back, 233
leaf rot, 232
leaf spot and bud rot, 232
Leptolaelia, 140
Leptotes bicolor, 140
light
  ailments associated with, 224–225

burning, 12, 21
  measurement of, 20–21
  relation to temperature, 17
  response of plants to, 19–21
  struggle for, in jungle, 3
  (see also requirements for each genus)
Linden, J., 47
Lindley, Dr., 36
Listrostachys, 134
Lord and Burnham, 222
Lueddeman, 45
Luisia, 134
Lycaste
  characteristics and culture, 199
  species
    L. aromatica, 199
    L. Deppei, 199
    L. Dowiana, 199
    L. Skinneri, 199–200
Lycaste Tribe, 198–200

Macrophoma, 232
marketing blooms, 260–263
Masdevallia
  characteristics, 205
  species
    M. coccinea, 205–206
    M. chimaera, 206
    M. elephanticeps, 206
    M. muscosa, 206
    M. Roezlii, 206
Maxillaria Houtteana, 201
  M. Sanderiana, 201
Maxillaria Tribe, 201–202
Mendel, 60
Mendel, Samuel, 45
Mesospinidium sanguineum, 189
Miltonia
  characteristics and culture, 176
  species
    M. candida, 177
    M. Clowesii, 177
    M. Phaluenopsis, 177
    M. Roezlii, 177–178
    M. spectabilis, 178
    M. vexillaria, 178
  hybrid, *M. Bleuana,* 178
Miltonioda, 187
mineral nutrition
  absorption of minerals, 212–214

mineral nutrition, ash, 212
  chemical analysis of osmundine, 214
  dry weight, 212
  experimental feeding, 215–216
  major elements, 213
  mineral deficiencies, 213–215, 226
  minor elements, 213–214
  photosynthesis, 213
mitosis, 74
  and colchicine, 75
monopodial, definition, 122
Mormodes luxata, 192
mosaic disease, 234–235
Moss, Mr., 46
Mystacidium, 134

nectary, 100
Neogyne Gardneriana, 194
nicotine, 27, 238
Nun's Orchid (see Phaius Tankervilliae)

Odontioda, 187
Odontocidium, 187
Odontoglossum
  characteristics and culture, 178–180
  species
    O. bictoniense, 180
    O. citrosmum, 180
    O. crispum, 180–181
    O. grande, 181
    O. Harryanum, 181
    O. Insleayi, 181
    O. luteo-purpureum, 181–182
    O. nobile, 182
    O. odoratum, 182
    O. pulchellum, 182
    O. Rossii, 182
    O. Schlieperianum, 182
    O. Uro-Skinneri, 182
Odontoglossum Tribe, 175–187
Odontonia, 187
Oncidium
  characteristics and culture, 182–184
  species
    O. altissimum, 184–185
    O. ampliatum, 185
    O. excavatum, 185
    O. flexuosum, 185
    O. incurvum, 185
    O. Kramerianum, 185

    O. Lanceanum, 185
    O. ornithorrhyncum, 186
    O. Papilio, 186
    O. pumilum, 186
    O. sphacelatum, 186
    O. splendidum, 186–187
    O. tigrinum, 187
    O. varicosum, 187
orchid beetle (weevil), 235
orchid cases, 252–253
orchids as house plants, 251–252
orchids in the garden, 254
osmunda fibre, 4, 26–30
osmundine (see osmunda fibre)
ovary, 100, 105–106
ovules, 102, 105

Palumbina, 188
Paphinia cristata, 201
  P. grandiflora, 201
  P. rugosa, 201
Paphiopedilum
  characteristics and culture, 155–158
  genetics, 164–166
  hybridization, 162–164
  species
    P. Argus, 159–160
    P. barbatum, 160
    P. bellatulum, 158
    P. Boxallii (see P. villosum)
    P. callosum, 160
    P. Charlesworthii, 160
    P. concolor, 158
    P. Dayanum, 160
    P. exul, 160
    P. Fairieanum, 160
    P. Godefroyae, 158
    P. hirsutissimum, 160
    P. insigne, 161
    P. insigne, var. Harefield Hall, 161
    P. Lawrenceanum, 161
    P. Lowii, 161
    P. niveum, 158–159
    P. preastans, 159
    P. Rothschildianum, 159
    P. Sanderianum, 159
    P. Spicerianum, 161–162
    P. Stonei, 159
    P. villosum, 162
Parathion, 238–239

Percival, R., 46
Peristeria elata, 195
petal blight, 234
*p*H, 26
  of flask medium, 116–117
Phaio-Calanthe, 203
Phaius
  characteristics and culture, 202
  species
    P. grandifolius (see *P. Tankervilliae*)
    P. maculatus, 203
    P. Tankervilliae, 203
Phaius Tribe, 202–205
Phalaenopsis
  characteristics and culture, 122–127
  species
    P. amabilis, 127
    P. amethystina, 128
    P. Aphrodite, 127
    P. cornu-cervi, 128
    P. Esmeralda, 128
    P. intermedia, 128
    P. Lowii, 127
    P. Lueddemanniana, 128
    P. rosea, 129
    P. Schilleriana, 127
    P. Stuartiana, 128
Pholidota chinensis, 194
Phoma, 232
Phragmopedilum caudatum, 166
  P. Sargentianum, 167
Physothrips xanthius, 237
Phytomonas cattleyae, 232
Phytomonas oncidii, 232
Phytophthora omnivora, 233
  P. palmivora, 233
placentae, 105
plastids, 66
Pleione praecox, 194
Pleurothallis ornata, 206
Pleurothallis Tribe, 205–206
pollination, 99–102
pollen, 99, 102
pollen tubes, 104–105
pollinium, 99–102
Polyrrhiza, 134
Potinara, 73
Potting, care after potting, 30–31
  methods for Cattleya, 26–30
  (see also methods under other genera)
prices, 8, 97, 262

propagation, general methods, 15, 33–35
  (see also culture of other genera)
pseudobulb, definition, 14
purple pigment, 66
Pythium, 234

Quekettia, 189

rain forest, tropical, 3, 39–41
rats and mice, 240
red pigment (see anthocyanin)
red spider, 35, 238–239
reduction division, 60
Reichenbach, Prof., 45
relative humidity (see humidity)
Renantanda, 131
Renanthera, 131
reservoirs, 4, 14
rest period, 40–42
  (see also under culture of each genus)
Restrepia, 206
rhizome, definition, 12
rhizome, infection, 233
Rhynchostylis, 134
Rodriguezia secunda, 197
  R. venusta, 197
roller blinds, 20, 248
roots, 3, 15
  mineral absorption by, 212–214
rostellum, 100
rotenone, 35, 238
rusts, 234

Saccolabium coeleste, 134
Sander, 46, 53
Sarcanthus, 134
Sarcopodium amplum, 174
Sawyer, H. D., 57
scale insect, 27, 237
Scaphosepalum, 206
Schimper, A. W. F., 40
Schomburgkia Lueddemanii, 140
Schroeder, Baroness, 46
Sclerotinia fuckeliana, 234
Sclerotium rolfsii, 233
Scuticaria Hadwenii, 202
  S. Steelii, 202
seedlings
  community pot to flowering size, 89–97
  flask culture, 81–88, 108–109, 114, 116–117

seedlings, general information, 8–9, 15
   gravel culture, 218–223
   (see also Cattleya and other genera)
Selenipedium Chica, 167
shade, 20–22, 247–248
sheath blackening, 234
sheath, definition, 14
slugs, 35, 239–240
Sobralia
   characteristics and culture, 207
   species
      S. fragrans, 207
      S. leucoxantha, 207
      S. macrantha, 207
Sobralia Tribe, 206–208
soft rot, 231
Sophrolaeliocattleya, 72–73
Sophronitis
   characteristics and culture, 58
   in hybrids, 72–73
   species
      S. cernua, 59
      S. grandiflora, 59
      S. violacea, 59
sow bugs, 237
Spathoglottis, 205
Stanhopea
   characteristics and culture, 195
   species
      S. oculata, 196
      S. tigrina, 196
      S. Wardii, 196
stigma, 100–102
stomata, 227
Swainson, 36
sympodial, definition, 122

temperature
   ailments associated with, 225
   function in plant growth, 17–18
   relative humidity and, 18–19
   (see also culture of each genus)
terete, definition, 129
Tetranychus, 238
tetraploid, 165–166 (see also colchicine)
thrips, 35, 237
Triana, José, 47

tribes, explanation, 120–122
Trichocentrum albo-purpureum, 198
   T. panduratum, 198
Trichopilia suavis, 208
   T. tortillis, 209
triploid, 165–166 (see also colchicine)

V-bottom benches, 222
Vanda
   characteristics and culture, 129–131
   hybrid, *V. Miss Joaquim,* 131
   species
      V. caerulea, 131
      V. Hookeriana, 131
      V. Kimballiana, 131
      V. Roxburghii, 131
      V. Sanderiana, 132
      V. suavis, 132
      V. teres, 133
      V. tricolor, 133
Vandopsis, 134
Vanilla planifolia, 209
Vanilla Tribe, 209
varietal names, explanation, 38–39
Veitch, Messrs. and Sons, 43, 52
ventilation
   in disease control, 226, 229
   principles of, 22–23
   (see also treatment for each genus)
viability tests, 107–108

Warscewicz, 43
water
   general rules for watering, 24–25
   in disease control, 226, 229
   *p*H, 26, 249
   (for specific treatment see culture of
      each genus)
wilt, 233
wire loop, 117

Zygopetalum
   characteristics and culture, 209–210
   species
      Z. crinitum, 210
      Z. Mackayi, 210–211
Zygopetalum Tribe, 209–211